ANUS MUNDI

ANUS MUNDI

1,500 DAYS IN AUSCHWITZ/BIRKENAU

Wieslaw Kielar

Translated from the German
by Susanne Flatauer

Times
BOOKS

Published by TIMES BOOKS, a division
of Quadrangle/The New York Times Book Co., Inc.
Three Park Avenue, New York, N.Y. 10016

Published simultaneously in Canada by
Fitzhenry & Whiteside, Ltd., Toronto

First published in Poland in 1972
by Verlag Wydawnictwo Literackie, Krakow
Also published in West Germany in 1979 by S. Fischer Verlag

Library of Congress Cataloging in Publication Data

Kielar, Wieslaw.
  Anus mundi.

  1. Ośwoęcom (Concentration camp)   2. World War,
1939-1945—Personal narratives, Polish.   3. Kielar,
Wieslaw.   4. Prisoners of war—Poland—Biography.
5. Prisoners of war—Germany—Biography.   I. Title.
D805.P7K5213   1980   940.54'72'43094386Z   80-5129
ISBN 0-8129-0921-6

Manufactured in the United States of America

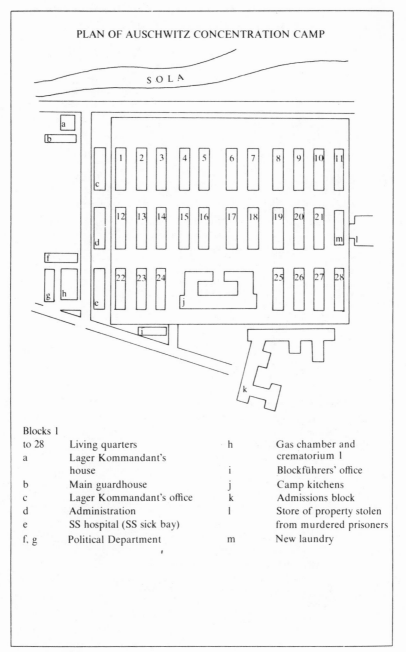

PLAN OF AUSCHWITZ CONCENTRATION CAMP

SOLA

Blocks 1			
to 28	Living quarters	h	Gas chamber and
a	Lager Kommandant's		crematorium 1
	house	i	Blockführers' office
b	Main guardhouse	j	Camp kitchens
c	Lager Kommandant's office	k	Admissions block
d	Administration	l	Store of property stolen
e	SS hospital (SS sick bay)		from murdered prisoners
f, g	Political Department	m	New laundry

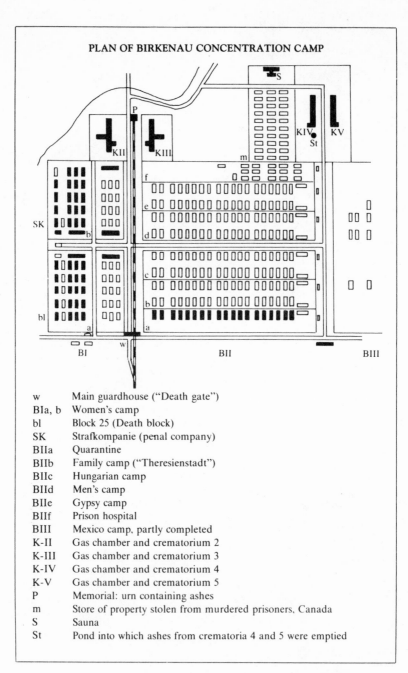

PLAN OF BIRKENAU CONCENTRATION CAMP

w   Main guardhouse ("Death gate")
BIa, b   Women's camp
bl   Block 25 (Death block)
SK   Strafkompanie (penal company)
BIIa   Quarantine
BIIb   Family camp ("Theresienstadt")
BIIc   Hungarian camp
BIId   Men's camp
BIIe   Gypsy camp
BIIf   Prison hospital
BIII   Mexico camp, partly completed
K-II   Gas chamber and crematorium 2
K-III   Gas chamber and crematorium 3
K-IV   Gas chamber and crematorium 4
K-V   Gas chamber and crematorium 5
P   Memorial: urn containing ashes
m   Store of property stolen from murdered prisoners, Canada
S   Sauna
St   Pond into which ashes from crematoria 4 and 5 were emptied

ANUS MUNDI

CHAPTER I

WE TRIED to stay together and until now, we'd been lucky. This time, too. Here we were, just as we had been in our prison cell: Tadek Szwed, Djunio Beker, Romek Trojanowski and I, sitting on a bench, each clutching the small bundle they had allowed us to bring from Tarnov prison. I had brought too much stuff, and worst of all was this winter coat, a real nuisance, which, heaven knows why, my parents had thoughtfully sent me before our departure. It was summer, for God's sake! Whatever could the old people have been thinking about? Perhaps they'd imagined that I might have to spend the winter in prison or doing farm work; anyway, that's where we thought we were going. I must have looked preposterous with this heavy coat in this heat.

The policemen escorting us were decent. They allowed us to talk to each other and to smoke if we wanted to. But we were not permitted to go near the windows. No one wanted to escape anyway. Although we didn't know where we were going, we didn't think it would be worse than prison. Our escorts, whom we tried to question several times about our destination, remained stubbornly silent. In the end one of them relented enough to inform us that we were being taken to a place to do laboring, but where this place was he wasn't allowed to say. We'd find out soon enough. . . . So our speculations had been correct.

The weather was splendid. Not surprising, since it was mid-June. Cornfields that were still green, shady woods, villages and small towns rushed past the windows. People working in the fields looked up and waved. There was nothing out of the ordinary about our train.

We arrived in Cracov about midday. The whole station was

3

festooned with swastikas. There was excitement and undisguised rejoicing among the Germans. From the loudspeakers came the blare of military music and strident speeches: Victory! Paris had fallen. It was June of 1940.

We traveled on. Our mood was subdued. Not surprising, with news like that. Our German escorts, on the other hand, were bursting with delight.

We stop for a long time at some station. It turns out that this is the frontier between the *Generalgouvernement* [Polish territory under German rule, 1939–44] and the Reich. We continue our journey. Next we stop at what, judging from the number of trucks on either side of the train, must be a major station. The name of the place, written in large letters on the station building, is: AUSCHWITZ. Someone explains that this is *Oswiecim*. Some dump or other. We don't think about it any more because now our train has started to move again. Presumably we're being shunted into a siding since the train curves sharply so that the wheels squeal remorselessly. Now we're not allowed to move at all. We mustn't so much as look in the direction of the windows. We sit still. Our train seems to have got the hiccups. Now it moves a few yards, now it stops. From the other side of the window come the sounds of voices shouting in German, of feet running and stamping. Suddenly the doors of our carriage are flung open. Someone on the platform shouts at the top of his voice: "Everybody out! Get a move on, you shits." Our escorts assist us to climb out of the train in their own way. They bring the butts of their carbines down on our backs with resounding blows. We all dash like mad towards the one and only exit. One by one we jump down from the high carriage and land directly at the feet of scores of SS men; they are lined up in rows leading towards a high fence which encircles a large building. Beaten, pushed and terrified by the SS men yelling at us, we rush like a flock of panicking sheep through the open gate.

Outside the building we must run yet another gauntlet, this time made up not of the SS but of tall, sinister-looking men who are strangely dressed in what look remarkably like striped pajamas. Each one holds in his hand a large stick which he waves

4

continually to right and left. I catch a blow on my hand, but luckily the coat I carry softens it a little. I jump out of the way only to receive a kick from another tall fellow in stripes.

At last the beating stopped and they began to line us up. One of the stripeys, with a swarthy complexion and penetrating black eyes, ran down the rows shouting, shoving and making people stand in straight lines. The rest of them, however, stood in line with us. We noticed that on their trousers and jackets were sewn black or green triangles, and below them the numbers 1 to 30. Number 1 was a wide-shouldered and dark-skinned fellow with the face of a highwayman. He was busy counting the rows, after which he took up a position facing us and, standing to attention, commanded in a sharp voice: "Company, halt! Caps off! Eyes right!"

We had not the least idea what this was all about, but just to be on the safe side we stood quite still. Suddenly the striped man commanding us stepped smartly up to a group of SS men standing a little to one side. At a short distance from them he came to attention, clicking his heels and taking off his cap in one swift movement; then he proceeded to talk rapidly in German, none of which we understood. One of the SS men, pointing at a nearby building, muttered something in reply without removing his pipe from his mouth. As soon as he had finished, Stripey once more clicked heels, put on his blue sailor's cap, did a regulation about-turn and returned to his previous position. Another command rang out. All the stripeys fell out and lined us up near the building.

After we had been divided into small groups, we were led into the basement where all our personal belongings were taken away; this included the removal of hair from every part of our body, followed by a bath in ice-cold water. We were handed a cardboard tab with a number which was to replace our names from now on. My number was 290, Romek Trojanowski's 44, and Edek Galinski's 537. Thus, in a perfectly simple manner, we became numbers.

After some time our clothes were returned to us and we were herded back into the yard where we had to form into rows of five.

5

Two of our number who could speak German well were appointed interpreters. It was their first job to translate the words of a weedy SS officer who informed us that as of this moment we were in preventive custody and sentenced to spend the rest of our lives in the concentration camp of Auschwitz.

And precisely what a concentration camp was we were about to find out.

CHAPTER 2

Caps off! Caps on! We had come to learn what this meant. The command had to be executed quickly and smartly. Heaven help anyone who lagged behind. Since the majority of our transport was young people, it was easier for us to cope with the hardships of exercises like hopping, rolling, dancing and similar harassments, which were invariably accompanied by beatings and ill-treatment. It was worse for men of advanced years. They were conspicuous and thus the more persistently ill-treated. Thanks to them we young people managed to snatch a few moments of peace and quiet whenever the SS turned their attentions to the elderly.

We had already learned that those wearing striped clothing were prisoners like us, who came here from Sachsenhausen where they had been held since 1933. This made it all the more difficult for us to understand why they treated us so viciously, even when there were no SS men about. Often they were worse than the SS, pursuing us wherever we went and beating us with their sticks. That was why many of us had black eyes or bruised heads.

We were instructed that we must address all stripeys as "Mr. Kapo, sir." When addressing a Kapo one must stand at attention, execute a "caps off" according to regulations—although, in fact, none of us possessed a cap—and after that recite the phrase: "Number [giving one's camp number] begs respectfully to report." If one succeeded in reporting quickly and correctly, one might escape blows. But one would almost invariably get some-

6

thing wrong somewhere, and as a result endure a blow or, if one was lucky, a well-aimed kick.

Things did not ease up until it was almost dark. However, before we were allowed into the building, we were made to undergo another thorough initiation. At the command of Kapo No. 1, all of us—and we were more than seven hundred—had to enter the block through the narrow door, after which we had to make our way to where our sleeping quarters had been prepared. Taught by bitter experience that any command had to be carried out instantly, we flung ourselves towards the door. The Kapos had already started to beat the slower ones. Consequently, everybody wanted to get as quickly as possible to the door, which might provide some cover. But at the door the crush was indescribable. People were shoving one another, pushing, choking, squashing, trampling. And from the rear, wild with rage, the Kapos were assaulting us, beating and kicking and hitting us with bars on heads, backs and hands.

Screams, groans, curses. At last the door to save me. Suddenly I am catapulted along a short corridor, only to get my foot caught in some unexpected stairs. People fall on top of me and from somewhere blows keep raining down on us. As fast as we can we get to our feet and race up the stairs. I am utterly out of breath, but with one final leap I reach the last step. There is a huge Kapo standing right across the corridor, his legs wide apart. His blows are aimed with the skill of the expert: my ears ring, in my mouth is the taste of blood and—why not admit it—tears are in my eyes. Summoning up my last strength, I run into the large room at the end of the corridor. Terrified out of my mind I fall to the floor which is spread with straw.

After a while the room is filled with prisoners lying side by side, battered, beaten, breathless, humiliated, frightened and utterly exhausted. Romek is lying next to me. He breathes heavily and does not speak. But Djunio mutters: "You bastards," in an attempt to relieve his pent-up feelings. It does absolutely nothing for us. We lie on the straw, trying not to think of what is to come.

Not for long, though. Soon the corridor reverberates with the sound of heavy boots. They go from room to room. After a while

Kapo No. 1 as well as the SS man with the pipe between his teeth appear in our doorway. Someone shouts: "Attention!" We leap up with alacrity. However, not everybody manages to leap up at the same time.

"You bloody lot of shits! You motherfuckers!" the Kapo yells.

Slowly The Pipe removes his pipe from his mouth; white teeth gleam between full lips. In a whisper, his voice almost gentle, he commands: "Lie down." We lie down slowly, not all at once. Before the last ones have lain down, a new command, more energetic now: "Up!" We jump up. Somebody is late again, but The Pipe does not seem to notice. Calmly he knocks the ash out of his pipe, knocking it rhythmically against the doorframe. Suddenly he shouts at the top of his voice: "Lie down!" We drop to the floor. "Up! Lie down! Up! Lie down! Up! Lie down! Up!" And so on; there is no end to it. We can no longer breathe. For some time now there has been no straw on the floor. Instead there is a great deal of chaff everywhere. In our noses. In our throats. In our eyes. The Kapo and The Pipe have virtually become dissolved in this chaff. From out of a cloud of dust comes the indefatigable voice of the SS man: "Lie down! Up! Lie down! Up!" When will it end? My knees are made of cotton wool, my body grows heavier and heavier. One can no longer see anything. Mercifully one can no longer hear any command either; they have gone.

We drop to the floor, which, only a short while ago, had been spread with straw. Someone runs to the window and tries to open it. Facing the windows, not far away, stands the SS guards' hut. "Shut the windows!" a German yells. When the one who opened the window fails to hear him, he fires a burst from his machine pistol by way of a warning. That does it. No one dares any longer to go near the windows.

It is getting dark. Everybody tries to find a place wherever he can. Our Tarnov lot keep together. From one corner of the room comes a loudly whispered prayer. The others join in. An earsplitting yell from the corridor: "Shut up!" It grows quiet, and we fall asleep. Only Djunio Beker tosses about, banging his fist on the floor in impotent rage, and, his tears almost choking him, he mutters: "You bastards!"

CHAPTER 3

THIS IS my third day in the camp. Three slices of bread, three bowls of soup, three small pieces of bacon, a few bruises, dozens of kicks, thousands of humiliations. But I am unhurt and alive. And I want to stay alive.

It was today that, for the first time, I saw someone die. I never imagined that one could take so long to die. But then perhaps the Jew was exceptionally tough. Although he didn't look it, that old, short-sighted, emaciated little man. Propped against the wall of the block, he lay in the hot June sun. The skin of his bald head had burst open in several places. Whole clouds of flies stuck to the blood mingled with sand. Heavy lids covered his deeply sunken, purple-black-rimmed eyes. Sometimes he raised them, but it seemed to be too great an effort, for he lowered them again at once. Black, chapped, thirst-scorched lips moved convulsively. "Water, water," he croaked. The Kapos formed a close circle round him. When they went way, the old Jew no longer gave any signs of life.

Our daily program was thoroughly varied. Our Kapos and the SS men saw to that. They outdid each other in inventing ever-new tortures. For days on end we engaged in what was known as "sport": hopping, rolling, dancing, knee-bending.

Hopping involved a distance of dozens of yards across the square and back. Rolling, on the other hand, took place only where there was a lot of dust. Dancing was for relaxation, to cheer things up a bit, while knee-bending was carried out to the command of: "One, two, three," to a standing position and down again to knees bent.

Legs turned to jelly with tiredness. A shorn head, swollen from the sun, and heavy as lead. Thirst burning the entrails. Did someone faint? They took him to the building; there the Kapo managed to bring him round. Cold water, a well-applied kick, off you go, back into your line.

The Pipe was with us all the time. Legs apart, he stood in the shade of the one and only tree, smoking his pipe or, when he put away his pipe, whistling a melody from an opera. Sometimes he beckoned someone to come closer, and then there would be a solo performance. Not too long though, on account of the June heat which tired the Pipe. "Come here, you! Come here! All right, that'll do. What's your job?" he inquired innocently. "Oh, a student? Great," he said admiringly. And then suddenly he hit him full in the mouth. "Fuck off, you Polish shit."

Actually The Pipe had more imagination, and as behooves an SS officer, was more refined and intelligent than the sergeant; fortunately, *he* only turned up occasionally. It had been the sergeant's idea yesterday to produce something like a religious spectacle. He selected a Jew and ordered him to climb onto a huge, upside-down barrel by the building and to recite his prayers. The Jew sang loudly and bowed according to orthodox rite which made SS men as well as Kapos fall about laughing; for us, though, it provided a breathing space. However, the spectacle did not end with this display. Plagge, the one with the pipe, remembered that there was a priest among us.

"Where is the minister?"

The priest stood on the barrel next to the Jew and began to pray. Quietly at first, but with a voice that was growing increasingly louder and more confident. The joke ceased to be funny, which was why they decided to continue with sport instead.

We drilled without a pause. The Jew and the priest hopped towards the tree, helped by Kapo No. 1 who kept hitting them with his stick. *Lagerführer* [SS leader in charge of one or more sections of the camp] Mayer, nicknamed "Dolly," ordered them to climb the tree in whose shade Plagge loved to sit. They climbed clumsily; as soon as one got a little higher, Dolly's dog pulled him down. The entertainment might have lasted longer, but the dog grew tired of it.

Now we were ordered to do the same. With the Kapos' sticks providing the necessary encouragement we began to climb. A huge joke! Several dozen people, beaten and kicked by the Kapos and snapped at by the dog, tried to climb the wretched tree. At last I, too, got hold of it. Stepping on someone lying under the tree, I held onto the trunk with one hand and pulled myself up with the other, clutching a foot dangling in front of me. The owner of the foot thrashing about was looking for a foothold; finding it on my head he put his weight on it. I pulled more strongly. He fell down. With one leap I was above the heads of several other people.

I must get higher up on the tree. Someone is pulling at my foot from below, pressing his nails into my thigh. With my free foot I kick really hard at someone's head. Still those nails dig deeper and deeper into my flesh. A head is raised higher and higher; I can already hear the whisper: "You bastard!" That's Djunio. I pull hard, my hands trying to hold onto the bark of the tree, but I'm down. Dozens of feet trample on my head, back and hands. Wildly I crawl on all fours, to get away, away from the tree. Out of reach of the frenzied feet I struggle to stand up, but in front of me is a wall of striped, impassable bodies. Again blows rain down on me. I face about and fling myself like one demented on the crowd milling round the tree, biting, scratching, pushing, desperate to get away from the blows. But I no longer have the strength to force my way in between the others. I fall back, face about again, turning round and round like a madman while from all sides blows come down on me. My head is bursting, my ears ringing.

With difficulty I open my eyes. I am lying propped against the wall of the building. Someone is bending over me. A Kapo, No. 2, a green triangle on his striped jacket. No stick, a friendly look, snub-nosed, the cap tilted rakishly. Ah yes, he's the kind Kapo, Otto, the *Arbeitsdienst* [vaguely equivalent to trusty. Trusties were responsible for assigning prisoners to work teams]. Come along; he beckons me and the others lying next to me. Djunio is one of them. He now has two black eyes. "Don't be afraid. Good work. Fetch food," Otto says in a kindly voice.

CHAPTER 4

TODAY PROMISES to be better. Perhaps this is because some of the people are needed for work. Several prisoners go to the former barracks, together with two SS men and Kapos. Rumor has it that

11

we are all to be transferred there soon. Otto keeps inventing new jobs. That is better than sport or the latest fashion, singing. Singing was introduced by Kapo No. 30, Leo Wietschorek. He is one of the worst villains, a broad-shouldered giant, with hands like shovels. Many people could not speak German; hence it was hard to remember words the meaning of which one did not understand.

"Here in Auschwitz I must stay," I shouted at the top of my voice, because that was all I knew. When it came to the "trala tralalala" the choir rose to a mighty crescendo, an occasion which Djunio used to vent his rage by changing the words to "bastards, bastards."

As soon as Leo approached, Djunio sang properly again. Opening his mouth wide, he sang horribly off key and thus attracted Leo's attention. The Kapo stood in front of him, legs apart, bending forward as if listening to Djunio's singing and then with all his might hit him on the chin with the side of his hand. Djunio teetered, his teeth clashed together, but he remained on his feet. As a rule, after a blow like that, it was wise to fall down even if one did not actually faint. Everybody knew that. It was well known that then, proud of the force of his blow, Leo would leave his victim alone and proceed to the next one. Djunio endured the blow. The blood rushed to Leo's face. Tight-lipped he got ready to strike again. Djunio remained standing. From the corner of his mouth came a small trickle of blood. Leo flung away his stick. And now he used his hands to thrash Djunio, first the right, then the left, again and again and again. Djunio staggered but remained standing. More blows. Now his legs gave way under him, but he did not fall, he knelt. A kick in the belly with the boot. Djunio roared, doubled up, red foam at his mouth. One more kick and Djunio keeled over backwards.

Leo pulled down his striped jacket, wiped his hands on his trousers, picked up his stick and walked away contentedly. He walked past me just as I was singing a full-throated "trala tralalala," and was gone. This time I had been lucky.

Fortune continues to smile on me. Now I am with the team which pulls out grass round the building. Otto has appointed one of our crowd who speaks German to be our foreman. Standing next to us he keeps a lookout for approaching Kapos or SS men. As soon as one approaches he shouts at us to get on with the work. When no enemy is in sight we have a rest. There is not much grass anyway, only odd tufts here and there, scorched by the hot June sun and trampled by hopping prisoners.

Beyond the wire, not far away, is a cottage. People must live there, because there is always some movement around the house. A woman keeps looking in our direction, giving surreptitious signs of wanting to make contact with us. But we are afraid to respond. One of the more courageous among us says the word "Tarnov." The woman must understand, for she gives a slight nod and disappears inside the cottage. After a while she returns and begins puttering around in her garden.

"Look out!" the foreman warns us. "Get on with your work. Come along." We crouch and crawl on all fours. With our nails we pull out the few remaining blades of grass, enveloped in a cloud of dust. The foreman clicks his heels and reports to Plagge The Pipe: "Team Three at work."

I can only see his legs. His green uniform is tight and reveals his thighs. Tan boots, elegantly polished, beat time with the tune he whistles.

Our good spot near the cottage, on which we already pin certain hopes, is perfectly cleared of grass. We move on. In this place there is more grass. Plagge stays with us all the time. Oh! He has stopped his whistling. Now he calls for the foreman. Another command. He wants us to pull out the grass with our teeth.

In my mouth there is the bitter taste of grass. There's sand between my teeth, dirt in my nose, and the sun beats down on the back of my head. I have a pain in my back, my neck is going numb. I'd even prefer "sport" to this. Laughter can be heard from afar. A group of Kapos loudly express their admiration for the SS man's brilliant idea. Pleased with himself, Plagge lights his pipe. How funny we must look, a flock of human beings browsing at the feet of their good shepherd. Nobody has laid a finger on anyone, nobody has kicked anyone, and yet someone collapses, unconscious. Fortunately the gong interrupts this entertainment. Midday meal.

13

Some of us already have lice. They torture us mercilessly; the whole body itches. At roll call it's almost impossible to stand still and not to scratch. Impatient as always, Djunio scratches with abandon. Needless to say, Bruno notices him at once.

"Have you got lice?" he asks ominously.

"Yes, camp senior, sir," Djunio replies honestly, fear in his voice.

Well, this is it! He'll finish him off, that's for certain. Djunio is insane. Bruno orders him to stand to one side.

"Anybody else?"

Silence. It would appear that lice love silence. I can feel them crawling all over my body. One is tickling me under my arm. I can't stand it any longer. Another one is crawling down my neck. Against my will and against all reason my hand reaches towards my neck. There! I've caught it. What a monster.

Of course, Bruno notices it at once.

"You too! You filthy beggar!"

"Yes, camp senior, sir," I reply, terrified.

With the pole he holds in his hand he pulls me out of the row and stands me by the wall next to Djunio. After a while there are quite a few of us. The Kapos confer among themselves. We stand like doomed men, expecting the worst.

Half-way along the corridor on the first floor is a narrow little room. We are taken there and the door is locked behind us. We go without supper, but at least there are no beatings.

In the morning everybody is driven into the yard for roll call. Not us, though. Through the glass pane in the door Bruno and Plagge peer at us. Bruno counts, using his fingers.

"Correct. Carry on!"

We sit down. We kill the lice in our clothing. We do it carefully to avoid accidentally killing the lot.

Dear old lice! Thanks to them Kapos and SS men avoid our cell. We enjoy peace and quiet. Grub comes regularly, and it even seems that the portions are larger than usual. We laze about for days while outside the heat, sport and blows continue. Life is beautiful.

On our door is a warning notice: BEWARE LICE! And from the

other side of the glass door the envious glances of our mates, tired out by sport and work. They implore us to let them have at least one louse. Next time we go to the latrine we manage to pass on a few. Before long our group from Tarnov is together again. They tell us that many prisoners have been transferred to the second camp, the barracks. Things are supposed to be much better there. Over there they work, whereas here there's only "sport."

Today a remarkably large number of volunteers reported with lice. But they're too late. Now anyone reporting that he has lice is given five on the arse. Probably by now they have all got lice, but no one will admit it any longer.

CHAPTER 5

ROLL CALL. We stand in rows in a large square behind the hospital block. The Kapos are having a hard time counting us. The SS men, too. The roll call won't tally. Maybe someone has escaped. They keep counting, but don't get the correct figure. They're furious. They vent their fury on us. We stand to attention, side by side, at arm's length, hands folded behind our heads, elbows turned back as far as possible. Thus we stand for an hour, maybe more, maybe less, because time has lost all meaning. Each second seems to be an eternity. Hands grow numb. Elbows gradually move forward. But "they" see everything. At once someone stands next to you and hits you in the mouth. Knee-bending as a punishment, but with hands kept at the back of the neck. It is hard to keep it up in this position. A group of SS men approach. Among them is *Rapportführer* [an NCO member of the SS, in charge of one section of the camp and responsible to the administration] Palitzsch. Young and slim, in a beautifully cut uniform, his unpleasant face covered with pimples.

"Interpreter!" he bellows.

In response to his bellowing the prisoner Count Baworowski sprints forward. Awkward, lanky, emaciated, he listens to the Rapportführer's abrupt barking.

Pale with fear, Baworowski interprets: "A prisoner has escaped—Wiejowski—the person who helped him to get away is to come forward.".

Silence. No one comes forward.

"You're going to stand here until someone comes forward."

Silence.

"Damn bastards! I'll show you!"

Baworowski, who has received an unexpected kick on his backside, staggers towards our row; on the way he loses his spectacles. He steps back, looking round helplessly. He crawls on all fours, feels about with his hands. There they are! The broken frame refuses to stay on his nose.

The SS men have left. Now Leo is practicing sport with us. It is getting dark. Consequently we manage to cheat. The Kapos, who seem to have grown tired, slope off, one after the other, back to the block. After a while Leo returns, smacking his lips noisily. He hasn't quite swallowed his food, but already he's shouting: "Knees bend!"

I sit comfortably on my heels. The others do the same. Not all manage to cheat.

"Up!"

How hard it is to get up. Leo uses his stick to help anyone who cannot do it by himself. We are tormented by hunger. Now we stand to attention with raised arms. Night has fallen. From the river, dampness, sticky and cold, comes creeping towards us. Our hands have gone dead, our shoulders hurt like hell. Leo disappears, I don't know where. We lower our arms. The pain, as the blood rushes in, is excruciating; minutes become eternities. It grows colder all the time. We shiver as if we have an attack of malaria. And this burning in our stomach. If one could only get some coffee. Someone asks for permission to go to the toilet. Permission refused. We piss in our trousers.

Dawn. Now the cold is so cruel that our teeth chatter loudly. When will it end? Perhaps they'll catch the fugitive? Suddenly the sun appears behind the block. It turns warm. For a change they make us fold our hands behind our heads. The longed-for sun now grows into a hated tormentor; it's a good job that our folded hands protect our shaven heads from its scorching rays. Some-

16

thing to drink! Somebody collapses. Leo rushes over to him. He beats him with his stick, but it no longer has much effect. After a while another man passes out, and still another. From the sky a veritable fire pours down. The pain is in one's hands and feet. It is impossible to stand any longer in this heat. Many pretend to faint. Before Leo has a chance to apply his own method of bringing them round, they may rest for a while. I decide to try the same trick. I fall down on my face. What a relief! However, there's the thought that at any moment Leo might come. I can hear the gravel crunching under the approaching feet. A hand pushes something under my nose. That's not Leo. It's the sick bay Kapo. His small penetrating eyes blink at me with understanding. Before Leo arrives they carry me to the sick bay. In the room some dozen bodies are lying on the floor. There's coffee, too. Bock, the sick bay Kapo, gives me some tablets. I swallow them and fall asleep immediately.

Stehappell [literally: standing-up roll call; a punishment] continued until 2 P.M. Thus I managed to get out of four hours of it. We might have had to stand even longer, but somebody is supposed to have confessed to having helped with the escape.

Next day we were transferred from Quarantine to Block 2. The block senior was a German wearing the green triangle of the criminal and the number 6. His name was Bonitz. His deputy was a Silesian called Jasinski.

CHAPTER 6

WE WERE standing side by side on a temporary scaffold. Each one had in his hand an iron cramp of the kind used to hold together girders. Day in, day out, we worked on the walls of blocks in order to remove the rendering down to the brickwork. The work was not hard, but from the sun-warmed walls the heat hit you as if from an oven. Besides, one could always be seen and had to work properly so as not to attract attention. At any rate it was better than sport or beatings.

However, it was not always possible to smuggle oneself into the same *Kommando* [work team; squad]. Sometimes I carried bricks to the crematorium which was being built; at other times I wheeled rubble to the big square which once had been a hippodrome and was now being made into a parade ground. Here all work had to be done on the double. Here one also got the most blows from Kapos and SS men. With envious eyes I watched the prisoners who worked right at the entrance to the camp, building the guardhouse. And I resolved to get into this Kommando.

Next morning, immediately after roll call, at the command: "Form into work teams," we ran towards the joiners' and carpenters' group.

The tall Kapo in charge knew very well who was a member of his team, as, incidentally, did anybody else who led a Kommando. Shouting and pushing, he quickly drove us away. We tried to join another team by running from one group to the next. But there was nothing doing. The teams marched out to work, and the camp Kapo began to catch those who were hanging about without an assignment. They were mainly the clumsy, the old, the sick, and the beaten; in a word, those who had already become *Mussulmen* [camp name for prisoners who had lost the will to stay alive]. These Mussulmen were given the worst work, mainly with the handcarts, where they were mercilessly goaded and beaten. Now we were Mussulmen, too. Kapo Leo was just about to take "care" of us, when Otto, one of the Arbeitsdienst Kapos, put in a timely appearance.

Otto surveyed the motley crowd of "unemployed" and chose a few of the younger and better looking ones, me among them.

The unfortunate Djunio had to go with Leo. Forever beaten, his face a mass of cuts and bruises, he constantly drew attention to himself. Djunio was unlucky.

Accompanied by Otto we marched happily in the direction of a single-story block at the entrance gate of the camp. There he took us to a large room on the ground floor where wooden planks were stored, and ordered us to sort them. He stayed for a bit, then he lightly tapped the nearest prisoner with his stick and walked towards the exit. At the door he uttered a few words which he tried to say in Polish: "Get cracking, *robota* [work]!"

And he was gone. A splendid fellow, this Otto. We began to work fast, especially because outside it had started to rain and it was getting rather chilly. It didn't take us long to sort the planks. Not long enough, as it turned out, because presently there was nothing left to do. We didn't want to stand about idly, so we carried the wood from one corner to the next, taking our time over it, of course, in order to spin out the work. In the end, having grown weary, we sat down on the planks and talked.

That's how Palitzsch, of all people, came upon us. He had been standing at the door for some time without any of us noticing him. Behind him lurked the dark figure of camp senior Bruno. Kazik Szumlakowski saw them first. He did shout: "Look out," but it was already too late. We were caught red-handed and by the worst of the whole lot.

There were seven of us. We stood in a row. I was the first and lay obediently on my stomach on the stool. Bruno held my head between his knees and pulled up my trousers to stretch them tightly across my backside. Palitzsch raised the strap.

"Count," Bruno barked.

"One." A short, sharp blow. A dull pain across the area where the strap had come down.

"Two." What a diabolical pain! I tried to wriggle loose, but Bruno had a lot of practice and held me fast.

"Three." My God, I can't stand it. It burns. It tugs, it swells; I can feel it swelling. Once more, four. And again, five. I jump up like a madman. Bruno sends me to the end of the line next to Romek Trojanowski.

"Next!"

Kazik Szumlakowski lies down.

One, two, three, four, five.

To anyone just watching, the beating doesn't seem to last very long.

"Next!"

Miecio Popkiewicz, followed by Tadek Szwed, then Edek Galinski, and after him Bolek Szumlakowski.

"Next!"

There's only one left. I hadn't noticed that Romek Trojanowski

19

has pushed behind me so that I find myself last. I look around, puzzled.

"What are you gaping at, you stupid git. Come along."

Bruno pulls me by my collar, while I shout that I've already had a beating. I resist, I explain, I gesticulate, all of which results in the Germans getting still more furious. After three blows I realize that I've forgotten to count aloud. Now I scream at the top of my voice: "Four!"

Not likely. Bruno corrects me: "One!"

I yell: "Five!"

And Bruno: "Two!"

I flung myself about, because instead of the blows landing on the buttocks, they came down on my back, even more agonizing. By some miracle I managed to free my head from the vice-like grip of Bruno's knees and, in an attempt at evading the blows of the enraged Palitzsch, I put my hands round his legs in their highly polished jackboots. He brought down his stick as if he were threshing wheat with a flail, now hitting the floor, now me. Gradually the blows became fewer, nor were they quite as vicious as before, because his strength was flagging. He couldn't kick me either because I was desperately hanging on to his boots with both hands. One more blow and then the stick broke in half.

I let go of his boots. One final kick and it was all over. At midday roll call I could barely crawl. The rain stopped and the sun came out from behind the clouds. At once it grew hot and sticky. I felt that I was going to faint. Although I was starving I could not finish my meal. In the afternoon I did not go to work. Bonitz, the block senior, gave me special permission to stay in the block. I lay on my belly. My buttocks were swollen and terribly painful. It seemed to me as though the flesh was coming away from the bones. At supper I only drank my coffee; the bread I hid under my head. I nodded off and when I awoke the bread had gone. Next morning I was absolutely whacked. But I did crawl to roll call. The day was comparatively uneventful.

On the following morning I felt much better. Otto detailed me to work with the joiners' team. In part I had to thank Romek for this. He was trying to make up for my sufferings of the two days before, which he had unintentionally caused.

CHAPTER 7

NEXT MORNING I was sitting astride a tree trunk removing the bark with a special knife. Next to me a prisoner was busily at work. Because he did his work so deftly I took him for a joiner, but he laughed when I asked him. He told me in confidence that he was a Capuchin monk but did not want anyone here to know.

Wolak was a young man, a little older than myself. He was a favorite of Kapo Balke, because he tried to do his work well. After my encounter with Palitzsch I was so weak that Wolak, who had noticed this, not only did his own work but mine as well. That was why I clung to him. Besides, he was at all times full of optimism and confidence. In the evening, after roll call, we sat with a large group of prisoners and watched enviously those lucky beggars from Silesia who, because they had been sent money from home, were able to buy food in the canteen. We, who had come from the Generalgouvernement, had no news whatever from home, let alone money.

Wolak had an idea. "Listen, we, too, can get money."

He took me to one side so that nobody would be able to eavesdrop and explained his plan to me. Among the joiners there were two or three prisoners who were skilled in the use of machinery. Every day they went into the town escorted by a guard. There they worked in the workshop of the Salesian monks, planing boards required for building the block leaders' office. He would himself talk to the Kapo and introduce me as an expert joiner conversant with woodworking. In this way we could establish contacts with the Salesian monks and obtain money.

There were three of us "experts." Otto took us to the camp gate where he handed us over to two SS guards. We marched past the building site of the new guardhouse, past a barrier where a *Scharführer* [lance sergeant] checked our passes, and then we were outside the camp area. We marched along an embankment flanking the river; at this hour of the morning the road which ran alongside was almost deserted. In a meadow near the bridge leading into the town, cows were grazing peacefully.

Once we had crossed the bridge, we entered the little town.

Here traffic was much heavier; the SS men ordered us to walk in the middle of the road. We marched on, followed by the anxious glances of passersby.

We arrived at the monastery past the market square. One of the SS men informed us that we were not allowed to speak to anyone during working hours nor to leave the workshop.

Several civilians were already at work in a large room. They did not appear to notice our arrival. Our guards took up positions by the open door leading into the yard and, leaning their carbines against the doorframe, proceeded to roll cigarettes. The foreman came in and saluted them with his arm raised. Then he beckoned me; I took off my cap and approached.

He said something to me in German, but I could not understand what he wanted of me. The machines were making a frightful din. He then spoke in Polish, trying to shout down the noise.

"Are you a joiner?"

"Yes," I replied hesitantly.

"Do you know how to work these machines?"

"Not terribly well," I replied, a little more boldly because the foreman was talking to me pleasantly.

"All right then. Start on this machine, putting grooves in these boards, and we'll see how it goes."

I began to work. I handed the planed boards to a young worker who placed them under the rotating cutter. I held the boards and then pushed them in such a way that one board after the other came to rest on the other side. Then I ran round the worker, took hold of the grooved boards, one by one, and stacked them in a corner of the workshop. The work became easier as time went on: nobody beat me, nobody goaded me. The morning passed quickly. I did not even notice that it was almost midday.

A car arrived from the camp. The finished boards were loaded in a great hurry because our midday meal was waiting.

Hastily we gulped down our camp food without, however, feeling really full. The foreman began a conversation with the SS men and walked casually out into the yard with them. Now there was a chance for us to talk to the civilians. My fellow worker gave me a bacon sandwich which I accepted with gratitude, looking round anxiously to make sure the SS men hadn't seen anything.

"Don't be afraid, eat your food in peace and quiet," he said.

"The foreman went off with them on purpose. The fat SS man comes from Silesia, and the other one isn't too bad either. It's different, though, when a good-looking young blond guy comes in this place. You have to watch it with him."

The worker asked me about the camp. He had learnt something about it from my predecessor. Beatings, starvation—he'd heard about them. His wife always gave him extra sandwiches to take to work, and he had shared them with my predecessor. He showed me the place where he put the food so that no one would see it. I thanked him. During our conversation I mentioned in passing that in the camp there was a priest, a monk, who through me wanted to get in touch with the Salesians. I explained to him that there was a canteen in the camp, but that only those who had money could buy things there.

He promised to talk to the foreman and to let me know his reaction next day.

The foreman returned with the guards. End of break. Back to work. The workers left at three, we puttered about until five, and then the SS men took us back to the camp. We took the same route. It was still very hot. Immediately past the bridge we turned left and ran down the bank in order to get to the meadow. One of my fellow prisoners asked the guards for permission to relieve himself.

"Well, be quick about it," the fat SS man replied in Polish, and began rolling a cigarette.

The prisoner ran to a little fence close by, where he searched around. After a while he picked up a small parcel and returned immediately.

Everybody received a fairly large slice of bread and streaky bacon.

"Eat up quickly," said our benefactor, "before we get anywhere near the camp. You must not take anything back into camp. There may be a search, and then we'll be in the soup."

While I ate I looked for the girl I had noticed in the morning herding the cows. She was nowhere to be seen. But I was certain that it was she who had hidden the parcel.

An SS man on a bike was coming towards us. Our escorts raised their right arms in salute: "Heil Hitler!"

As soon as he was past, the fat one said: "Well, how about it?

23

Have you finished? Every crumb? Mind that no one takes anything back into camp. And not a word to the others. Off we go now. Forward, march! Left, and left!" We entered the camp area.

CHAPTER 8

DURING THE next few days nothing really changed. The same group of us went to work. My civilian workmate gave me plenty to eat. Furthermore there was always some food on the way back. But no money. At last Wolak decided that he would write a note with a request for money. Perhaps this would be more effective. On the following morning I was to ask my civilian mate to pass the note to one of the Salesian monks. Wolak wrote this stiff [prison slang for a clandestine letter] in Latin. I rolled it up and slipped it in the seam of my striped jacket.

Next day we had a change of guards. What bad luck!

The two SS men were young, arrogant and self-assured; the worst thing was that they treated us with the utmost callousness. On our way to the workshop they even forbade us to talk to each other. And when, as we passed a cornfield, I picked an ear of corn, I was punished by having to hop all the way to the meadow where the cows grazed.

I only hope the girl doesn't hide any bread today, I thought, or she'll catch it as well, and we shall be punished, too. In the workshop we did our work nervously. The SS men never let us out of their sight, goading and abusing us constantly. Nevertheless I tried to find an opportunity to slip the stiff surreptitiously to my civilian mate, with the eyes of the Germans on me the whole time. I was determined to get rid of the message at all costs because I feared that these eager beavers might search us on the way back to camp.

In the afternoon, when I realized that the civilian workers would finish quite soon, I had to risk it. While pushing the boards forward on the machine I fished out the stiff and quick as a flash slipped it in between the shavings of the grooved board when I was quite close to my workmate. The worker noticed immediately,

24

and as I went to fetch the next board he brushed the shavings into a box which he put in a corner of the joinery. After a while he took the box into the next room, collecting all sorts of rubbish in it on his way.

I breathed a sigh of relief.

Encouraged by this spectacular success, I was resolved not to forego my bacon sandwich, which the worker would leave behind for me. Wrapped in paper, the bread was lying on a board among various tools. All I had to do was to reach for it. Had it not been for our new guards, I would have eaten it long since. But this damned lot was watching us like hawks. In fact, it seemed to me that they were only waiting to catch me doing something forbidden. Perhaps they had already noticed the small packet and were expecting me to stretch out my hand. Although I was hungry, I didn't want to run any more risks. Maybe tomorrow things would be a little better.

Closing time. Come along. Get a move on.

As we left, one of the guards glanced at the board. The packet still lay there, untouched. All the same, they searched us on the way, in the meadow by the fence, exactly at the spot where the girl used to hide the food for us. She was watching from afar. While I marched I thought all the time of the bread left behind in the workshop. All I could expect back in the camp was a small portion of bread and a little margarine. Whereas in the canteen . . . But it was better not to think about food because it only made your stomach rumble still more loudly.

Left, left and left: we were entering the camp.

After roll call Wolak came to see me. "Well, how about it, have you got it?"

I shrugged my shoulders. Not yet. Tomorrow, perhaps.

The next day appeared to start auspiciously. Apparently the two young SS men had left with another group of prisoners, since we had our old guards back again. The fat one was in a very good mood. On the previous day he had gone to Khorzov to visit his family. He offered us some tobacco. My pals accepted immediately, but not I because I hadn't started to smoke in those days. The girl herded her cows on the meadow and watched us from afar as always.

25

At the workshop the workers had already started. My civilian workmate pointed to the board where there were now two small packets.

"Today you'll have to do twice the work," he said cheerfully.

As was his custom, the foreman involved the guards in conversation and managed to maneuver them out into the yard. Now I could eat my fill in peace and quiet.

I asked what had happened about the note. Okay! He had handed it to the foreman, and the foreman had passed it on to the director of the Salesian monks. Working hours passed quickly. During the morning one of the guards handed his carbine to the other and went away for a few minutes. When he returned, the other one went. They smelled of beer. We were given sweetened coffee. We were thirsty. It was hot, after all, and we were quite content.

The foreman gave me a funny look. After a while he came up to me and said, trying to make himself understood above the screeching of the machine: "You'll get the money for the priest. But, for heaven's sake, be careful." He pointed to my civilian fellow worker. "He'll give it to you." During the lunch break I saw the director of the Salesian monks. He walked through the workshop, tall and earnest, and stopped for a brief talk with the foreman. He did not appear to see the SS men. As unexpectedly as he had come, he was gone again.

So, it was from this priest that the eagerly desired money would come: I realized this in a flash. Before he left, my civilian workmate gave me a clear sign. Concealed in the wood shavings was a roll of notes. I looked at the door. Okay. The SS men seemed engrossed in conversation and paid no attention to what went on in the workshop. Unnoticed by my comrades I hid the roll in the seam of my jacket. No one had seen anything. I was nearly bursting with happiness. What a good day I'd had today. No doubt about it.

On our way back we stopped by the little fence, as usual. The girl herding her cows watched us from afar. The small packet was in the same place, as usual.

I wolfed down my bread in large mouthfuls. But there was one thought going round and round in my head. I had expected one banknote, and there were several. Wolak had told me he'd asked for ten or fifteen marks. That was the amount German citizens in the camp were allowed to receive.

Perhaps the monks had sent more than that? If so, I shouldn't harm anyone if I were to keep five marks for myself. Surely I was entitled to something for taking the risk. Only I must find out how much there was before I met Wolak.

Deep in thought I did not notice that we had reached the camp. There was the gong for roll call. Perhaps I'd just make it across to the latrine between Block 2 and Block 3. It would be empty now because everybody was running to attend roll call.

CHAPTER 9

THE LATRINE was indeed empty. Splendid. I drew out the bank-notes and counted. There were four five-mark notes. Fantastic! I pocketed one note and rolled up the rest again.

Suddenly I felt a heavy paw on the back of my neck.

"What are you doing here?"

I ducked. If there had been any hair on my head, it would have stood on end.

"Where did you get the money, you thief?" he yelled, glancing at my number.

He guessed at once that since I had been in the first transport I could not have received any money from home. He took away the money, even the note which I had managed to hide in my pocket.

Kapo Grönke was himself an old thief. I thought he'd leave me in peace once he had taken the money. But he led me by the collar across the parade ground to where the inmates of my block were standing. He gave me a hard kick and block senior Bonitz gave me another one for good measure.

During roll call Wolak sidled up to me. "What happened?"

"The shoemakers' Kapo pinched twenty marks from me; he says I stole them."

After roll call I was to report to the block senior. Jasinski, the clerk, took me to the block seniors' room. They were waiting for

27

me. The money lay there on the table. I stood on the threshold, trembling and full of dreadful forebodings. The expression on the Kapo's repulsive face did not promise well. Bonitz smiled ominously and beckoned with his forefinger.

"Come a little closer, you old thief! Don't be afraid, come on!" he yelled.

I approached fearfully and at that moment received a slap in the face from the tall Kapo. Before I could collect myself, I got one on the other side of my face. I bet he would have continued hitting me, had not the block senior stopped him magnanimously.

"Quiet! Come here, clerk." He called Jasinski over.

"Interpret for me."

"Where did you get the money?" was the first question.

"I found it."

"Where did you find it?"

"In the latrine."

"You're lying!" The block senior was getting worked up. Nobody in the camp could possibly have so much money. Fifteen marks at the most.

"That's a load of bull! You silly cunt! Twenty-five marks!" He pointed at the table.

So there were. Five five-mark notes. In my hurry I hadn't noticed.

"Let's have a look at your jacket. I bet you used this hiding place before." Triumphantly the Kapo produced the long tear in the seam of my striped jacket. Again he hit me in the face. Bonitz joined in. Now they were both hitting me.

"Tell the truth. Tell it as it was," Jasinski, out of pity, advised me. "Be quick about it, or they'll kill you."

"In which team do you work?" was the next question.

"In the joiners' workshop?"

They sent Jasinski to fetch Kapo Balke.

Balke arrived. On the way Jasinski had quickly told him what it was all about. The three went into a huddle. I didn't understand much of what they were discussing. I only hoped that they would divide the loot among themselves and that would be the end of it. No such luck. Now the investigation began in earnest. They were already on the right track, for Balke had reported that I was work-

28

ing outside the camp in the Auschwitz workshops of the Salesian monks. That meant contacts with the civilian population.

After Wiejowski's escape a short while ago, which had allegedly taken place with the help of workers outside the camp, the Germans had become particularly sensitive on this point. Balke attempted to make light of the whole matter and suggested dealing with it internally. But Kapo Grönke, seeing himself as the main hero in having uncovered this affair, advised an official report to the camp authorities. Finally, by way of concluding the investigation, block senior Bonitz slapped my face yet again and announced that a report would be made immediately after morning roll call.

Completely shattered after so promising a day I related the course of events to Wolak. I merely concealed the matter of the five marks I had meant to make for myself.

I was tormented by pangs of remorse. Wolak tried to comfort me as best he could, taking half of the blame himself. The mere thought that tomorrow morning I would have to report to the dreaded Rapportführer Palitzsch for punishment made me shudder. That night I did not sleep a wink. Wolak, who was lying next to me, did not sleep either. I could hear him praying. And I prayed too.

Gong. Coffee. Roll call. I am standing there feeling as if I have been sentenced to death. Wolak reaches for my hand and squeezes it tightly. "Everything is in the hands of God," he says. "If they hit you again, tell the truth, that this money was meant for me."

Roll call is nearly over. "Prisoner 290," shouts camp senior Bruno. Everybody joins in the call according to camp custom. The call "290" echoes from mouth to mouth. My feeble legs seem to be rooted on the spot. Somebody pushes me out of the line; the block senior comes rushing up and pulls me after him. I am standing in front of the Rapportführer. Stammering, my voice barely audible, I report to him. In passing Palitzsch casts a glance at me. Then he shouts: "Form into work teams!"

I stand forlornly by the main gate. Before me the teams march out to work. Has my team marched out? I ponder. Probably. They don't know anything yet.

The camp senior ostentatiously rattles the chains in his hands. It is with such chains that cattle are tethered in the stable. A tall, gaunt *Blockführer* [SS man supervising two or three blocks and responsible to the Rapportführer], with a face like a squeezed lemon, pale and slightly bored, is with him. He looks as if he had T.B.

"Come along now!" he says to me in fluent Polish. "You're going to swing a little."

We walked along the camp street in the direction of Block 3.

"Tell me, how was it with these bank notes?" he asks deadpan.

"I found the money, Herr Blockführer."

"Ah, you're stupid. With whom have you had contact? First the money, then contacts with civilians, and finally—escape. Once you've been hanging from the post for a while, the Political Department will extract the whole truth from you, never fear . . . You're suspected of planning to escape," he added in German for Bruno's benefit. I looked at the two of them, horrified.

Again Bruno rattles the chains ominously.

"That's it," says Bruno with mock-pity.

CHAPTER 10

WE ENTERED the loft of Block 3. They stood me under one of the many beams in this loft. This beam was different from the others merely because it had a hook quite high up. Underneath stood a stool. The camp senior forced my arms back, tied them expertly with a chain and ordered me to climb onto the stool.

Unperturbed, the SS man lit a cigarette. A firm tug at my arms, an upward pull and I was fastened to the hook. I screamed, more from fear than pain, because my legs were still standing on the stool. Half doubled up, I saw the SS man take out a notepad. Bruno stood poised, ready at any moment to kick the stool from under me.

"Come now, tell the truth. What's all this business with the money?" The Blockführer's question rang in my ears. "You'll sing all right, make no mistake. The sooner the better for you. Swing for a little while and you'll curse your mother for having given birth to you. So, come along, let's have the whole story."

I reflected for a while, sweat pouring from my forehead. I knew already that I was going to tell all. I tried to excuse my cowardice somehow. Wolak did say I should tell the truth if they started beating me.

"Come on, quickly," the SS man tempted, bending over me. Bruno seemed to think that the SS man was looking at him and pushed the stool away. Intense pain in my twisted shoulders, increasing every moment. With my heels I tried to prevent myself from dropping by pressing firmly against the beam, but it was no good. Slowly my strength was ebbing away.

"I'll tell, I'll tell everything," I gasped.

"Well, you didn't take long to make up your mind, did you? Camp senior!" the SS man said peremptorily, and with his foot pushed the stool towards me. Bruno helpfully placed the stool in position.

Massaging my aching wrists I began to talk: "Wolak . . . the letter . . . the civilian . . ."

"Is that all?" The SS man closed his notebook.

We went down to the ground floor. For a time the Blockführer conferred with the camp senior. I caught only a few words: "Political Department . . . Wolak . . . light work." When they had finished, the SS man walked away in the direction of the building site of the Blockführers' office. Bruno took me to the kitchen next to Block 2. I fetched buckets of water from a well. The work was not hard, but carrying the full buckets was laborious. My shoulders hurt. Nobody shouted at me, nobody hit me, and that was something to be thankful for. I thought of Wolak. He kept coming back into my mind. Probably at this moment he was making his statement in the Political Department.

The news went round the camp like wildfire. There were some who were amazed that I could have hung from the hook and still have the strength to carry buckets of water. Others thought unkindly that they hadn't taken long to make me talk in the attic and that afterwards I even managed to get a light job. One of the older prisoners came up to me and said angrily: "You've betrayed the priest, you swine."

31

He went on berating me in great agitation, but his Kapo came running towards us and, beating him across the shoulders with a stick, chased him to a group of prisoners who were carting rubble from neighboring blocks.

I did not see Wolak until after evening roll call. He had been interrogated in the Political Department. He had made a statement about the letter and its contents. All he had asked for was some financial help. They implied that the letter might have contained other matters, but he persisted in his statement, saying that the truth of it could be checked quite easily.

"Wiesiu! Cheer up! It'll be all right. They're not going to hang us for a lousy twenty marks."

Twenty, I thought. There were twenty-five, weren't there? What was the matter with this money?

The next day the same Blockführer took me to the single-story building outside the wire fences where the Political Department had its offices. Wolak stayed in the camp. Probably he was carrying water to the kitchen. As I went down the long corridor on the first floor I thought I was walking past the fat SS man. I was led into a room where a good-looking officer sat at his desk. Next to him, behind a typewriter, sat a young prisoner wearing clean, striped clothes. The officer gazed at me curiously for some time and then put his first question. The young prisoner was an interpreter. The first few questions had nothing whatever to do with the matter in hand. He asked about my home, my family, my father's profession, my mother's profession, where I came from, and so on.

Then he came to the point. I was made to describe in great detail the manner in which I had passed Wolak's message to the civilian workers, as well as the manner in which I had received the money; how I had brought it into the camp and how I had let myself be caught while counting the money, in order to put aside five marks for myself. All he wanted to know in addition was whether this letter written in Latin had been the only one I had smuggled out or whether there had been others. Of course I denied this. In the end he found that, on the whole, what I had said tallied with what Wolak and the workers from the Salesians' workshop, who had been interrogated already, had said. For

32

smuggling money into the camp and for making contact with people outside the camp, I would receive the punishment I deserved. On the same day, after roll call, Wolak's and my numbers were called out. Rapportführer Palitzsch ordered the camp senior to take us away to the quarantine station, which was in a block within the hospital complex.

I was astounded that everything had gone off without beatings.

"There you are," said Wolak. "Providence watches over us."

CHAPTER I I

ON THE steps of the quarantine station stood several personable prisoners. They were the first staff members of the camp hospital which was in this block.

"Why did you get caught," one of them inquired. "Because of Wiejowski? No? Because of the banknotes?" He made a sceptical face. "Leo'll show you what's what."

Kapo Leo was in charge of the eleven prisoners who were under suspicion of having helped Wiejowski to escape. I gazed in fear and trembling at Leo's huge frame as he walked towards us. As always he held in his hand a wooden stick; his little eyes, screwed up as though he were laughing, appraised our emaciated bodies.

"At the double, march!"

We ran to a square where, not long ago, we had had to undergo the notorious Stehappell as punishment for Wiejowski's escape. Eleven prisoners in a row were crouching in the knee-bend position. Leo ignored them completely; instead he lavished all his attention on us.

We ran round and round the square until he issued a new command: "Halt! Knees bend! Hands up! Hop!"

Down the square, back and forth. When our legs threatened to give way, he changed the command to: "Roll!"

We rolled in the dust of the yard, our sweaty bodies covered with dirt. Having grown completely hoarse from constantly shouting commands at us, Leo ordered us to join the eleven men who all this time had been squatting with knees bent. From this moment there were thirteen of us.

We were given a moment's respite because Leo had been called to see the sick bay Kapo. At the time we didn't quite understand that Bock had called Leo deliberately to let us have a quick breather.

The eleven prisoners bombarded us with questions.

"Why are you here? Is it because of Wiejowski? Or on account of the banknotes?"

"How much longer is this likely to go on?" we asked in turn.

"It's long past roll call."

The conversation came to a halt abruptly because Leo had returned.

"At the double, march!"

The sun had long since gone down, but we were still exercising, in turn hopping, dancing, rolling, or doing knee-bends.

"A song! In Auschwitz camp I had to stay . . ." Leo began. With this song on our lips we returned to Block 16 where we were to live from now on. End of sport—at least for today.

Supper. Wolak and I did not get any supper. Utterly shattered, we lay in the straw. From the corridor came the sound of a mouth organ. It was Leo playing it.

After a few days of sport I became so weak that I could no longer keep up with the others. Leo did not like weaklings, or perhaps he thought I was malingering; at any rate, he began to exercise with me on my own whenever he allowed the others to rest. When I collapsed, completely exhausted, he dragged me to the pump, poured water over me and resuscitated me with a few blows. After such an interlude I continued exercising, and after a short time the whole process was repeated. I saw no way out of this situation and thought desperately what I should do in order to get myself into the sick bay, which I regarded as my only salvation. While "hopping" I found a few small glass splinters, but I could not bring myself to swallow them. And yet I had to do something like it, for I felt that I would not last out until evening. With one of the larger pieces of glass I slashed the skin on my chest. It did not hurt, but I bled profusely. At last Leo noticed the bloodstains on my shirt. He called one of the medical orderlies who was looking out of the window of the block. The man produced a bottle of iodine with which he treated my wounds. After which Leo, with redoubled energy, resumed giving me "solo" exercises. Finally he stopped and after some brief thought said resolutely: "Come along!"

I trailed slowly behind him. He took me to the bathroom in Block 16. On the corridor we met Mietek D., one of the medical orderlies. Leo ordered him to bring a stool. Having put down the stool, Mietek D. wanted to leave. But with a movement of his hand Leo held him back. Then he ordered me to lie on the stool. Mietek held my head between his knees, but not very tightly so that I managed to break away at the first blow. And then Leo went berserk. He lashed out wildly. I writhed on the wet concrete floor, trying to dodge the blows without success. Although I did not lose consciousness I could neither get up nor defend myself. Lying on my back, I gasped for breath, my mouth wide open. Leo stopped hitting me. Instead he poured large quantites of cold water over me. All at once I felt that the water which Leo was pouring into my open mouth threatened to suffocate me. I saw his livid face bending over me. At last he thrust his stick into my mouth, twisting it round, first one way and then the other. Then he peered closely at me, obviously trying to ascertain whether I was still alive, and then he went away.

I did not have the strength to get up. All I could do was to roll over onto my stomach and, a little later, onto my side. Then I was sick. I no longer felt any pain, but I was terribly cold. An attack of the shivers followed. Hands lifted me, placed me across their shoulders, and after a while I lay in my room covered with blankets. The sick bay Kapo gave me some tablets. Mietek D. brought a jug of hot coffee. Before long I felt much better. I went to sleep.

I was awoken by many voices and the stamping of boots in the corridor. It was my twelve fellow prisoners on "punishment" returning from their exercises. Outside it was growing dark.

"Well, you've been lucky today, haven't you," one of them said with envy in his voice. He was unaware that I had had one foot in the grave or that Leo would have finished me off in the bath if sick bay Kapo Bock had not turned up in time. As was his wont, Leo was at this moment sitting on the steps leading to the block, soulfully playing sad tunes on his mouth organ.

Lying next to me was Wolak, all tired out. He was praying. His faith gave him strength. Despite the adversities of fate he was at all times cheerful and completely certain that everything would turn out well. As I was falling asleep I thought of the next day with dread.

That night a large transport arrived from Pawiak prison. This was the so-called first Warsaw transport. For the majority of them it was the worst and, at the same time, the final phase of their lives. For the 1,500 prisoners in the camp, their arrival provided a breathing space because the entire attention of the SS and the Kapos was concentrated on these new arrivals. For Kapo Leo Wietschorek it meant promotion, for on that day he was transferred from Quarantine into the camp as second camp senior to assist Bruno Brodniewicz.

And what did it mean for me?

The arrival of this transport saved my life. Of the thirteen on "punishment," I was intended to be Leo's first victim. But his timely transfer prevented him from finishing me off.

CHAPTER 12

AFTER LEO's departure, Wolak and I became cleaners in Block 14. One day Dr. Popiersch, one of the camp doctors, carried out an inspection. The sick bay simply sparkled, it was so clean. The credit for this went to Wolak and me, and we were duly rewarded. At first I was terrified when Mietek D., a secretive expression on his face, led us to the loft where Bock, accompanied by one of the chief medical orderlies, was waiting for us. We were given half a loaf of bread, a piece of sausage and some margarine. That was for working so well. If we continued working satisfactorily, Bock informed us, we would be appointed auxiliary medical orderlies. We had to eat our gifts there and then, for no one must know that we had received extra rations.

Similar incidents occurred from time to time.

"See," Wolak would say, "Providence watches over us."

In fact, we might say we were lucky in adversity; the camp authorities seemed to have forgotten the thirteen prisoners on "punishment." After the arrival of the first Warsaw transport Leo went elsewhere, and we came under the authority of Bock. Although, like Leo or Bruno, Bock wore the green triangle of the habitual criminal, he was quite a different person. He was entrusted with the organization of the hospital block, which cannot have been an easy task in those difficult days.

One night there was a great commotion in the camp. The second transport from Warsaw had arrived. The medical orderlies helped with the reception of the transport and the operation of the clothing depot.

In the morning I cleaned out the temporary hut right behind the sick bay block which had been specially built for the reception of this transport. Among the heaps of rubbish and refuse of all kinds I found many things to eat. Slices of bread, cake, onions, garlic, a little sugar mixed with sand, a jar with a scrap of lard—not worth taking to the camp kitchen, but a feast for the likes of me.

I ate secretly. My stomach could stand anything. Half an hour later I was hungry again, so hungry that I could hardly wait for the midday and evening rations. At lunchtime it was my job to clean out the soup buckets. Bits of congealed soup would cling to the sides of the buckets. I scraped them out carefully so that sometimes I got two full plates. Soon the cleaning of buckets became my speciality, and I did not do at all badly from it.

I regained my strength quite quickly and even put on some weight. When writing a letter home I no longer had to lie when I told them that "I am well and in good health."

During this time conditions in the camp went from bad to worse. Autumn came. It was cold. From the window of our room I could see a large area of the camp. The parade ground was being rolled. A few dozen prisoners were harnessed to a roller. Barefoot and dressed in flimsy drill trousers, they waded in the sodden ground, pulling the roller with difficulty. They were all said to be priests or Jews. Fat Kapo Krankemann directed this group stand-

37

ing on the roller handles. Every time he jumped off there would be one pulling prisoner less, lying in the mud dying. After roll call they would take him to the hospital block; often he was dead on arrival.

Roll calls took ages. We, the hospital block staff, held roll calls inside our block; they lasted barely a few minutes. I thanked heaven that I was one of the thirteen on "punishment."

In about mid-October, during roll call, Leo came running to our block, quite out of breath. In his hand he held a list. We had already finished our roll call.

"Fall in, the thirteen!" he yelled at the door. We leapt up like madmen. He proceeded to check our numbers. Miracles will happen: Wolak and I received merely a kick, after which Leo ordered us to stay in the block. The remaining eleven were driven to the parade ground.

We were able to watch the punishment from our window. A stool was brought from Block 11. At the same time they fetched five civilians who had been involved in Wiejowski's escape. They were followed by Kapo Bock carrying cotton wool and his iodine bottle. The whole camp was to witness the punishment.

The youngest of the eleven screamed piteously. One by one they all had to lie across the stool. They were beaten on the bare buttocks. Bock treated their bruised backsides with iodine. After roll call they were taken to Block 11, from where they were sent to Flossenburg Labor Camp.

Only the two of us were left in the room. That same day Bock summoned us, and in the presence of all the medical orderlies we were appointed auxiliary orderlies. I was happy, but in my heart there remained a nagging worry: what did fate have in store for us?

CHAPTER 13

AUTUMN WAS here.

Since the early morning a persistent drizzle had been coming down. I was waiting impatiently to hear the loud voice of the runner from the camp kitchen shouting "Come and get it!" before rushing off to another block.

It was a pity, really, to leave one's warm place by the stove. But one must eat as well; already the block senior was hurrying the orderlies to fetch the soup from the kitchen.

Outside the kitchen a number of orderlies from various blocks stood waiting. The handing out of soup buckets took place with due ceremony. To begin with, Leon the cook would check that everybody was present. Then he gave the command: "Caps off!," reported to Kapo "Ma" and gave the command: "Caps on!"; only then, after the number of buckets for any particular block had been counted out, was the orderly allowed to take them away. One had to be quick about it, too, because Ma, despite the kindly nickname bestowed on him by the prisoners, was waiting for a chance to ill-treat any slow ones.

The hot food bubbled in the buckets. I was working out in my head how much of this soup would be left over. After all, in our block there were so many people down with diarrhea. For my room there was a bucket with 50 liters of soup for 50 persons. Nothing was left over apart from what I managed to scrape from the sides. I ran quickly in order to collect the buckets from the other rooms in our block. Before returning them to the kitchen they had to be cleaned and rinsed. I always managed to scrape out a whole bowlful, including some for Edzio Ferenc, for whom I tried to obtain as much extra food as I could. Edzio was in a rotten team and therefore had deteriorated to a Mussulman; his head was covered with boils. He was near death. In the room where many had diarrhea, half the soup was left over. I got a second helping, and then the block senior ordered me to take the rest to the surgical block.

In the afternoon it rained and snowed. The cold was damp and persistent. Even before we arrived at the store to fetch the food we were wet through and freezing. How about the teams working in the field, I thought with a shudder. In charge of the store was an innocuous SS man, who was short, thin, bony and funny. We nicknamed him "Schwejk." His right-hand man was a prisoner called Adolf, who had several good-looking fellow prisoners to help him. This Adolf and I knew each other very well, and together we began to do a little pilfering. Gradually our thieving activities came to be on quite a large scale. Some mates of the store workers were lying ill in our hospital block, and the workers regularly sent them food through us. Of course, we, too, were given something for our trouble.

Schwejk covered any shortage from a subsidiary store. He didn't do all this because of his kind heart; he stole, too. He stole because he wanted one of the Polish doctors to treat him, and he paid for his services with food from the SS stores. You scratch my back and I'll scratch yours. Thus it was not surprising that he paid no particular attention to our light-fingered practices.

However, this afternoon he had a premonition. Obviously he thought that we had been taking too many liberties, and he began to count the loaves that had already been put on the stretchers we used to carry our food supplies. Patiently he counted several times, arriving at a different figure every time because we used his preoccupation in order to put the stolen bread back on the shelves. At long last he gave up and said resignedly: "Okay." Then he told us to get lost, which we did.

When we returned from the store it was already quite dark. It was still raining and snowing. The teams were returning to the camp. The prisoners, wet through and frozen stiff, dressed merely in dark drill overalls, barefoot or wearing heavy wooden clogs, waded through the slush, out of step, and paying not the least attention to the Kapos' shouts of "Left, left." They marched supporting each other, the stronger carrying the unconscious and the ones who had died or who had been killed during the course of the day. They lined up for roll call on the parade ground. We ran quickly with our stretchers laden with food and felt the gaze of hundreds of starving prisoners. Happily we managed to reach our block safely. Our roll call took place as usual in the corridor. It was short, and afterwards we went to our rooms.

In the camp roll call was still going on. Two or three hours had passed since its start. In the furious snowstorm thousands of prisoners were slowly freezing solid. One could see that death was reaping a rich harvest.

"All medical orderlies fall in. To your stations," ordered Bock.

The hospital block was getting ready to admit the sick, of whom

40

hundreds were expected. I was detailed to help the gatekeeper who guarded the entrance to the block.

Roll call was over. The clatter of wooden clogs, the shouting, the squelching of mud mixed with snow, the stampede of hundreds of prisoners, frozen to the marrow, seeking refuge in the small hospital block. There they were. First came the strongest who had overtaken the others, the ones who really needed immediate help. The door was closed. They ran against it. Several of us were holding it shut from inside. What would happen when this horde forced its way into the outpatients' department?

The little block senior pushed us firmly away from the door, then he flung himself, shouting and hitting out, into the seething crowd. We were in his wake. After a while some sort of order had been restored. Priority was given to the weakest, those who could barely stand on their feet, the ones who were already lying in the mud and sometimes no longer gave any signs of life. We carried them into the block and laid them in the corridor, one by one, just to give them a place. There were so many. Now the people who had been first to storm the door actually helped us. But that was only a ruse. Once they had carried the sick inside they dropped them anywhere, completely crowding the outpatients' clinic so that neither doctors nor orderlies were able to get on with their work. Bock was furious. We had to force people outside and organize them into a line. Dozens of new patients were already lying at the entrance to the block. Before we managed to carry them inside, half of the ones standing in line had collapsed. There were malingerers, too, but they were only discovered in the shower. We did not yet have any hot water.

There were so many sick people that the doctors did not have time to examine them carefully. Corpse bearers took the corpses through another door out of the block, while we carried those who were still alive into the washroom. Here we had to undress them all, which was by no means easy work. It was difficult to get the wet rags off the motionless skeletons that were covered with boils and soiled with excrement. Each one had his number written on his chest in indelible pencil; the barbers shaved off their head and body hair; the shaved places were disinfected. Then we laid them on a board in front of the shower and sprinkled them with cold

41

water instead of giving them a bath. This was, of course, against regulations, but we saved valuable time and saved the sick additional suffering. Only now could they be taken to their rooms. Some had to be transferred upstairs because they had pneumonia; the majority stayed downstairs where they were laid side by side on straw mattresses. They were given charcoal or *Bolus Alba,* which they washed down with herbal tea or a beverage euphemistically known as "summer coffee."

That particular evening the corpse bearers had to work overtime. They had the additional difficulty of not always being able to decipher the numbers on the chests of the dead, which had become blurred and illegible and which had to be entered in the death register. It was essential that next morning at roll call everything tallied.

Slowly the corridor grew empty. Now we let in all those who had been patiently waiting their turn outside the block. Most of them were moribund, too. All the same, that day only some of them were admitted to the sick bay, for the sick bay was full. The others were merely given a dressing, some charcoal or a tablet and sent back to their blocks. Any who survived the night might try again next morning to get into the hospital block.

I washed the corridor, the outpatient clinic and the latrines, and ran a bath for myself. I was horribly tired. Suddenly I remembered that I hadn't seen Edzio all day. Probably he could not get to the sick bay on account of this crowd. But perhaps? Surely not, though. I should have noticed him.

Before going to sleep I felt hungry. I finished the bowl of cold soup which had been meant for my mate.

CHAPTER 14

QUITE UNEXPECTEDLY Wolak went to Dachau with a transport of priests. I feared that at the last moment they might fetch him out of the transport. But nothing happened. This surely meant that our case had been forgotten. I was greatly relieved, for I had been constantly afraid that we might have to share the fate of those eleven who had been sent to Flossenburg. After Wolak's departure I was officially appointed medical orderly. Nevertheless my tasks were the same as before. But at least I no longer had to fear that at any moment I might be transferred into the camp; I felt more secure.

As for the boys from my hometown, I saw them only rarely. On the whole they seemed to manage somehow. Before the onset of winter each of them had succeeded in joining a reasonably good Kommando, at least one that worked under cover. Edzio Ferenc was the only one out of luck. Not only did he fall ill, but he was sent to the *Strafkommando* [penal company; abbreviated in German as SK], from where no transfer to the hospital block was permitted.

Djunio Beker had died a few days earlier. Towards the end he lost a lot of weight. He was plagued by severe diarrhea and had completely deteriorated into a Mussulman. The fate of a prisoner like that was sealed from the very beginning. No doubt he died on that evening I mentioned before, together with hundreds of prisoners like him.

The ninth of December was the name day of Wiesiek Piller and myself. Wiesiek worked as an assistant in the lab, and his two colleagues decided to celebrate the occasion. From somewhere they organized [camp euphemism for stealing or scrounging] some sugar, which they used to concoct strange mixtures in their test tubes. Thus we came to drink our first drop of alcohol produced in the camp, all in strict secrecy, of course. Their brew was disgusting, tepid but strong. In fact it was undrinkable until our pharmacist added a few drops of something or other. After some of this "booze" I seemed to be floating on air; it was most agreeable and life in the camp appeared to be less frightful.

Often I went to the mortuary for a little chat. Gienek Obojski from Warsaw had organized raw potatoes from somewhere. In the cellar there was a small coke-burning stove where we would fry potato pancakes. We used to sit on "coffins" round the hot stove, the pancakes sizzling, their delicious aroma tempting to the nose and palate and overpowering the revolting stench of chlorine with which the corpses had been sprinkled. We had become so accustomed to the presence of the corpses that they no longer had

43

any effect on us. I would play on the mouth organ and Ali would sing. The mood was jolly, not unlike a boy scouts' campfire. We need have no fear of discovery. Neither the SDGs [the abbreviation stands for *Sanitätsdienstgrade,* meaning higher-ranking nursing staff] nor the camp doctor ever came here; even Peter, the block senior, would not enter the mortuary. They all avoided the cellar. It was exclusively our place. Nothing threatened us here. Here we felt most at ease.

Gienek had been arrested by the Germans when he was a boy of eighteen while crossing the Hungarian border. He arrived in Auschwitz as early as June 14, 1940. Athletically built and exceptionally strong, he caught the attention of Palitzsch who turned him into a corpse bearer. Anyone watching him at work would find it scarcely credible that this boy, with his pink cheeks and the innocent gaze of his blue eyes, continued to be the epitome of all things gentle, kind and even naïve, or, to put it another way, the epitome of everything that was in direct contrast to the hateful occupation he had been ordered to carry out. There had been no time for him to get to know a normal life, and here he was made to experience a life of the very worst. And yet he remained true to himself.

Teofil Banasiuk was, strictly speaking, the opposite of Obojski. He was short and insignificant, but with the hidden strength of an ox and with small, darting eyes. A typical product of suburban Warsaw, he knew about life. Beneath the veneer of good humor, there lay a hard, ruthless and vengeful being. He openly hated the Germans and had sworn cruel revenge for Warsaw, for himself, for all those whom he had to carry into that mortuary with his own hands. He was determined to survive the camp at any price so that he might seek revenge. Teofil and Obojski complemented one another splendidly.

Obojski and I were friends. I got to know him more intimately during our joint expeditions to collect corpses, those corpses whose numbers increased alarmingly from day to day.

It was one of the tasks of corpse bearers to remove the dead bodies from the blocks before morning roll call. As they had a great deal of work, whereas I had not very much at all, the block senior appointed me their assistant. Both Obojski and Teofil re-

44

ciprocated by helping me cart the full soup buckets and other food from the kitchen. After a while we organized the work in such a way that we derived a certain amount of personal benefit from carrying corpses as well as food.

It was the duty of block seniors to report the actual number of persons in their block to the main orderly room each morning. The number of portions of food which would be issued to the block on that day depended upon the count. There was not a single block where not at least a few persons had died during the night. Consequently, if the corpse bearers had collected the dead bodies before roll call, the block senior was forced to report the actual number of persons, that is to say, minus those who had died and who were now on the mortuary register. For obvious reasons the block seniors preferred the corpses to be collected after roll call; in that case they could count them as alive in their returns and pocket their food rations. The block seniors were able to carry on these machinations until Obojski and Teofil noticed that on some blocks the number of corpses increased every night. Those block seniors murdered prisoners, not out of lust to kill, not out of sadism or perversion, but out of greed. After a time there was a serious quarrel between a block senior and the outraged Obojski. But up to that moment the blocks were ruled arbitrarily, and block seniors were masters over life and, particularly, death of any prisoner because, with the tacit approval of the camp authorities, a prisoner's death meant another small slice of bread for them.

CHAPTER 15

IT WAS still quite dark outside. There must have been a severe frost during the night, for the snow under our feet made a crunching noise. Obojski walked ahead while I brought up the rear. We were carrying a stretcher on which lay two dirty, rolled-up blankets. Above the dark silhouette of the theatre building countless stars glittered coldly. From somewhere in the distance beyond the frozen river Sola came the barking of dogs.

45

Miki's block was nearest to the sick bay; therefore we went there first. Since his hands were not free, Gienek opened the door with a kick. Clouds of steam came from the sparsely lit corridor. A warm, dank stench wafted around us. There was the clattering of hundreds of pairs of wooden clogs, groans, curses, an indescribable din, and above it all the strident voice of the block senior.

Dressed in the blue jacket of the camp élite, Miki Galas, a German criminal prisoner (Number 11), and one of the thirty villains Palitzsch had fetched from Sachsenhausen, was engaged in administering "punishment" to a prisoner. The prisoner, held fast by two sturdy orderlies, was lying across the stool. Onto his skinny backside fell blows which the block senior gauged with a practiced hand. With each blow the maltreated prisoner screamed more loudly: "It wasn't me. I didn't steal it."

Upon seeing us Miki interrupted the beating. The prisoner, taking advantage of this, freed himself from the grip of the orderlies. But Miki was faster. Grabbing him by the collar, he turned the man round to face him and struck him a tremendous blow with his left hand.

"I'll teach you to steal the bread of your mate, you fucking thief. That's the last bit of food you'll ever eat."

And in order to emphasize the last sentence he kicked the man, who was lying on the ground, in the stomach.

Then he turned to us, quite calm now, and said in his broken Polish, "Well, you two body snatchers," slapping Obojski on his broad shoulders at the same time. "Go and fetch those shits." He pointed into the washroom where the orderlies were hastily ripping the lice-infested clothes off the corpses. Noticing that some of the corpses had already been stripped, Gienek remarked to the orderlies: "Of course, no numbers taken down. Forgotten," he added sarcastically. Obojski knew the methods of certain orderlies. Sometimes they found a decent garment which later they would sell for food to ill-clad prisoners.

"The clerk has the numbers of the stiffs," the orderlies justified themselves in chorus.

Obojski went for a moment into the block senior's room, which was also the block orderly room. After a while he emerged holding a piece of paper with the numbers of the dead prisoners. Now, using a pencil, he began to write the numbers on the chests of the dead, one by one, reading out the numbers from his list. However, the indelible pencil would not write on the dry skin. Without hesitating, and in order not to lose any time, he spat, smeared the spittle with his finger and once more traced the figures with the indelible pencil. Okay! The four-figure numbers were clearly legible now. What did it matter that, when alive, the dead person had had a different number. The main thing was that names and numbers of the dead were struck from the register of the living and entered into the register of the dead. What happens afterwards is nobody's business. In the crematorium all the ashes will be mixed up anyway.

We loaded the corpses onto the stretcher, laying them side by side, head to foot, in order to distribute the weight. We covered the four bodies with blankets, buckled the straps which were fastened to the stretcher handles, threw them across the back of our necks where they rested comfortably and lifted the heavy load simultaneously. Obojski did this effortlessly. I, on the other hand, was not yet quite used to this work. My knees shook, and everything went black. It was worse on the stairs leading into the yard. At the door we were once more enveloped by steam and I felt for the stairs in the dark. Gienek urged me on; he carried the entire weight by himself because he was in front.

At last! Now we walked in step slowly, the stretcher creaking and rocking rhythmically. We took the shortest route back, across the yard between the SK block and our block, where the mortuary was. At the door leading to the cellar we met Ali and Teofil. They had managed to complete their first trip.

"Have you got anything?" Teos asked as he went past.

"Yes, there are four of them!" Not everybody was able to carry that many. Only when you worked with Gienek were such feats of strength possible.

"You stupid nit," Teofil cut me short. "When I'm with Gienek we can take six in one go. What I meant was, have you got any grub?"

"Two portions," Obojski replied and dragged me vehemently down the stairs.

Once in the cellar, we tipped our burden onto the concrete

floor. In the cold air the corpses had stiffened, so that it was difficult to pull the blanket out from under them. Gienek lifted the lid
of a coffin just a little and, taking from his jacket two portions of
bread, put them inside where there was already half a loaf and a
jar of jam, most probably the haul of Ali and Teofil. Quickly we
returned to Miki's block. We managed to get them all away before roll call. Our food store inside the coffin was growing steadily
more lavish.

"Well, my dear old friend," Theos expounded as we ran together to attend roll call, "like hyenas we feed on corpses. But at
least we fill our bellies before we go up the chimney. Isn't that
right, eh, Gienek? Up the chimney, anyway."

CHAPTER 16

ROLL CALL was over, and we were about to have our supper when
Bock's shrill voice shouted: "Obojski! Teofil!" The two corpse
bearers swallowed their last morsels of bread and rushed to the
door. We all knew well what this meant: if these two were summoned during camp roll call, it meant a liquidation. A short time
ago executions had started, during which Obojski and Teofil had
always been present. But today something more sinister was in the
offing. Bock ordered them to select a few helpers from among us.
Naturally I was included in this group.

Outside the block a Blockführer was waiting for us. We were
made to load coffins and stretchers onto a truck. Clinging to the
truck, we made our way to the camp gate, harried by the SS man,
the frightened looks of thousands of inquisitive and at the same
time fearful prisoners following us, while on the parade ground
roll call was continuing. As we were being counted by the guards,
roll call finished. Amid yells and blows everybody was hurried
into his block. Strict camp curfew was imposed. Directly opposite
the guardhouse, on the other side of the fence, there was a small
gravel pit from which sand and gravel were brought for the construction of new blocks in the camp. A few dozen SS men, hel-
meted, with ordered arms, were lined up in two rows on a piece of

flat ground. We had to stand aside by the embankment. When the truck had been unloaded we were ordered to turn our backs to the trench; it was easy to guess that the executions were about to begin. We stood opposite the two rows of SS men, from whom an officer selected three or four for the firing squad. Now we were facing the place of execution. The first doomed man arrived, his hands tied behind his back. He was being roughly pushed forward by a young SS man.

The prisoner was barefoot, dressed in a pair of torn trousers and a rag which at one time might have been his shirt. The SS man stood him facing the steep wall of the gravel pit and left. The firing squad lined up on the opposite side. To the left, on a small hill, stood a group of officers, one of whom began to read out the verdict, while a second, at the very moment the first one had finished reading, gave the command: "Fire!" The first volley resounded, echoing from the buildings around us. The prisoner keeled over into the sand. From the embankment small stones rolled down to the feet of the executed man, which were twitching convulsively. An SS man drew his pistol and gave him the coup de grace.

"Corpse bearer!" Gienek pulled me firmly along. We rushed into the pit carrying the stretcher. Urged on by the SS men, we placed the corpse on the stretcher and ran up the side of the pit as fast as our feet would carry us. On the way we passed the next victim who was being led to his doom. Before we had got rid of our burden, the next volley rang out. This time Teofil and another fellow prisoner ran down. Meanwhile the medical orderlies who had been standing idly next to the truck lifted the first corpse into one of the boxes. After the third volley it was our turn again to run down and fetch the dead body.

The dead man's entrails were pouring out. In great haste we gathered them up, warm and steaming as they were, with our hands. As we made our way to the top, blood streamed from the tilting stretcher. We worked without a break. Down and up, down and up, it is hard to say how many times. Only the firing squad took turns. Next! Another volley. Next, next, next. The shots echoed monotonously from the walls of the buildings close by. Fire! Next! Into the coffins. There was no room left, so we packed

49

two into one coffin. "Take this rubbish away!" one SS man shouted at us. "Come on, faster, you stupid bastards."

Our ears were ringing, our hearts beating wildly. The sickly, nauseating stench of blood made us retch. Our hands and feet refused to obey us, our bodies were almost collapsing with fatigue. How many more, for heaven's sake?

At last the shots ceased. Accompanied by the clicking of carbine bolts, we scrubbed the stretchers with sand. Traces of blood on the ground were covered with gravel. Meanwhile the others loaded the truck. Thin rivulets of blood dripped from the boards, spilling onto the platform, cascading over the wheels and splashing us before disappearing in the sand.

Now we were commanded to line up and to turn round. Once more the carbine bolts clicked. Holy Mother of God, this is the end. Someone next to me began to pray. Dear God, save me, I prayed. But instead of the shots we had expected we felt blows from rifle butts and the fists of the SS men.

"Be off! Get on with it!"

Obojski and Teofil sprang forward to take the shaft, while we braced ourselves hard against the sides of the truck. The wheels of the overloaded truck sank deep into the gravel. Accompanied by blows, shouts and yells, we started almost at a gallop. We reached the crematorium at the double. The unloading did not take long. It was getting dark when we returned to the camp. From the town, far away, floated the measured, melodious sounds of church bells: the Angelus.

That evening we had extra rations for having worked well.

CHAPTER 17

IN SPRING Himmler himself came to inspect the camp. The camp was sparkling. The Mussulmen were tucked away somewhere. Only well nourished prisoners in clean clothes were walking around the camp. Our sick bay began to look like a real hospital, at least outwardly. The sick, each in his own bed, on sheets, under clean blankets. Standing under the bed were bedpans, bottles and chamberpots. The diet kitchen supplied milk soups for people with stomach complaints, saltfree diets for kidney sufferers, white bread for patients on special diets. The corpse bearers had to keep their occupation secret.

Some slight benefit resulted from this visit by Himmler: a few of the sham improvements were continued. What did not change was the mortality among patients; on the contrary, it rose. Death spared no one, not even the hospital staff. Epidemics broke out. Among camp inmates the reputation of the sick bay deteriorated steadily. Unfortunately, this reputation was quite justified. The majority of patients in the hospital block never returned to the camp. Several times each day transports of corpses were delivered to the crematorium. What was the use of the most expert medical treatment available when there was nothing with which to treat the patients? We possessed a black ointment for the itch and painkillers galore, as well as *Tanalbin,* charcoal and *Bolus Alba.* But none of these things had ever cured anybody. There were a few who were discharged as cured, but they were really exceptions. It was therefore not surprising that the prisoners avoided the sick bay whenever they could.

One day fate would have it that Teofil could not be found at the very moment when he was wanted. The car was waiting, the SDG was agitated, and Bock appointed me instead of Teofil since he could see no other way out. After we had loaded the stretchers the SDG locked us in with them and sat next to the driver. We drove in the direction of the town, along the street which I remembered from the year before when I had been a joiner in the Salesians' workshop. We stopped for some time in the marketplace. Passersby gazed curiously at the ambulance because they could see prisoners inside it through the half-open door. I, on the other hand, was impressed by the traffic, by people walking about freely, by open shops with all sorts of goods and foodstuffs for sale. This was not surprising, since it was the first time in a whole year that I had a chance to get a glimpse of the free world.

The ambulance was parked outside a baker's shop with the delicious smell of freshly baked bread wafting towards us. This tempting aroma gave us no peace. Gienek invented a reason and asked the SDG for permission to step outside the ambulance. The SDG graciously assented and put the driver in charge of us, after which he departed. The driver, probably a Silesian, began to talk to us in Polish. A girl, hearing Polish being spoken, asked the SS man—pretending at the same time to be flirting with him—whether she might give us some bread. The driver, taken with the pretty girl, had no objections on the condition that she did it unobtrusively.

Thus it came about that after a short time we had a load of fresh bread, which we hid on the stretcher under the blanket used for covering corpses. After the return of the SDG we continued our journey, and on the way we ate the crusty new bread with relish.

We were driving along the large chemical works, the construction of which had begun a short time ago. Wherever one looked there were prisoners at work, mainly doing excavations. A tall Scharführer standing by the side of the road under construction stopped the ambulance. Peeping out from behind his back was armless Siegurd, the Head Kapo of this large Kommando. The SS man pointed at a meadow a few hundred yards away where a prisoner had been shot. We picked up our stretcher and walked together in the direction which had been pointed out to us. In the open meadow stood a solitary willow tree, hiding in its shade the corpse of the man who had been shot dead. Its leaves rustled gently, high in the sky the larks were singing and over the flower-strewn meadow butterflies were dancing; the fresh grass smelled good.

What a different world is this from that in which we are forced to live, I thought, and how beautiful it is.

It seemed that at that moment Gienek felt as I did, for he failed to hear when the SDG spoke to him, ordering him to turn over the corpse lying on the ground facedown. The inspection began. The SDG made a note, so did the Scharführer, and the SS man who had shot the prisoner dead signed the document. In conclusion of this official act, the Scharführer patted the SS man on the shoulder in appreciation of his first class marksmanship, and then he told us to load the corpse on the stretcher.

The prisoner had been shot through the back three times. There was very little blood, only the shirt tinted a delicate pink, and a line of congealed blood from the open mouth of the dead man. Gienek looked meaningfully at the man's unbuttoned fly. It was obvious that the prisoner had been shot while he was urinating. We knew what was written in the report: shot while trying to escape.

As we walked back, the dead man's legs dangling from the stretcher swung in time with our steps. The larks were still singing high in the sky. We arrived at the ambulance.

"Put the stretcher inside," the SDG snapped.

The ambulance door closed behind us with a bang. The engine started up. We sat next to the corpse, silent, each engrossed in his own thoughts. In my imagination I saw the meadow full of flowers. Nothing else, only this meadow, the butterflies, the larks, the flowers. There was no prisoner's corpse in it.

We were approaching the camp. Just before we reached the guards Gienek suddenly remembered the half-eaten bread under the corpse lying on the stretcher. His concern had been unnecessary; there was no search.

Gienek promised to take me along again when the opportunity should present itself. And I did not have to wait long. One day when it had been exceedingly hot, straight after evening roll call, we drove to the river Sola in order to retrieve the corpse of a prisoner who was supposed to have drowned while trying to escape. The fast flowing waters of the mountain river had flung him on some bushes growing by the water's edge, and he had got caught on a protruding tree stump. The corpse was in a state of complete decomposition. The terrible stench of the putrefied flesh and the clouds of flies nearly drove us crazy, despite the fact that we had ample experience with corpses. With difficulty we collected these human remains and loaded them into the ambulance. We stank so badly that, as an exception, the SDG allowed us to have a bath. What good was that, though? After the bath we had to put our clothes, saturated with the smell of decomposition, back on again, and then we still had to take the corpse to the crematorium in the closed ambulance.

This excursion hadn't been a very happy one. But then the previous one had been altogether delightful, hadn't it?

CHAPTER 18

IN THE summer the shootings of prisoners increased. For some unknown reason the camp administration no longer favored the ditches of the numerous gravel pits in the neighborhood of the camp. The volleys of the firing squad had made too much noise. Rapportführer Palitzsch, a zealous implementer of every cruel order of the SS, and always full of "good" ideas, produced a small-bore rifle from Katowice's slaughterhouse. After some slight adjustments, including the mounting of a silencer—which had been made in the camp locksmith's shop—this proved to be eminently suitable for killing thousands of prisoners in a noiseless production-line process. The person implementing the verdicts of the "court-martial" was, needless to say, the moving spirit of the project, Palitzsch himself.

Palitzsch delighted in frightening prisoners by strutting up and down outside the entrance of the yard of Block 11, where the executions took place, brandishing his carbine. Before each execution he fetched the corpse bearers from our block. Obojski and Teofil had to assist at every liquidation. The rest of the Kommando waited in the corridor of Block 11 until the executions were over. We were needed merely for loading the truck and for taking the corpses to the crematorium. Since liquidations occurred with increasing frequency, the corpse-bearer Kommando unit was enlarged and Teofil was appointed Kommando senior. My occasional help was no longer needed, at least not during liquidations. There was only one more occasion when I stood in for Teofil in his absence, on a beautiful July day.

I was standing at the window of my room, watching the SK at work. Their workplace was in the very gravel pit where, not so long ago, masses of prisoners had been shot. My window was an excellent observation post. While pretending to clean the windows I saw very well what was going on there. Two days earlier the penal company had been enlarged by several new arrivals from Czechoslovakia. They were all Jews. At the express command of the Lagerführer they were all to be finished off here. Both SS men

54

and Kapos applied themselves enthusiastically to the job in hand. Two days later there were only a few of the Slovak Jews left. One of these Jews, a man of athletic build and tremendously broad, was still holding out, although the SS and the Kapos had made him the main object of maltreatment. Working doggedly, he tried not to provide any cause for complaint. It was as if he still believed in what was written above the entrance to the camp, only a few steps from his work place: ARBEIT MACHT FREI [work will set you free].

Thus it was that he pushed heavy handcarts; the Kapos made sure they were piled high. He pushed them on the double, running a gauntlet of villains who beat him with sticks. Then he tipped the gravel where he had been told and returned the same way with his empty cart, constantly beaten, shoved and kicked. Each time he tried as fast as he could to get past the trap which had been prepared for him—a plank which had been laid across a deep pit. He knew that it was at this place that most of his fellow countrymen had been finished off. Anyone unable to keep his balance on the plank fell into the pit with his cart, and there was no way out from there. Once down in the pit, the cruelest among the Kapos beat their victim to death with sticks. But if there was one among them with enough strength to climb up the side of the pit in spite of the gravel which was constantly slipping away from under his feet, the SS man stationed at the top would fling him back into the pit with a well-aimed kick.

The athletic Jew was still on his feet, but he was growing visibly weaker, and one could feel that he was using his last reserves of strength. He must have realized that he was surrounded on all sides and that he could not get away. But he fought for his life to the very end. He tried to work, but his movements were growing slower, increasingly uncoordinated. Groping about like a blind man, he looked for the cart, which was lying upside down at his feet. It might well be that he really could not any longer see very well. As he turned round and round helplessly, his feet got caught in rough places, and whenever he fell the Kapos would fling themselves on their hapless victim like hungry wolves. At the spot where earlier there had been only one SS man there were now

55

several, even higher-ranking men among them. This was good fun. It was taking three days to bring one prisoner to his death. Either this was due to lack of competence on the part of the executioners, or this Jew was an exceptional case. At any rate it was worth watching.

The Jew had been lying in the pit for some time now, completely covered with dust, drenched in sweat, bleeding. When one of the SS men saw that he no longer gave any sign of life, he shouted in the direction of the gate: "Camp senior, forward!"

Bruno came running. With one expert glance he evaluated the situation and returned quickly to the gate. Gienek, who had been standing next to me for a while, grew agitated.

"I bet they'll call for me presently. As if there wasn't anyone else to do it," he said bitterly. "And Teos is fit for nothing. He's stoned again." Lately Teofil had been drinking rather heavily. He had found a source where he could quench his thirst. I had taken his place. The SDG came along with us.

When we got to the scene it turned out that we had been called too soon. The tortured Jew was still making a superhuman effort to fight against death. At that moment he was attempting to climb out of the pit; he tried and tried, but the sand slipped away from under his feet. Once more he fell to the bottom of the pit, only to succeed, after a while, with equal perseverance and stubbornness, to get almost to the top—in vain, for he slid back to where he had come from. The SS men were having a wonderful time.

We wanted to turn back, but Lagerführer Fritsch yelled at us, and we were rooted to the spot. The camp doctor, who was also present, was nonchalantly cleaning his spectacles with a handkerchief. Now Fritsch turned to a small group of spectators and said something in a raised voice. This seemed to concern the Kapos, for two of them—without waiting for him to finish—leapt into the pit. There was the dull thud of blows and the heartrending groans of the tortured man. The Jew dropped on his knees and doubled up in order to protect his head. However, in so doing, he unintentionally exposed his back to the blows. The Kapos knew where they must aim—at the kidneys. They were experts. Once more the tortured man rose; he gave one tremendous scream which stopped the Kapos in their tracks and then keeled over. It was the end. Suddenly one of the Kapos bent over him.

"Would you believe it, he's still alive," he said, turning to the spectators with undisguised surprise and as if to justify himself.

"What?" the Lagerführer screamed, positively foaming with rage. That was enough. The Kapo laid a stick across the powerful neck of the dying man; then he rocked on it for a while until something cracked. This time there was no doubt that it was the end.

We had a job getting the corpse out of the pit; the Kapos had to help us get to the top. There was barely room on the stretcher for the dead body. After consultation with the camp doctor the SDG dispatched us directly to the crematorium. While he accompanied us there he explained: "They're going to do a post mortem on this fat pig." We carried the body to the room where Georg Zemanek had been working for a short time. Georg was busy mounting a piece of human skin which was distinctly tattooed, a special commission from somebody in the SS. Our SDG was quite carried away. His artistic contemplation was interrupted by the arrival of the SS doctor who ordered him peremptorily to take us back to the camp at once.

In the gravel pit the penal company was working at a slowed-down pace. Apaprently the Kapos were tired from their three-day struggle. Besides, there was no one in front of whom they could show off. The spectators, who had seen enough, had drifted away. The last Slovak Jew had been dispatched to his reward and the task with which the Lagerführer had entrusted them duly completed. Meanwhile the "fat pig" was being cut up on the autopsy table of the crematorium.

CHAPTER 19

RECENTLY I had noticed that, whenever he returned from delivering corpses to the crematorium, Teofil was remarkably excited and exceptionally talkative. He would hold forth about the meaning of life in general, using the characteristic language of suburban Warsaw whence he came. If he could not raise much interest in his unappreciative audience, he would give a resigned wave of his hand and finish his speech with his favorite saying: "Up the chimney, come what may."

It was not hard to guess that he had been drinking, and I began to fancy a drop myself. Therefore I asked him whether I might not also use his source of supply. Teos winked knowingly, and that was it. I was to help him next day to take a full truck to the crematorium.

I had been inside the crematorium on several occasions, but I should never have thought that it would be there, of all places, that I was to find the opportunity of getting sloshed for the first time in my life.

Only the initiated were allowed access to Zemanek's workshop. This time there were four of us, with me the only newcomer. I vaguely remembered the room where Georg carried out autopsies from my previous visit. Now, while he concocted the brew, I was able to take a good look around. With its concrete floor and big metal-topped table, the little room looked rather like a butcher shop, except that it was not meat hanging from the hooks, but jars of assorted sizes, in which there were specimens of almost every conceivable human organ preserved in formalin. One glass vessel contained the specially prepared liver of the huge Jew. This liver was gigantic and completely black. That Jew, so Zemanek attested, had been one of the wealthiest Czech industrialists. In the last analysis he had been murdered because the SS doctor had earmarked his body for his research even while the Jew was still alive. He wanted to know what the liver of such a giant would look like after three days of constant beatings. In yet another container was the whole head of a prisoner whose skull was said to be of particular anthropological interest.

Lying on the table were several pieces of human skin with "interesting," many-colored, neatly executed tattoos. It was quite a collection which Zemanek had mounted for one of the VIPs in the SS. He also showed us a small tattoo which did not seem to be different from any of the others. It was not even very carefully done, but on the other hand, it was witty. A prisoner had this design tattooed on his penis, a part of the anatomy not normally exposed to public gaze. It consisted of a swastika and next to it a death's head, such as the SS wore on their caps. For this joke he had to pay with his life.

I remembered the owner of this tattoo. One day when he attended the outpatients' clinic, luck would have it that SS *Untersturmführer* [Second Lieutenant] Dr. Entress was admitting patients in person. While examining the patient who was standing naked in front of him, he apparently noticed the little tattoo without letting on that he had done so. He ordered the man to be admitted to the isolation ward where, with the assistance of an SDG, he died of heart failure in the "treatment room." Thus Zemanek was able to show us the formalin-preserved part of this joker's body which had been the cause of his death.

The impatient Teos glanced nervously at the door—at any moment someone uninvited might come in—and demanded something concrete. George flung the tattoo into a corner and poured him a glassful. Teofil emptied the glass without blinking. Gienek took a sip, no more, and left the rest for me. I sniffed at the liquid, and it nearly knocked me sideways. It stank of formalin, petrol and something else, but, at any rate, very little of alcohol. Teofil advised me to hold my nose if I couldn't get it down any other way. Even though I had to force myself, I drank the whole lot down because I was ashamed. After all, I had demanded to be taken to this drinking session. The revolting stuff burned like fire in my throat and stomach. With commendable foresight, Zemanek gave me very strong coffee and sugar as a chaser, which reduced the abominable burning, but then the petrol made me burp. As a practiced drinker, Teofil advised me to return to the camp as quickly as possible before the alcohol began to take effect. Even now I felt my legs go strangely numb. We clung to the empty truck instead of pushing it and stopped outside the guardhouse in order to report our return to camp. It was the duty of Teos, as Kapo of the corpse bearers, to make the report. As always, he mixed up his German words, but nobody minded, since all the SS men knew him and his occupation. They let us into the camp with a laugh. Before we reached our block I saw everything double. And then I was sick. God knows, I paid very dearly for this booze-up.

Marian Tolinski, our pharmacist, saved me with various remedies from his pharmacy. I revealed, out of gratitude, my source for the alcohol. A few days later we went there together. Thanks to Marian we managed to drink this mixture of Zemanek's. As we returned from the crematorium we were stopped by the guards, who told us to collect another batch of corpses from the gravel pit. This time it was a group of Soviet prisoners of war who had been taken to the camp straight from the battle area in the east and quickly killed. The Germans were victorious on all fronts, even here in Auschwitz. These "defeated" enemies of the Reich took us back to the crematorium, where we celebrated the "act of heroism" in our own way. What else was there for us to do? Up the chimney, come what may.

CHAPTER 20

ONE SUMMER'S day it was announced that all invalids in the camp were to assemble outside the block of the clothing depot. The same order was issued in the sick bay, except that the SS doctor had used his discretion to select a certain number of patients who were to be added to those selected from the camp. Rumor had it that they were to be taken to a hospital or sanatorium in Dresden where they would receive special nursing care. Among these lucky people were a few young men from Jaroslaw who had TB and who were looked after by Staszek Hedorowicz in his room. The boys were happy about this lucky chance, which enabled them to escape the harsh conditions of the camp.

And then it seemed that the fate of this "fortunate" transport was beginning to darken. Staszek, who sensed that danger was threatening his comrades, tried desperately to get them out of a potentially perilous situation, but in vain. It was impossible to remove anyone from the list. Towards evening some five hundred prisoners were loaded into a waiting train that took them into the interior of the Reich. Within the next few days our worst suspicions were confirmed. All the patients had been liquidated in Dresden, allegedly with poison gas. That they had perished emerged when their clothes were returned to the camp clothing depot. Furthermore, the camp office systematically removed them from the register of the living over the next few weeks.

The fact that the Germans dared to destroy five hundred lives, in one fell swoop and in so unconventional a manner, had a very depressing effect on the prisoners. From now on anything might happen.

Some weeks passed after these events. One day a few hundred newly arrived Soviet prisoners of war were herded together in Block 11. That same afternoon Dr. Entress appeared unexpectedly and, as he had done a few weeks earlier, went through all three sick bay blocks, carefully inspecting every room where patients were accommodated.

He ordered the seriously ill he had selected to be taken to the square outside Block 16, from where the nursing orderlies transferred them to the penal company whose inmates had previously been removed to another block. The majority of these patients were stretcher cases.

We returned to our various occupations.

After evening roll call, a new camp curfew was announced. Consequently there was no more work in the outpatients' clinic, and everybody went to bed earlier than usual. Before going to sleep there were noisy comments concerning the day's ominous events. It was said that the patients had been herded into the bunkers with the Soviet prisoners of war, where they had been locked up in inconceivably crowded conditions. General despondency spread among us.

That evening nobody felt like reminiscing about the pre-war years, as was the custom in our room. Next day no one could cling to his illusions any longer. Teofil and Gienek had reliable information: everybody had been gassed. Palitzsch had been seen in the camp, walking about with a gas mask dangling from his neck. Allegedly the previously sealed windows and the door to the bunker rooms were again open. They had to be aired before the corpse bearers began their work. And there was to be plenty of work—about a thousand corpses. The tragedy of Dresden was nothing compared to what the SS men had done in our camp, literally before our very eyes.

Next evening there was another camp curfew. We lay in our beds; as usual, someone was entertaining us with stories from his life. Suddenly the entrance door of the block banged, and we could hear the ominous tread of military boots.

"The fiend is coming," someone said with fear in his voice.

"All nursing orderlies line up! Quick!" Palitzsch's sharp voice echoed in the empty corridor.

We shot up quick as lightning. Flinging on our clothes, we rushed outside into the lit corridor. Peter, the hospital block senior, was already downstairs; quickly he lined us up in twos. I squeezed myself into the second row in order to be as unobtrusive as possible. But Palitzsch had no wish to pay attention to anyone in particular. There were more important matters to attend to, for he needed us this time. He issued brief orders to the block senior standing next to him, who in his turn called out to the corpse bearers: "Obojski, Teofil, pick your men for two trucks. To the SK, at once."

Outside Block 11 Palitzsch was waiting for us. It was getting dark.

CHAPTER 21

THE HEAVY wooden door to the yard of the penal company opened. We pushed the trucks into the yard and turned them round, facing the gate. Waiting in the yard was the entire SS retinue, with Lagerführer Fritsch and camp doctor Entress at the head. We stood expectantly while the SS men conferred for a time, after which they summoned Gienek and Teofil.

They were handed gas masks. Palitzsch and several Block-führers also put on their gas masks. Together they approached the entrance to the block cellars. They stayed down there for rather a long time. We waited in silence. Night fell. In the yard it was now quite dark. Only above the entrance to the bunker a naked bulb cast a feeble gleam of light over the group of SS men waiting by the steps.

Palitzsch was first to reappear, behind him the rest of the SS men. They had taken off their gas masks, which meant that the gas was already diffusing. After a while Obojski and Teofil returned as well.

Now we were divided into groups, each with its own special task. Some went down into the bunkers in order to fetch the corpses out of the cells, others carried them up the stairs where yet another group of nursing orderlies undressed them. The rest were ordered to haul the naked corpses a little farther into the yard, ready for loading onto the waiting trucks.

I managed to get into the first group because I wanted to be as far away as possible from the SS and, in particular, from Palitzsch, of whom I was very much afraid.

Downstairs it was stifling and reeked of dead bodies. All the cells were open, and in them we saw the corpses of the gassed, crowded together and standing up. It was a little less crowded where the sick had been. A few corpses lay in a heap directly behind the door. We began with them. It was difficult to pry apart the bodies that were clinging together. One by one we dragged them into the corridor, from where the others carried them up the stairs. The deeper we penetrated into the cells, the harder it became to fetch out the corpses. Pressed together in the small cells they stood, although they were dead, with the same countenance they had had, presumably, two days earlier. Their faces were blue, almost purplish. Wide open eyes threatened to pop out of their sockets; their tongues protruded between their open lips; their bared teeth gave an eerie appearance to their faces.

To begin with, two of us carried one corpse. As a result there was confusion on the narrow stairs, people getting in each other's way. We made only slow progress; we began to work singly. Instead of carrying the corpses, we each dragged them behind us by a hand or a foot. Now our work progressed much faster and more smoothly. The whole bunker was disinfected with chlorine, which made our labors easier still. True, the strong smell of chlorine made one's eyes smart, but at least it reduced the stench of the putrefying corpses. The greatest problem was getting the bodies up the stairs. Their heavy heads bumped against each step with a dull thud; their limp extremities caught on protruding steps and thresholds.

Upstairs, in the corridor next to the washroom, we flung the bodies on the floor; here other prisoners undressed them while we turned back to fetch another load. Before very long I discovered that the air up there was considerably better; moreover, the work of undressing seemed to be less arduous.

Therefore, having dragged out another corpse, I began to un-dress it. However, it turned out that taking garments off limp and distended bodies was not at all easier than transporting them; but at least there was a little more fresh air here, and it was somewhat cooler.

Out of pockets fell money, notes, letters, photographs, several bits and pieces, keepsakes and cigarettes; in other words, the sort of things one was allowed to keep in a prison camp. All these belongings now lay on the floor, mingled with excrement and wet chlorine, forming a veritable rubbish heap. From time to time, one of the SS men would rummage with his boot in this junk, which had been the prisoners' most cherished keepsakes, perhaps the only ones they had left.. Whenever an SS man discovered something valuable he would pick it up in mock-disgust, play about with it for a bit, and when he fancied himself unobserved, quickly slip it into his pocket. All we helped ourselves to were belts, which we needed for work and which, anyway, we had offi-cial permission to take.

The first platform loaded by members of Teofil's group left the yard. Now Gienek replenished his own team which, needless to say, included me. The naked corpses, once they had been dragged across the steps out into the yard, had to undergo a special treat-ment. Closely supervised by SS men, dentists peered into the mouth of every corpse. When they found gold crowns, gold teeth or other gold work, they pulled them out with forceps. It did not take long for a small wooden box to be filled, to the undisguised satisfaction of the SS men. Proudly they passed the box from hand to hand, appraising its weight and marveling that those "Asiatic savages"—as they called the murdered prisoners—had carried so much gold in their mouths during their lifetimes. Drunk and very pleased with themselves, they intensified their rummaging among the heaps of clothing and rags in search of watches, rings and gold chains. If they found any, they simply stole or—more rarely—flung them ostentatiously into the box.

One of the Blockführers was struggling with the hand of a huge prisoner in an attempt to remove a wide wedding ring from his finger. The German was so drunk that he could not manage it. He stood there, cursing obscenely and looking around helplessly. Suddenly he detected a shovel by the wall, which someone had apparently forgotten to take away. Here was the solution to his problem. With one blow he chopped all five fingers off the blue hand. The wedding ring rolled along the floor. With a coarse laugh he picked it up and dropped it virtuously into the box, not without first having kicked the hacked-off stumps in the direction of the heap of corpses. These mutilated fingers made a far more harrowing impression on me than dozens of dead bodies being loaded on platforms.

CHAPTER 22

WE KNEW that we should have to do it again. At night the same team was on the march to Block 11. Instructions were no longer necessary. Without being told we harnessed ourselves to the truck. Tonight the yard of the penal company was swallowed up in darkness earlier than usual; it was cloudy and a penetrating rain was coming down steadily. Dirt and chlorine combined to form a foaming slippery surface. The stench hung heavily in the air, permeated with the nauseating reek of putrefied bodies.

After their drunken revelry of the previous night, the Blockführers were in a foul mood, hustling us as if we were slacking off. Come on! Get a move on, faster, faster!

We tried to finish this revolting job as quickly as possible, but we were only half-way through. We worked nervously but faster and more deftly than before.

The corpses were already decomposed. We made our labors less objectionable by fastening leather straps round arms, legs or necks of the gassed so that we would not have to touch them; then we dragged the sticky and bloated corpses along the floor to the platform. There, using a well-tried technique, we flung them onto the truck. The truck was almost full, but we piled it still higher in order to take away as many corpses as possible at one time. Why go twice? Let's put on another few, one more. Already the pile was much too high. There was no question of carrying on.

"Obojski, have you done?" the SS man asked. "How many? Eighty! Oho, that's a good piece of work." He noted down the figure with satisfaction.

Off we went. We braced ourselves against the sides of the truck. The others fastened straps and chains and, in their turn, pushed with all their might.

"Heave ho," Gienek shouted, struggling with the shafts. Simultaneously the SS man opened the heavy gate. We had forgotten to cover the load with tarpaulins.

"Step, stop, take the tarpaulins, you idiots," the Scharführer yelled, livid with rage.

Quick as a flash Gienek threw a few tarpaulins over the bodies, but the covers were barely enough to hide the protruding limbs.

The truck creaked, and with a crunching sound the wheels slowly began to move, cutting deeply into the rain-softened gravel. Suddenly one wheel got stuck in the mud. A blow from the sharply moving shafts flung Obojski against the wall of the next block. The overloaded truck teetered dangerously to one side. Noticing this, a few of the orderlies managed to jump out of the way in time. With a loud crash, the truck overturned amid swearing and cursing and the moans of those who had been unable to save themselves and were now buried underneath. From the bloated, crushed bellies of the gassed corpses the gases began to escape, hissing loudly and intensifying the already intolerable stench.

Out of the confusion of bodies, intertwined arms and legs, there came a low groan. Somebody was right at the very bottom, buried under a thick layer of corpses. Quickly we began to remove the bodies in an attempt to get to the unfortunate man who was calling for help with a steadily weakening voice.

First we uncovered his head and face, which was terrified and distorted with pain.

"Malina, are you alive?" someone asked fatuously.

An SS man approached, his interest aroused. "What's going on here? One more for the crematorium?"

"Help! Save me!" the almost suffocated Malina implored.

All at once the SS man, arms akimbo, shrieked with laughter. This excessive merriment was in fact caused by a macabre sight: by pure accident the body of a huge prisoner was literally forcing Malina into the tangle of corpses, the muscular arm of the dead giant clutching the half-throttled man in a tight embrace and seeming to choke him. Someone laughed hysterically and we—we just stood there gaping instead of going to his aid. It was precisely this eerie spectacle which amused the SS man. Obojski was first to pull himself together.

"Have you all gone mad? Save him, for heaven's sake, can't you see he's suffocating?"

He leapt on top of the pile of corpses and began pulling at the dead man's fat legs so violently that the skin burst, exposing the purple rotting flesh.

Poor half-choked Malina was taken to the hospital with several broken ribs. This time we did not put all the corpses back onto the trucks, to avoid a repetition of the accident.

"How many, Obojski? Seventy. Very well, off you go." The SS man, having checked the number of bodies on the truck, ordered us to be off.

This time we proceeded without difficulty. Close behind Marian I pulled the truck, a strap across my shoulder. Past the gate Gienek turned the shaft to the right. We got into the camp street. It was still raining steadily. From his tower a curious watchman pointed his searchlight in our direction. The infuriated Scharführer darted up to the fence.

"Lights out, you idiot!"

67

That did it. The searchlight went out immediately. Once more it was dark all around us. We pulled in silence, the only sound coming from the wheels crunching on the gravel path of the sleeping camp.

At the Blockführers' office we went through the usual routine. The SS man on duty counted us rapidly but carefully. The Scharführer reported the number of corpses brought in. We were allowed to proceed.

The water gleamed on the rain-wet concrete at the entrance to the crematorium. Obediently we stopped outside the open door. Gienek vigorously removed the wet tarpaulin from the load of bodies because here there was no longer any need to conceal them. With a practiced hand I threw the loop of a strap round a head which was protruding from among the corpses. The others did the same. Now we all pulled in a joint effort. A few lying right on top came sliding down first. The huge, well-built bodies of the Russians hit the hard concrete, their shaven skulls seeming to burst from the force of the impact. Only the lightweight, emaciated skeletons of sick prisoners who had been gassed caused no difficulties. As we had done in the bunker, we tied straps round one of their extremities and pulled the bodies inside the crematorium. The SS man was driving us on nervously.

"Quick, quick, quick!" He glanced with a worried expression towards the building of the SS sick bay which was situated in close proximity to the crematorium.

We needed no goading, for this was the last transport. In double time we dragged the bodies by their straps, first across a large hall, then to the right past the room where autopsies were conducted; past a recess with urns stacked in corners and, at the end, a long room already almost half-full with corpses. A second door led into the room where the ovens were. Prisoners stripped to the waist were running everywhere. The small crematorium could no longer handle the incineration of so many corpses. For this reason each oven was loaded with two bodies at the same time. Our work was finished, but for the crematorium workers there was strenuous labor for days to come.

One of the prisoners who worked in the crematorium was

Mietek, a boy from Cracov and an old prisoner. He looked indifferent. He said something we could not understand. But then there really was nothing to talk about. At that moment we felt exactly as he did. Indifferent, without feelings, unutterably tired and thinking only of the moment when "this" would at long last come to an end. Automatically, and almost collapsing with fatigue, we pushed the empty truck back into the camp. We were saturated with the revolting stench of corpses. The SS man on guard duty turned away with revulsion, covering his nose with a handkerchief.

"Go away, you stinking skunks! Be off with you!"

The block senior had kept our supper for us. Today there were extra rations again.

The mere thought of food made me want to throw up. Let's get to the washroom, quick. A bath. Hot water. I longed to scrub away all traces of these terrible nights.

The dirt came off in the hot water, but the traces remained. Marian's hair turned quite white. Despite our tiredness, nobody could go to sleep except for Teos. He must be dreaming, for he was flinging himself about restlessly, muttering, "Up the chimney, come what may," every few minutes.

CHAPTER 23

FROM THE beginning of autumn conditions in the camp grew steadily worse and with them the prisoners' mood. An increasing number of liquidations; roll calls that went on forever; hard labor in connection with the constant extensions of the camp, always to be carried out on the double; beatings; harassments; dirt, scabies, fleas and armies of lice, which created huge epidemics; hunger and diarrhea also took its toll among prisoners who were still alive; as well as the introduction of a new method to get rid of the very ill through injections of petrol or phenol—all this created an atmosphere of general depression, a feeling of despair. We realized we were in a hopeless situation from which there was only one way to freedom, and that was, according to the generally quoted words of Lagerführer Fritsch, up the chimney of the crematorium.

Up the chimney, come what may, the only German phrase Teos knew, became for camp inmates synonymous with freedom.

People in the camp lived from day to day, their only concern to stay alive till the next day. But in order to live through this day one needed a great deal of toughness, courage and luck. Anyone who collapsed physically would die quickly or else he would be finished off within a few days by Kapos, block seniors and SS men, all of whom were experts in their trade. The ones who stayed alive were, as a rule, young people, but there were also some older prisoners who had gotten used to camp conditions, who knew camp life and thus managed as best they could. It was worst for new arrivals who had no idea at all as to what a concentration camp was like. The more fortunate among them were those who, in this alien atmosphere, met friends, relations or acquaintances who looked after them during those first and worst days until they had become "independent" and grasped the rules of the difficult art of staying alive in the camp. And it really was an art, unless one was exceptionally lucky.

Those who were best off were the people who had no scruples at all. They advanced rapidly. They came to power, not squeamish about the means they chose, at the cost of human suffering and even of human life. The important thing was that, in this way, one made sure of one's own position, one filled one's stomach with the stolen rations of one's hungry fellows. Completely corrupted by the example of German criminals and ruthless SS men, these men, through their own bloodthirsty instincts, came to be criminals themselves.

Mercifully, there was only a handful of these depraved prisoners. There were also others who, although initially cruel and ruthless, changed in time, under the influence of a sudden pang of conscience.

Many were so desperate about the hopelessness of their position that they put an end to their own suffering. They ran into the electrified barbed-wire fence or hanged themselves with their own belts. A few prisoners attempted to escape, but this was doomed from the start to failure. They died of starvation in the bunker, but before they did, they jeopardized the lives of fellow prisoners from their Kommando or block, who were put to death by the dozen. But even in these circumstances there would, occasionally, be a prisoner who possessed the strength to sacrifice his own life for humanitarian reasons in order to save someone with a large family and children from death.

I often thanked God that I was one of a small group whom fate had spared. I worked under one roof, felt neither hunger nor cold and was not tempted to harm others, a temptation to which any prisoner fighting for his life in the camp was invariably exposed. When I sent my periodic letter home, I was always able to add to the stereotyped sentence "I am in good health and feeling well," the words "and I hold my head up high."

CHAPTER 24

IT WAS unusually cold for early October, and it was raining. Typically rotten autumn weather—rain and snow. Camp senior Bock had detailed me to the "disinfecting team." Beyond the last buildings, in a large meadow which had been fenced in temporarily with watch towers rising at each corner, stood prisoners of war crowded together. They had been hustled to this spot a short while ago.

A large number of SS men, Kapos and block seniors were bustling about among this crowd, lining them up in rows of five with the help of blows from sticks and rifle butts.

To begin with the Russians were ordered to undress. In silent obedience they took off their soaking wet drill suits and threw them into a large heap, which grew before our eyes. They retained only the tin plate bearing their number, which hung down from their chests. They were hungry, emaciated, frozen and incredibly filthy. One by one, their heads shaved by the camp barbers, they approached a vat which had been sunk into the ground. This vat

71

contained water in which some disinfectant had been dissolved. The prisoners, naked and shivering, now had to endure this compulsory bath.

Everyone had to immerse himself in this old, smelly liquid, which in time came to be as thick as a mudpack. Anyone who recoiled was made to suffer worse than the rest. The SDG in attendance and an SS man who assisted him watched carefully to see that "disinfection" took place according to regulations. With his boot he held the prisoner's head under water until there was a gurgling sound from inside the vat and air bubbles rose to the surface. After such a procedure the prisoner, frightened and choking, would jump out of the vat, always assuming that he was still strong enough to do so. There were some who were so weak that they had to be pulled out. When they had run a few paces—almost blinded because their eyes were gummed up with the dirty and stinging disinfectant—they were stopped again and had to undergo yet another ordeal, this one, too, a disinfection, as if they had not already had a bath in lysol.

"Hands up!"

They stopped, bewildered, and obediently raised their arms. I brandished a small atomizer filled with another disinfectant called *Cuprex* in order to moisten their freshly shaved armpits.

"Bend down!"

They did not understand. "Ass up," said Antek, showing off his knowledge of the Russian language. The prisoner eagerly extended his scrawny rear, and I squirted him vigorously until the next one came along. However, this kind of purposeful squirting took too much time and caused a congestion; the SS men hurried us along. Consequently we discarded our posh atomizers, and we wiped armpits and the area between the legs with a rag moistened with Cuprex. Now we made great progress, but the whole exercise failed in its objective. Instead of disinfecting, all we did was to spread the vermin which had escaped death in the quick dip in lysol. But the SS men were pleased, for speed was of the essence.

"That's the way to do it," the SDG said contentedly, hitting an already "disinfected" prisoner with his stick, under the pretext of wanting to make room for the next man. Those who had been "deloused" were lined up in rows of five, accompanied by yelling, cursing, shouting and constant ill-treatment at the least excuse. Now the SS were no longer in a hurry. They waited until they had collected a group of a hundred, and only then did they take them, at the double, into our camp, which was a few minutes away.

The prisoners of war ran naked, their bare feet making a splashing sound in the dirty puddles, which, here and there, were covered with the steadily falling snow. And still more people were arriving all the time to be disinfected. The hours passed slowly. A strong wind brought whole clouds of rain mingled with snow. I was soaked to the skin, the sticky, wet cold penetrated to the very marrow; I began to have shivering fits. The naked prisoners huddled close together in an attempt to keep their frozen bodies warm. They trembled with cold and uttered inarticulate noises in unison which sounded like a single dismal groan.

"Shut up! Bloody Bolsheviks! Shut up!" the Germans shouted, but without success. The Russians, exhausted and frozen, no longer took any notice. Neither blows nor curses had any effect. This spontaneous groan escaped from their throats quite unconsciously. It was expressing lament, pain, helplessness.

Towards morning the last group of a hundred naked prisoners left the fenced spot. The stronger ones were carrying their totally exhausted comrades on their shoulders. The ground, covered with snowflakes, was wet, trampled by thousands of feet. Piles of prisoners' clothing were lying about: boots, metal bowls, leftovers of more than ten thousand people who had been driven into the camp.

We reported our return to the guard, utterly exhausted from the work which had lasted throughout the night. I was afraid of being searched because I had found a small piece of perfumed soap, which I had hidden on myself. No need, though, for nobody was interested in me. The SS men were busy with the prisoners of war, preoccupied with a fraction of the vanquished army, in front of whose survivors they swaggered with their superiority, and whom they maltreated in a sophisticated way, in a way worthy of the knights with the SS insignia, who were bravely fighting in a dangerous sector of the front, the newly set-up, so-called prisoner-of-war labor camp.

Within the next few weeks these "brave" SS men achieved such outstanding "success" with the Soviet prisoners of war that they could no longer cope with the incinerating of corpses in the crematorium and, for that reason, were forced to bury thousands of dead bodies in long ditches by the forest of Birkenau, where presently the construction of a new camp was started.

CHAPTER 25

THE PRISONER-OF-WAR camp came into being in a specially segregated part of our camp. Several blocks had simply been partitioned off by barbed-wire fencing, after which thousands of prisoners of war were forcibly herded into this enclosure. The most zealous Blockführers and block seniors were employed in an endeavor to introduce "exemplary" order. These "experts" set to work with a will. The corpse bearers could no longer keep up with the removal of the dead. As a result, gigantic heaps of corpses began to pile up in front of each block, illustrating the frightful mortality rate among the prisoners of war.

It seemed like bitter irony when the camp authorities began to build a hospital there. In charge was block senior Peter, who thus became camp senior of the prisoner-of-war camp's hospital. Peter seemed to be pleased with this promotion and strutted about in the block wearing his new armband. The intention was that he would be finally transferred to the prisoner-of-war camp together with the orderlies he had selected.

The aroma of fried potato pancakes tempted me into the diet kitchen, which would occasionally prepare this delicacy for the sick bay élite. When I saw the block senior in the kitchen, for whom the pancakes were apparently being cooked, I tried to retreat.

"Wait a minute." Peter held me back with a peremptory movement of his free hand. For in the other he held a crisply fried potato pancake, dripping with fat and done to a turn. He pointed at a plateful of potato pancakes on the table and commanded: "Take those to Jurek. He is ill in bed in my room. Understand?"

What was I do do? Since I did not wish to get on Peter's bad side, I picked up the plate of potato pancakes and went to take them to Peter's favorite. That's not for you I told myself, full of envy.

Why the devil did I have to go to the kitchen, I thought, gnashing my teeth as I walked up the stairs. Because of my gluttony I now had to wait on "Little Miss Arse," as Dr. Dehring had once called Jurek, unkindly but aptly. One might excuse Peter's weakness for Jurek. Basically Peter wasn't a bad fellow, but what about Jurek? Still on the stairs, shortly before I got to the block senior's room, I quickly managed to gulp down two crisp potato pancakes.

Poor Jurek is ill, therefore he doesn't need to eat a lot. Let's hope Peter didn't count how many there were on the plate.

I found the door locked. I knocked. Silence.

"Peter's asked me to bring you something to eat," I shouted, hastily swallowing the last mouthful. The bed creaked, slippers slopped, the key was turned in the lock. Over his naked body Jurek had thrown a multi-colored dressing gown, under which one could see slim, hairless legs and a pair of silk panties. With small steps he walked back to the only bed in the room.

"Oh, I don't feel at all well." He coughed delicately and put his hand to his hollow chest. He was supposed to be consumptive, at least that was what Peter suggested. Everybody knew that not long ago he had undergone a minor surgical operation, really more in connection with his extraordinary relationship with Peter than with his lung trouble.

When he had got back into bed, he tore off a small piece of potato pancake with his thin delicate fingers. He seemed bored.

"Help yourself, Wiesiu," he invited, pushing the plate towards me. "I'm sure you must be hungry. I've no appetite at all," he complained.

His well-shaped head, wearing some colorful turban-like headgear, dropped heavily back onto the soft pillow. He had a pretty, almost girlish, face with large blue eyes fringed with long, thick lashes, and peach-skinned cheeks. Now he grimaced like a petulant child.

"Did you know, Peter wants me to be block senior at his Rus-

75

sian camp? I've heard it's simply dreadful there. But I suppose I'll say yes. I'm fed up with the tactless remarks by some of these doctors. And as for this stuck-up Dr. Dehring, this horse doctor, he's too cheeky."

I picked up the plate and wandered to the door.

"Are you going already?" With feigned tones of regret Jurek bid me farewell.

Elite, bloody hell! You tart, you dirty bugger! I raged silently without, however, forgetting to close the door quietly behind me. As I walked towards the stairs I remembered my friend Wiesiek asking Dr. Jakubski one day: "How about homosexuality, doctor? Is it as good as with a woman?"

"Why do you ask me silly questions like that?" The doctor was indignant. "How am I to know? Why don't you ask you know who?"

We fell about laughing. No reason why we shouldn't; after all, there were no such boys on our block. But Wiesiek persisted. He asked again: "No kidding, doctor. There's been a lot of talk about these things lately. I've become interested from a scientific point of view," he added when he noticed discreet smiles on several faces.

"Of course," someone interjected facetiously, "one of the block seniors fancies Wiesiek."

There was general mirth.

"Well, a joke's a joke, but already the ancient Greeks . . ." Dr. Jakubski launched into a scientific lecture. It would seem that there were solutions for even this sort of problem.

CHAPTER 26

NEW TRANSPORTS of prisoners were constantly arriving. This led to a deterioration in the already disastrous conditions in the camp. Murder, starvation, sickness and epidemics played havoc among the utterly exhausted prisoners of war. Any that were considered fit for work were made to do heavy manual labor in connection with the building of the new camp in Birkenau. I found out what went on there before very long, when Gienek and I had to go to Birkenau to collect the corpses of men shot while trying to escape. It was the first day of frost, but here, in this marshy and swampy terrain, the ground was not yet frozen. In the wide, flat desert landscape one could already discern the outlines of the prospective giant camp, which disappeared far beyond the dark line of the forest in the early morning mist.

In order to get to the place where we were to collect two prisoners who had been shot while escaping, we had to walk along a road sticky with clay, which clung to our boots and made walking arduous. The bodies lay near a semi-derelict house, which formed an island surrounded by marshland.

The prisoners, who had been shot from behind, lay facedown on the ground. Their feet were bare; someone had taken off their boots. Their drawn-up legs and their arms, flung wide apart, had been stiffened by the frost. The laden stretcher hindered our progress across the marsh, which was covered with a light crust of ice. With difficulty we reached the ambulance. As far as the eye could see prisoners were at work everywhere, covered in mud, beaten and maltreated for trivial reasons. Dozens of dead and dying men were placed in a certain spot, from where they were loaded onto trucks and returned together with their Kommandos into camp for roll call.

The corpse bearers were run off their feet. First it had been the prisoners, now liquidations. No sooner had one pile of dead bodies been removed than there was a fresh harvest to be gathered in the hospital or in the blocks. The mortuary was packed with corpses. It was during this time that Dr. Entress carried out selections from among the seriously ill. Consequently we would rush to Block 15, where Panszczyk was on duty injecting the patients selected by the camp doctor with phenol. And when we had just finished our work there, a call would come from the treatment room opposite the outpatients' department of my block for us to remove yet more dead bodies.

To make things worse, there was a frightening increase in the lice and flea population in the camp and, in consequence, an

77

explosive spread of typhus throughout the camp. One of the means—the only one at the time, to be precise—with which the epidemic was to be halted, was an order issued by Lagerführer Aumeier to the hospital staff to carry out what was referred to as louse checks in all blocks, one by one.

These checks were among the most diabolical harassments to which the prisoners were subjected by the camp authorities. Unless it rained, louse check would take place in the yard, regardless of the season. The prisoners, naked to the waist, would take down their trousers. We searched their underwear, where there would invariably be an infestation of lice. We dusted their armpits and the areas between their legs with Cuprex. The dirtiest and most lice-infested prisoners had their numbers taken and were made to have cold baths by their block seniors, while their underwear and clothes were being disinfected. As a rule, prisoners objected to this delousing campaign because during it block seniors maltreated them; moreover, the bath in cold water and the waiting—everybody was naked—for fresh clothing would often take hours and be unpleasant, especially if it took place in winter. True, there were no lice in the clean underwear, but whole colonies of nits were not destroyed by the disinfecting process and from them quantities of hungry lice would emerge a few hours later.

It was, needless to say, the Mussulmen who were most severely lice-infested. The lice were literally eating them alive. And if one of them had ulcers or sores dressed with a paper bandage, one might truthfully say it was not he who had lice, rather the lice had him. On one occasion I forcibly removed one of these stinking, pus-soaked bandages. Under the paper seethed thousands of lice, like a single, gray, moving mass, which had penetrated deep into the wound and eaten away the flesh almost to the bone. One of the doctors gave this Mussulman a note to take to the outpatients' clinic. I was convinced that he would never have reported of his own free will because he was afraid of being put to death after selection by an SS doctor.

It is not surprising that under these circumstances prisoners did not exactly welcome these louse checks and viewed us, the orderlies who had to carry them out, with dislike. We in our turn did this work without conviction but with revulsion, above all because we believed our efforts were ineffective. Moreover, we ran the risk ourselves of catching the typhoid lice, which we had so far managed to avoid. Our lice, which we had, as it were, bred ourselves, were harmless because they did not carry the typhoid infection. All the same, after each louse check we immediately changed our underwear and clothing, "deloused" ourselves carefully and took hot showers in our bathroom. Thanks to these precautions we succeeded in avoiding typhus.

I had another adventure while taking a shower after an ordinary delousing. Standing under a stream of splashing hot water, I heard the sound of a deep voice which I did not recognize. I could not catch the words, but I guessed that the conversation was about me. Curious, I turned to the door from where the voice came. Standing in the door was a short Kapo, who was notorious throughout the camp for his cruelty as well as for his predilection for young men. Pointing at me, he remarked to Bock, who was standing next to him: "Man, what a big ape!"

The two of them laughed and went away, arm in arm.

"Did you hear what he said?" a fellow prisoner, who watched the scene, inquired. "He said you were an ape, a big ape. You didn't please him, and yet you were so close to making your fortune," he added facetiously. "He comes here quite often, looking at whoever is taking a shower," he went on more seriously. "He's looking for someone new because somebody has enticed away his last boy."

I remembered Wiesiek's interest "for these things from a scientific point of view." Perhaps he had already received an offer and was looking for a way out.

CHAPTER 27

IN THE spring transports of Jews began to arrive, always at night, who were directed not into the camp but into a farmhouse situated in Birkenau woods. The house was arranged in such a way

79

that a very large number of people could be killed at any one time (after they had been taken there via a branch line from the Auschwitz station). Once a transport had been gassed in the gas chamber of this seemingly innocent farmhouse. A small group of young and strong Jews, some twenty who had been allowed to stay alive, were forced to remove the corpses of their fellows from the gas chamber and bury them in pits in a meadow close to the house. After all traces of the crime were erased, the young Jews were taken to the hospital and lined up outside the outpatients' department. This invariably took place in the late evening, after the lights-out gong had sounded, when there was no one about in the camp. In the outpatients' department, the light was still on although all the staff had gone, for I was still there tidying the place up. Bock and Stessel seemed deep in conversation. The Jews were told that after their exhausting work they were to be given pep-up injections. They were inside the hospital; why should their suspicions have been aroused?

Klehr, wearing a doctor's white coat, saw them one after the other in his "consulting room," carefully closing the door once the patient had stepped inside. After each treatment, which took a surprisingly short time, he looked out into the corridor and called in the next. At the same time, Obojski and Teofil walked into the room, placed the "sleeping" patient on a stretcher, covered him with a blanket and carried him inside the block. Unsuspecting patients entered the consulting room, until the last one had gone in. When it was all over, I scrubbed the floor.

CHAPTER 28

ALMOST HALF of the hospital's inpatients were transferred to the so-called convalescent block in Birkenau. The selection was carried out by Entress in person, accompanied by Klehr. The patients were not gassed, but their fate was sealed all the same. In the course of the next few days almost all of them died because they had been left entirely to their own devices, without nursing care or medical supervision, under appalling conditions, in the half-completed camp. Their corpses were cremated in our crematorium, four bodies being loaded in one oven at a time in order to catch up on the backlog. The cremation process, too, was shortened; this meant that the bodies did not completely disintegrate. Any bones that were not cremated were pulverized by means of a wooden stamper. And if the family of someone who had died asked for the ashes, some of the ashes were passed through a sieve, during which process the ashes of all the dead were mingled before they were put into urns. Thus, not only did the families not receive the ashes of their relative who had been put to death in the camp, but, to add insult to injury, they also had to pay through the nose for having the urn sent to them.

After the temporary fence separating the prisoner-of-war camp from our own camp had been demolished, a high concrete wall was erected, partitioning off one-third of the whole camp. Rumor had it that this partitioned-off section was to house female prisoners. Women in a men's camp! It was simply unbelievable. People began to make jokes, particularly concerning the subject of catamites, or *Pipels,* as they were called in the camp, who would presumably now fall into disfavor. It may seem strange but it was the German criminals of all people, those who, up until then had been known as "camp queers," who now displayed the greatest interest in the topic of women. Notwithstanding their Pipels, the camp élite and even the younger members of the hospital staff— excepting the majority of emaciated camp inmates who were not interested in this subject—were keenly looking forward to the arrival of women, even if they were only fellow prisoners.

It was unusually warm for March. I took advantage of the balmy weather and began cleaning the windows of my room. There was already a whiff of spring in the air, which once more raised our hopes of freedom. "Wait till spring comes" was the motto of every prisoner. All the signs in the sky and on the ground pointed to the longed-for spring. The sun's rays were warming, and a warm wind gently stirred the branches of the nearby poplar trees with their swelling buds; above them in the air hung an invisible lark singing merrily. Spring.

The excited voice of Zygmunt, one of the lab assistants, woke me from my reveries.

"Wiesiek, come quickly. Women! At the clothing depot."

He was gone before I had even set eyes on him. I ran after him. Standing outside the clothing depot was a group of people wearing civilian clothes, men and—for the first time in our camp—women. It was true, then, that there was to be a women's camp. Now they would be put into dresses, striped like our clothing, and then taken into the special section of the camp.

We watched them from afar, not daring to go closer, when we saw the Blockführers chasing away the more daring prisoners. Bock appeared at the door of Block 21 and drove curious nursing orderlies, who were hanging around by the steps of the hospital and near the clothing depot, back to work.

An SS man noticed Bock and beckoned him. It turned out that one of the women was not feeling well; permission was granted for her to be given something to drink. Obojski and the lab assistant ran to the hospital kitchen and returned after a time with a jug of peppermint tea. The women drank first. A pretty young girl took the full jug from Gienek and passed it round. She used the inattention of the SS men in order to exchange a few sentences with him and give him a nice smile. He was the first in the camp who managed, in the presence of SS men, to make contact with a woman. From time to time he cast triumphant glances in our direction which seemed to say: how about this then, you silly boys.

At last one of the SS men, noticing that Obojski was taking liberties by talking quite casually to the new arrival, shooed him away.

"Obojski, go away, go away," he repeated when he saw that the prisoner hesitated, unable to keep his eyes off the frightened girl.

In the block we crowded round Gienek. He was beaming happily. His cheeks were flushed and his friendly blue eyes shone.

"Did you see that?" he said emphatically. "I talked to her. She is beautiful, isn't she? They brought her by car from the prison in Myslowitz. She is seventeen. The youngest of them all. They are scared, so I reassured her. But did you see how she smiled at me?"

The new arrivals stood outside the clothing depot for a long time. I returned to my work. It was wiser to finish cleaning my windows, otherwise I might get into trouble with that louse Fred.

Despite all predictions the new arrivals were not admitted to the clothing depot but taken to the bunkers of Block 11. Lager-führer Aumeier, Rapportführer Palitzsch and Lachmann of the Political Department had been seen going there. It seemed that there was to be a liquidation.

And before long our suspicions were confirmed. There it was, the shout: "Obojski! Teofil!"

There was no longer any doubt.

"Dammit, where's that Gienek?" Teos was getting all worked up.

Meanwhile Gienek had crept into a corner and was busy packing a small parcel which he intended to smuggle into the bunker. "For the pretty girl, I expect her at a side entrance in the cellar." They returned an hour before roll call began. Silently they carried the empty stretchers. Teofil went in front, behind him, white as a sheet, his jaws firmly clenched, Obojski. I opened the door to the mortuary for them.

"Do you know what this lunatic wanted to do?" Teos began wearily and sat down heavily on the nearest box. "You imbecile! They would have finished us off as they did the others. Fallen in love he has, or the devil knows what . . ." Teofil wanted to add something else but broke off in mid-sentence when he saw Obojski's face change color.

"Shut up, you swine," hissed Gienek with clenched fists. For the first time I saw his usually gentle face distorted with rage.

"Forgive me, Gienek," Teofil corrected himself quickly. He rushed over to Obojski and put his arm round Gienek's broad shoulders, which were shaking with sobs. He wept and impotently hit the damp wall of the mortuary with his fists—a big child that had been badly hurt. "They ordered them to take all their clothes off. It was the first time I had seen a naked woman. And it was she of all people that I had to see, under these circumstances. The older ones taunted her before they shot her. They saved her for the last. With the barrel of his rifle he pushed back her hair, her long hair." Obojski could no longer control himself. He whimpered, dug his nails into the wall, writhed convulsively and almost choked with the tears which kept streaming down his cheeks. At last he began to speak again, incoherently, the words sticking in his throat.

"If she saw me there—she crossed herself before he fired—with his boot he turned her over—and then I wanted—then Teos—I'll be even with them!" he concluded passionately. Then he suddenly clutched his belly. And then he vomited.

After roll call camp senior Bock handed Teofil a loaf of bread and a cube of margarine—extra food for the two corpse bearers for "good work," from Rapportführer Palitzsch in person.

"Where is the other one?" asked Bock, looking round for Obojski.

"Bad, not good, the young lady," Teos replied in broken German with a deprecating movement of his hand. Bock seemed to understand him, for he nodded sadly, turned abruptly and walked away silently.

Since that time Gienek was changed. There was no longer that naïve expression in his gaze; the childlike smile had vanished from his face which now was full of bitterness. He became hard. Outwardly he began to be like Teofil: he was growing indifferent.

CHAPTER 29

THE OTHER women were not taken to the separate part of our camp until a few days later. After evening roll call a strict curfew was imposed. In order to be able to see at least something, we climbed up into the loft, where from a small window we had watched liquidations in Block 11, or, more precisely, in the yard of Block 11. The women marched in a body, dozens, hundreds of them. By the time they had all disappeared in their camp behind the fence, it was quite dark. The medical orderlies from Blocks 20 and 21 were luckier because certain windows of their blocks looked out onto the women's camp. In fact, they quickly made contact with the women on the other side of the fence with the use of sign language.

It was known that the female prisoners came from the concentration camp of Ravensbrück and that among the few thousand who had come here there were mainly Polish women as well as a few *Funktionsdeutsche* [or *Funktionshäftling:* German prisoners employed by the SS as trusties] who were criminals. Another transport arrived that same night. This time the arrivals were Slovak Jewesses. Day in, day out, new transports came, mostly Jewish women from Slovakia, so that in less than a week every block of the women's camp was occupied by female prisoners. They stayed completely isolated; they were not employed for work outside their camp, and their food was supplied by our "men's kitchen." The food was taken no farther than the gate of the enclosure, from where the women fetched it without having any contact with the men.

These were the beginnings. The regulations were strictly observed under threat of beatings or even confinement in the bunker. However, such a state of affairs could not last. First contacts of a closer nature were established by the main office and, of course, also by the sick bay, since on the other side of the fence a hospital was then only in the process of being built. Gradually even the fence no longer presented a major obstacle. Anyone who could established forbidden contact from the windows of his block if they looked out onto the women's side. Later the first letters began to find their way over the fence and later still parcels containing food or other presents. Sometimes the male prisoners would find, on the other side of the fence, their wives, mothers, sisters or sweethearts. The women gratefully accepted the men's help, which was motivated mostly by compassion and an understanding of their sufferings.

In the course of time and with the gradual stabilization (if one might use that term) of conditions in the camp, there crept into the contacts with the women another more intimate factor which began to play a major part: sex, no doubt from very natural instincts. "Those favored by fortune," a few doctors and nursing

85

orderlies headed by camp senior Bock, entered the women's camp daily, taking medical supplies, applying dressings and giving treatment. After some time the women turned up in our camp. Every day female guards would bring another group to the records department, where they had their photographs taken, full face and left and right profiles, as we had done shortly after our arrival. From there they would come to our Block 28 to be X-rayed. The medical staff in charge of the X-ray department now had to cope with the additional difficulties of prisoners who had assignations with women in the dark little room. And it was not only conversation that some of the men making such an assignation had in mind. It was therefore not surprising that all sorts of rumors circulated in the camp concerning these rendezvous in the X-ray room, some of them very piquant and embellished with lurid details by certain of the participants in these events, details which were based entirely on their vivid imagination, as I was subsequently to find out myself.

The fact that the X-ray machine was only a step away from my room, and that there were no guards with the women, led to my being admitted to one of these meetings in the dark. Unobserved I slipped into the darkened cubicle where, according to my instructions from the X-ray-room assistant, I was to position the women patients in front of the X-ray machine. Groping about in the dark I found the first, then the second and after her the third, and, one by one, led them to the screen. All this time I never said a word; neither did they. So much for the attractions about which there were all these legends in circulation.

"Well, and how was it?" one of my mates asked later with a knowing wink. "Is it worth going there?"

"Ah!" I replied enigmatically, which set him thinking for a long time. From now on his imagination would work overtime until, one day, he would be able to convince himself that he had been taken in by me, just as I had been taken in before. But yet . . . There was, for instance, Wiesiek, a frequent visitor to the X-ray room. He had got to know the Funktionsdeutsche very well who daily took women prisoners to be X-rayed. He seemed to be content. All this "men-only" business had long ceased to interest him "from the scientific point of view."

CHAPTER 30

WITH THE beginning of spring a great many transports of French Jews arrived. This time they were not, as on previous occasions, taken straight to the gas chamber, but into the camp. The SS had come to appreciate the labor potential of prisoners, who were needed for the construction of the great chemical works of I.G. Farbenindustrie. Conditions in the Buna works were so harsh that after a few days most of those lining up outside the outpatients' department after evening roll call were from the French contingent. In an attempt to test my knowledge of French, I walked about among them trying to make conversation. I made up a sentence from words I remembered, but unfortunately they failed to understand me, although I was so full of good intentions.

"Please, doctor," a young Jew addressed me timidly.

"I'm not a doctor," I replied gruffly; I was annoyed because I could not make myself understood in French. *"Pologne, Polonais, comprenez-vous?* Dammit."

"But your French is excellent," he said, delighted, trying to flatter me. "Look here, sir. This old man who can hardly stand up—he's so ill—he's an old acquaintance from Paris," he went on more boldly, when he had realized that I was not dangerous. "Just look at him now. Couldn't you do something to have him seen by a doctor, please?" Indeed, the old man could scarcely stand on his legs. He had a black eye, his swollen lip had burst, his shorn head was severely bruised. Tomorrow, I thought, they'll finish him off.

"Where does he work?" I asked, merely to confirm my suspicions. From the looks of him I was convinced that he worked at Buna. That was where they did most of the beating these days.

"At Buna. We're there together. You've no idea what goes on there, mate," the young Jew confirmed, trying to read from my face whether or not I was prepared to help him.

"Wait a minute, I'll ask the porter." I decided to speak to Kazek because he was responsible for admissions to the hospital. "For heaven's sake, don't," said Kazek, "they'll take him to the convalescent block straightaway. You've only got to look at him. He'll be much better off staying with the Kommando."

"But he works at Buna," I tried to convince Kazek.

"Of course, it's as broad as it's long; either they gas him here or they murder him at Buna. But what the hell. Come here, only you'll have to carry him in, otherwise the others will start a row."

The old man, meanwhile, had been pushed to the end of the line by the stronger ones. The young Jew talked to him earnestly, instructing him as to what he must do. It appeared that the old man caught on quickly, because a moment later he collapsed with a groan. Thereupon we dragged him, supporting him under his arms, to the overcrowded outpatients' clinic, where we managed to get him in with those waiting to see the doctor. The old man was admitted to the hospital, but the young man had to make do with Tanalbin, a drug which was prescribed for anyone with whom there was, strictly speaking, nothing wrong apart from incipient diarrhea. He thanked me profusely for my help and shook my hand firmly.

"*Merci beaucoup.* Thanks. My name is David. Perhaps one day I'll need your help, so please, remember me."

Once again he shook my hand and hurried away. In my hand I felt a cold round metal object. The corridor was full of people; without looking at whatever it was I had been given I thrust my closed hand into my pocket. Being intensely curious, however, to take a look at the young Jew's present, I rushed to my room, assuming that it would be empty at this time of day. There wasn't anybody there, except for Marian K., who was lying on a top bunk whining because he had a toothache, in spite of the fact that he did not have many teeth left. He lay with his back to me, and I took advantage of this fact in order to look at my present, intending to hide it in my bed afterwards. I talked to Marian in an attempt to divert his attention and slipped the gold watch under the blanket. Having done this I returned outside, pondering what I ought to do with it. There I ran across Stessel, who immediately found work for me helping with the handing out of anti-scabies ointment.

After the job was completed, I hurried back to my room and my bed, where my treasure reposed. The watch had vanished. So had Marian. Bloody hell! Furious, I stormed into the washroom.

"Marian, stop messing about. Come on, hand it back."

Marian smiled impudently, flashing his rotten teeth which suddenly seemed to have stopped aching. He took my arm and explained in reassuring tones: "Now, tell me, what would you do with it? I bet you'd have left the watch in your bed until someone would have found it, like Klehr, for example."

That hit home. Klehr was the one I feared most. Lately he had taken to making frequent searches in my room.

"And I'll make it disappear ever so quietly. I even know where. There'll be grub to eat, my lad, a few potatoes, a little marg, sausages. You'll not regret it."

Marian kept his word. For a few days the washroom smelled of things other than pus, filth and diarrhea. There was frying of potatoes and potato pancakes, and there was sausage, too. Everything was faithfully shared with me. Since my stomach was full, I spared a kind thought for David, who, having learnt that his old friend had been taken to the convalescent block in Birkenau, avoided the hospital like the plague. I convinced myself that the gold which was smuggled into the camp had its value. One could save one's life as long as one was able to pay.

CHAPTER 31

SUDDENLY AND unexpectedly I was transferred from the hospital block into the camp with a few other orderlies, supposedly in order to reduce the hospital staff. Fortunately spring had arrived and it was quite warm.

I was quartered in Block 18a, where the prisoners who worked exclusively at the Buna works lived. Quite an unpleasant prospect after almost two years in the hothouse atmosphere of the hospital. I was afraid of the camp and still more afraid of the notorious Buna Kommando. The men living in the block were almost exclusively French Jews. The block senior was a crazy German criminal, a troublemaker, vicious, with sadistic tendencies. The room orderlies, both Poles and Jews, vied with each other in complying with their master's every wish. This night I got hardly any sleep. I was being bitten by fleas, and hordes of lice were crawling all over me. I was convinced I would catch typhus. The camp was still asleep when we were hustled out of the block into the yard where the columns were lining up, ready to march off to the Buna works. I joined the nearest group and stood among the Jews of Block 18. I suppose I must have stood out from the rest because Head Kapo Pressen noticed me at once.

"What are you doing here among all these Mussulmen?" he asked, terribly surprised, for only yesterday he had seen me in the hospital.

"I see, I see, did they give you the boot at the hospital?" he said, amused. "Never fear. You'll not die here. I won't make you join the shovel brigade either. To start with, I'll give you a small Kommando, and you'll be a ganger."

Delightful prospects, I thought. I knew Buna well from the stories going round. Kapos, SS men and even foremen liquidated people in huge numbers there.

"Perhaps you could get me some lighter work, like Kommando nursing orderly?" I suggested timidly. "I can't speak German," I added, trying to indicate that I did not wish to become a ganger.

"Okay, okay." He dismissed me because he was in a hurry. "We'll find something suitable later. Things aren't at all bad around here, especially with a protector like myself." He pointed proudly at the stick in his hand. "What's your number?" He raced off, noting it down while he ran because his Kommando was already moving off. "Left, left and left," he bellowed, setting the pace for the marching columns. The orchestra was not yet there; that's how early we started out for work.

On a siding near the station stood a goods train ready and waiting for us. We piled into the wagons and after a journey lasting only a few minutes we alighted at a small station in the village of Dwory.

"Form into work squads!" ordered the *Kommandoführer* [SS man in charge of work squad], a tall Scharführer with a long hook-nose whom the prisoners called The Owl. At his command two thousand men lined up in rows as if they had been touched by a magic wand. I alone did not know where I belonged. One by one, large and small groups of prisoners with their guards left the big meadow and turned towards the road which ran alongside the

90

village, accompanied by the "Left, left and left" from Kapos and foremen.

All who remained in the meadow were a few dozen of the worst-looking prisoners, a few guards and myself. Only then did Pressen remember me.

"Here, you, nursing orderly, come here," he called out peremptorily. The Owl, with his unpleasant mephisto face, was still standing next to him. The head Kapo assigned ten men to me and the Kommandoführer two SS men, having informed them where we were to go. Thus on my first day with the dangerous Buna works Kommando I had been made a ganger.

Walking by the side of ten French Jews, who formed up in two rows of five, it was now I who set the pace: left, left, and left. We marched through a long village in clouds of dust which had been stirred up by hundreds of prisoners marching ahead of us. The dusty road forked at the end of the village. The majority of columns turned to the left, while we marched to the right, behind the two SS men who were showing us the way. One of the guards asked me something. I did not understand him. Nor could I talk properly to the Frenchmen. This won't do, I thought to myself. How on earth am I going to make myself understood?

After we had ambled across plowed fields we came to a newly built road heavy with traffic—cars, trucks, bicycles and pedestrians. Everyone was heading for the large site which was Buna. We halted by a widely branching willow tree. Beneath the tree stood a big toolbox: we only noticed it when, presently, a civilian, supposedly a foreman, arrived and unlocked it. Looking at me long and hard he asked me in Polish: "And what has happened to the other ganger? I'm always being sent new ones. How can one work like that?" He muttered while handing me the tools. Later, when he had calmed down a little, he explained to me what we had to do.

Alongside the road a special track for vehicles was under construction. Where a straight line had been marked out by means of posts and lengths of string, we were to level the terrain, getting rid of all uneven places, of which there were a great many, in particular the protruding roots of trees on either side of the road. "You've got to get to this place here today, understand?"

The stretch of road we were to level was not very long. In consequence, the work was not very strenuous, especially since our SS guards behaved decently. The Jews distributed the spades and pickaxes among themselves and began to work enthusiastically as they knew exactly what each one of them had to do. Obviously they had worked in this spot before, which made the whole thing that much easier. The foreman, having assured himself that the work was progressing satisfactorily, got on his bicycle and rode off. The sun began to scorch, so that the guards withdrew into the shade of the tree from where they watched the prisoners at work with indifference.

I began to be quite simply bored. I did not know what to do with myself, so I began to pull up some of the protruding roots. As the hours passed, it grew steadily hotter; the prisoners now worked more sluggishly. While I leaned on my pickaxe, pretending to be taking a brief break, I was watching the road where my attention was suddenly attracted to a young woman who had already ridden back and forth several times on her bicycle. On the last occasion, when she had gone some fifty yards, she got off her bicycle and turned round, leaving the bike along the side of the road. She stopped not far from us, pretending to be repairing something on her machine. At the same time she skillfully threw a small parcel that had been hidden in her basket, which landed next to the tree stump. Then she got back on her bicycle, rode slowly past the guards, who accosted her cheerfully and, as she cycled past me, gave me an inviting look. I nodded imperceptibly as a sign that I had understood her intention. She replied with another nod and, pedaling steadily, was soon out of sight.

I considered how I could get close to the tree without attracting the guards' attention. However, it turned out that the SS men had seen everything and were only waiting for the woman to disappear. They looked around carefully and immediately walked up to the tree where the small parcel lay. They unpacked it and, having examined its contents, one of them called me and said: "Eat this quickly, but watch out for the Kommandoführer."

I quickly gulped down the sandwich, filled with two layers of bacon, and in my mind I thanked the woman who had not been afraid to put the packet under the tree, under the SS men's very noses. From the way she behaved I deduced that she had done this quite dangerous sort of thing before on more than one occasion. She must have known my predecessor well, and it was with him in mind that she had put the food parcel down, after pondering for a long time whether it was worth sacrificing it for me. The SS men took out their own snacks and busied themselves with their food, not in the least concerned with the prisoners who were merely pretending to work and waiting impatiently for their lunch break and something to eat. At long last one of the guards consulted his watch and ordered us to put down our tools. Lunch time.

We were taken to a workshop and boiler room, some ten minutes away from our workplace. A few teams had already eaten. Most prisoners were resting, others were busy scrubbing their bowls with sand. Lunch was handed out by Head Kapo Jupp, who was tall and skinny and given to yelling. He felt it incumbent upon himself to hit at least every other one of the Jews lining up for their food smartly on the head with his soup ladle. The portions were distributed in such a way that there were second helpings for some on whom fortune smiled, above all for the Funktionshäftlinge. I too was given a second helping although of more modest size. The Jews were given the buckets to scrape. Famished, they flung themselves on the buckets and fought over them, while Jupp took advantage of their squabbling in order to clobber them, to the general delight of the SS men who were watching this scene.

The lunch break did not last long. Our guards, who during the morning had been so calm, began at once to urge the Jews on to work harder.

"Come on, come on, you fucking Jews, get a move on, can't you." From afar I saw The Owl approaching on his bicycle. He stopped on the road without getting off his bike. After he had received the SS men's report he asked for the ganger. I approached, clicked my heels and reported: "Road construction team with ten prisoners at work."

I managed it quite well, for he regarded me affably and said: "All right, very well." Then he asked suddenly: "Are you the new ganger?" and rode off without waiting for a reply, but shouting

"Carry on" to the Jews who were still standing at attention as he cycled past them.

Perhaps it's not so bad working with these outside teams after all, I thought. The sun was nearing the horizon when we were told to finish working. The foreman turned up in time to lock the cleaned tools in the box. Before he departed he checked how much we had done. He was dissatisfied and informed me that this was not enough. "With the other ganger the team did twice the work. You have to goad these lazy Jews to work harder. Otherwise I'll have to report to the Kommandoführer that you are just standing about here. My firm pays a lot of money for your labor. Get it?"

We made our way back through the village. A terrible dust rose up once more. My throat was dry, parched with thirst. In almost every Kommando they carried those who had been killed or beaten or who were too emaciated to walk. Roll call was held in the meadow. It took a long time because they were waiting for a late team. At last they came running, quite out of breath and dragging a corpse behind them.

Immediately after supper the block senior ordered a louse check. It lasted well into the night, so there was no time to wash. In my sleep I felt the lice crawling all over me.

CHAPTER 32

THE ACCURSED morning bell woke me from deep sleep. Outside it was still gray. A quick wash, coffee instead of breakfast. March to the station, get on the train. Although it was only a few miles to Dwory, today our journey took almost an hour and a half. We had to wait for large military and arms transports to get past, destined for faraway front lines. We were therefore very late in arriving at Dwory. As a result the lining up of Kommandos took place at an increased pace and in rather a chaotic manner. Perhaps that was why we were assigned different guards. I was pleased when I discovered that one of them spoke Polish. But he was the one who turned out to be a real bastard. He drove the Jews viciously, berating, beating and kicking them and then turning his attention to me.

"If you don't know how to be a ganger, you can work like them," he said furiously when he saw that instead of concentrating on work I was gazing down the road, expecting to see the woman who had brought the food yesterday. I was used to physical work; besides, I had also learned how to pretend to be working efficiently, unlike the newcomers who gave everything, using up their last strength in order to avoid mistreatment.

In this particular instance it availed them little. The foreman, wanting to make up for lost time, drove them on, while the SS men used every opportunity to beat everybody. Meanwhile the woman whom I had been expecting appeared on her bicycle. Exactly as she had done on the day before, she cycled past a few times, carefully observing the workers and the raging SS men. She gathered that something was not quite right, especially since I, too, was working without so much as looking at her. So she departed without throwing her small parcel. The SS men were rampaging, the sun beat down mercilessly, and I was starving. Time seemed to be standing still; we could hardly wait for the lunch break. It was on the double to the workshop and the same coming back. There was a hollow place in the trunk of the willow tree, exactly where we had put down our tools before going off to lunch. When we returned, a small parcel had been left in this hollow place. She had put it there, after all, while we were away. The prisoners picked up their tools, but I stayed behind trying to get to the parcel. The SS man, the one who could speak Polish, noticed that I was fiddling with something, and he was at my side like a flash.

"What are you doing there? Show me what it is," he screamed, tearing the bread out of my hand and slapping my face. The Jews, amazed to see an SS man hitting a ganger, stood gaping and forgot to go on working. Now the second SS man sprang into action. He hit the Jews, one after the other, without exception. At last he found a victim whom he tortured until the man collapsed. One of the Jews ran over to his prostrate fellow prisoner and tried to lift him up which, in turn, made the SS man belaboring me fly into a frenzied rage.

95

Leaving me to my fate, he ran to the man who was bending over his comrade and kicked him viciously in the backside. The Jew staggered, lost his balance and sprawled next to the one whom he had been trying to help up. All at once the SS men grew merry. The two Jews got up clumsily and with difficulty. One of them, still on his knees, looked round for his cap which had fallen off his head during the beating and had rolled between the feet of the SS man. At last the Jew noticed it and crawled over to pick it up. This was what, apparently, the SS man had been waiting for. As the prisoner stretched out his hand to get hold of the cap, the guard deliberately kicked it a few yards away with his boot. The prisoner got up, brushed the soil from his trousers and went back to his work quite calmly, as if nothing had happened, while the second SS man kicked the cap playfully far into the cornfield.

"Where is your cap?" the second SS man inquired, standing next to the prisoner and slightly nudging him with the butt of his carbine. The Frenchman did not understand the question, or at least he pretended not to know what it was all about. In any case, he replied something in his own tongue, pointing now at the sun, now at his head, as if to say that he did not mind not having his cap at work and that he was not afraid of the sun. The SS man, however, continued to talk to the Jew, politely but persistently, pointing the barrel of his carbine in the direction in which the Jew was to go. "Go and fetch your cap," he repeated, and it was obvious that he was suppressing an outburst of fury with difficulty. The prisoner, with a feeling of foreboding, hesitated. Realizing the sudden change in the SS man's mood and faced with the carbine butt raised, ready to come down on him, he obeyed the order and walked in the direction pointed at. "Go on, go on," the SS man urged him.

He found it. At the moment when he held the lost cap in his hand and was about to turn back, a shot rang out. First one, then another. The prisoner fell as if struck by lightning. Where he had keeled over, his twitching hands could be seen for a while, but in the end they, too, were lost in the green of the young corn. At the sound of the shot the astonished prisoners stopped work. Even the second guard seemed to be surprised.

"Did you see that?" The marksman turned to him. "The bloody Jew tried to escape," he explained succinctly.

"What are you staring at?" he shouted at me. "Get back to work. I'll show you." He turned to the Jews and hit the prisoner nearest to him. "Get on with your work, you mother-fucking Jews."

From the road came the sound of horses' hooves. An elegant SS officer on horseback was galloping in our direction, apparently in order to investigate the shooting. We worked with redoubled energy. The SS men stood at attention.

"Heil Hitler! What's going on here?" he asked, reining in his foaming horse. The SS man who had shot the prisoner a moment ago reported the incident. Grabner, chief of the Political Department—I remember him well—listened calmly to the account, then he turned to us and demanded: "Who is the Kapo here?" As no one moved, the guard quickly gave me a sign.

"Ganger, come here!"

I stood to attention and recited the formula I had learned by heart:

"Prisoner in protective custody number 290 reporting road construction team with nine prisoners at work. One has been shot."

"What?" Grabner expressed great surprise. "Not shot, ganger," he explained patiently. "He was shot while attempting to escape. Understood?"

"Yes, sir," I repeated obediently, "shot while attempting to escape."

Pleased, Grabner nodded his head; then, settling himself in the saddle, he said: "Carry on," after which, as far as he was concerned, the whole matter was at an end. Then he took up the reins, gave the horse a tap with his whip and galloped off, smartly saluted with raised arm and a crisp "Heil Hitler" by the two SS men.

About five minutes later The Owl and two more SS men appeared. There was an investigation, and a statement was taken concerning the course of the "escape" incident. As a formality I, as ganger, was also questioned. The guard who spoke Polish helped me eagerly with my reply as though he was afraid I might say the wrong thing. Fear not! Having been "instructed" by Grabner, chief of the Political Department, I would never again dare say anything else about the escape of the rebellious prisoner. Not shot, but shot while attempting to escape.

CHAPTER 33

A NEW team was set up at Buna which was to work in the village of Monowitz. It consisted exclusively of Jews, not counting the two Germans who worked as under-Kapo and ganger. Head Kapo Jupp expected to gain personal advantage from this team; it worked in the neighboring village among the Polish people who sympathized with the prisoners and helped them as much as possible. Therefore, he thought, it would be a good idea to employ a Pole, an old prisoner, to act as decoy, so to speak, and, at the same time, as an intermediary between the villagers and prisoners from other countries. He chose me, a choice, incidentally, which was inspired by Head Kapo Pressen, who also counted on my gratitude. They had put the matter to me quite plainly, without in any way mincing their words. Being the only Pole I would certainly be supported by the neighboring population.

In return for this good Kommando, it followed that I would have to hand over the best of what I was given. I was to be clerk; therefore I would not have to work, but concern myself only with food supplies. The two Funktionsdeutschen were informed of my role, as were the guards who received instructions from Head Kapo Jupp. Naturally, they, too, would have to receive their cut.

Thus everything had been worked out from the top with great ingenuity. I would be in this Kommando as a decoy. My low number and the red triangle with the letter P in the center were to wear down completely the soft hearts of the Polish villagers during the process of compulsory resettlement of Monowitz.

As the command "Demolition team Monowitz, line up" was issued by The Owl, I stood in the front row next to the under-Kapo and the ganger; it was with not a little surprise that I noticed three SS men from the company joining us, no doubt intent upon preventing anyone else from beating them to it. While we took a different route from the others, Jupp began talking to them like old friends. I supposed they were talking about me because I felt their appraising but not hostile glances.

In order to get to Monowitz one had to walk quite a long way. Part of the road led along the railway track from Auschwitz to Skawina; farther on, we climbed up a high embankment and, after marching a few hundred yards across fields where excavations had taken place, we reached the first houses of the village.

The village stretched along the two sides of a glen. Down the middle of the glen ran a road which led nowhere. Several buildings on the left-hand side of the large village had already been demolished. Only at the very end of the village there remained a brick-built house, which we were now approaching.

The house was empty, the inhabitants obviously having left it because, like all the other houses, it was due to be demolished. In one of the rooms, our team's tools had been stored: crowbars, pickaxes, spades, sledge hammers, and the like. After the Kapos had distributed the tools among the prisoners, they led them to a large barn, which was already partly demolished. Jupp, who as a rule raged and rampaged, was calm, cool and collected. The SS men were not interested in the work of the prisoners, but took up their stations and abandoned themselves to their sweet slumbers. Needless to say, the prisoners took advantage of this by pretending to be working while looking round in the hope of finding something to eat.

For some time now I had been hanging about in the vicinity of this solitary house, ever since I noticed a young girl who had come on a few occasions to fetch vegetables from the garden. Encouraged by the indifferent attitude on the part of the guards—the garden was beyond the line guarded by the SS men—I approached her and addressed her with the customary "Good morning." Whereupon she reciprocated with a charming smile, displaying healthy white teeth. It was in so simple a manner that, after more than two years in a concentration camp, I struck up an acquaintance with another human being outside the outer cordon.

The girl was young, sweet, pretty and shy. I liked her. I think she liked me too, but perhaps she also felt pity for me without, however, letting me know this. But ever since our first meeting she came more often, and every time she brought some food in a small basket. She would leave the basket in the cellar of the deserted house, thus hiding it from the SS men and Kapos. After a while she realized that I did not eat her presents all by myself but shared them with the Germans. I felt I had to tell her honestly on what conditions I had been included in the team. She must have appreciated my situation, for from then on she brought even bigger supplies of food.

In general the SS men kept their word. They discharged their duty to guard us by sleeping in the bushes or in the barn, rousing themselves only whenever the Kommandoführer paid us a visit. In time they learned how to forage for food on their own. The villagers paid their tribute voluntarily because they saw how decently the guards behaved towards us. At times a newcomer might try to blackmail a peasant into giving him food by threatening to have his house demolished immediately. If this sort of thing occurred, it was reported to me and I, in turn, informed one of the guards, a *Rottenführer* [Lance-Corporal] who was permanently attached to our team, an extremely decent SS man who promptly settled the matter by choosing another guard to accompany him next day.

After some time Head Kapo Jupp left our Kommando, but took care to see that we continued regularly to hand over his share of the tribute. I did this with the help of prisoners experienced in that kind of thing, who smuggled the loot into the camp. I handed some of these smuggled goods over to Gienek Obojski at the hospital, some I gave to the bath attendants in Block 28 as a token of appreciation for the use of hot water and also for clean clothing, for one had to change frequently in consideration of contacts with people outside the camp, in order not to infect them with typhus-infected camp lice.

Besides, my acquaintance with the young girl, with whom occasionally I spent a long time in the dark cellar, had caused me to be especially concerned with my appearance. This led to my leg

100

being pulled, not always very tactfully, by Kapos and SS men alike, without there being any real reason for their coarse jokes because I had never even touched her. Whenever the girl happened to hear any of these remarks she blushed with embarrassment and ran away. One day when I was sitting with her in the cellar having, for the first time, made up my mind to kiss her, I was called away by a prearranged signal; the signal indicated that The Owl, our Kommandoführer, was approaching. When he inspected the progress of our demolition work he expressed great surprise that we had spared a house which should have been demolished a long time ago. There was the ever-growing pile threatening to engulf the house, as more soil from the factory building site was unloaded there. The Kapo tried to excuse the omission by explaining somewhat vaguely that we used this house as a tool store. The Owl ordered the tools to be taken into the village and insisted that the demolition of the building was to be started at once. Luckily he did not peep into the cellar and thus failed to discover a frightened young girl with a basketful of empty lunch dishes.

Brick by brick we demolished the house of our young benefactress, the house in which she had been born and grown up, the house in which she secretly spent many hours with a concentration camp prisoner in innocent flirtation, perhaps the first in her young life. Now she stood leaning on the fence and crying quietly while I hacked furiously at the bricks with my pickaxe, trying to hide my emotion.

That evening the house was no more. A few days later what was left of it was covered with earth. The girl disappeared too. I never saw her again.

CHAPTER 34

CONSIDERING THE conditions which prevailed in the camp at that time, I was doing all right. There typhoid epidemics created havoc; selections, injections and liquidations were the order of the day. Under these circumstances I was content to be working at Buna, especially in the Monowitz Kommando. I wanted to stay in this Kommando as long as possible. Unfortunately, all good things come to an end, some of them very quickly.

One evening I returned from work with a severe headache. Despite the heat I shivered continuously. Even a hot bath did not help very much. The bath attendant, who liked to make diagnoses, pronounced that I had—no doubt about it—caught typhus. While I was taking my bath I had an argument with Fred Stessel, my block senior. He caught sight of me in the washroom and made one hell of a row. On this occasion the bath attendants caught hell as well because they had allowed several rogues and villains from the camp who were teeming with typhus-carrying lice to use the sick bay bath. Although he did have a point, I was deeply outraged that he should treat me, a former nursing orderly, like any old Mussulman.

I made up my mind that I would not succumb to this illness which plagued me, that I would not report myself as sick at the hospital, and that I would cope with the typhus by myself. I had heard of such cases in the camp. Moreover, I still nursed the hope that it might not be typhus but an illness which would quickly pass or just plain exhaustion. However, the next day I felt even worse. I suspected that I had a high temperature.

At night, after I had returned from Buna, I went to have another bath, and once more was caught by Stessel. This time, miracles will happen, he did not make a row, but actually suggested himself that I ought to have myself examined and perhaps admitted to the hospital. Since I felt not at all well, I reported at the hospital that same evening. By now I was quite sure that I had typhus.

"You have a temperature of nearly 101 degrees and spots on your belly. You've got to go to bed." Such was Rudek's verdict. Complete with admission card I was taken to the hospital washroom by Marian Tolinski. Bath, shave, clean underwear. The bath orderlies offered to carry me to the typhoid block on a stretcher. But I managed to walk there under my own steam. Obojski and Tolinski insisted on coming with me. It was a good thing that they

102

did so because I was no longer able to walk up the stairs to the first floor.

"There you are, so you've caught it, too," was the greeting I received from one of the doctors I knew. "We'll take a look at you presently. Put him down there, by the window; that's a good place." The doctor's concerned voice reached me from a long way off. Slowly I lost consciousness.

CHAPTER 35

I LAY, legs together, in one bed with Roman O., who had been in my transport. It was nighttime, hot and stuffy, and I was plagued by a terrible thirst. I could not go to sleep. In spite of the fever I remained conscious. Roman, on the other hand, was delirious. In the brief moments when he came round, he begged and begged, weak-voiced: thirsty, thirsty. In the end the night duty orderly was roused and brought him a cup of cold tea. In the next bed someone wheezed noisily. Towards morning he fell silent. That very morning another patient was put in his bed. I did not find the day as dreadful as the night, particularly as during the day people kept dropping in to visit me. However, I felt that I was growing weaker.

"It's your heart; I really don't know how much longer it will last," said the doctor as he gave me an injection. "But we'll ginger it up, don't worry."

How good it was to know people, especially here in the hospital. Not everyone was given injections. All the majority of patients could count on was the resistance of their own body.

Roman looked about him absently and did not understand when people talked to him. He wetted himself. I had just enough strength to call for the bedpan, but my condition worsened hourly. The crisis day approached. At last I grew so weak that I was not in a position to turn over to the other side or to pull up my blanket when I had an attack of the shivers. I was delirious, but my delirious dreams were not altogether unpleasant. In spite of everything I was not completely unconscious. I could clearly hear someone who was standing by my bed saying: "Considering it's the crisis, it really isn't too bad. Only 102.9 degrees. Maybe the heart will last out."

It must have lasted out because that same night I felt the fever abating. I was very thirsty but could not make a sound. I tried propping myself up on my elbows but I could move only my fingers. Suddenly I was conscious of somebody from the next bed—obviously trying to get closer to the window—crawling across our bed and groping about in the dark with his hand. When he had made me out, he sought my neck and began throttling me. With superhuman strength I managed to cry out. The orderly on night duty came running. With difficulty he managed to subdue the patient, who, as the result of a very high temperature, had become delirious. He must have given the poor wretch a sedative because presently he lay there quite still. But towards morning the duty orderly found him leaning out of the window. At the last moment he caught him by his shirttail; otherwise he might have fallen out. But death would not allow him to escape. He died a few hours later, before he had got over his crisis.

For my bed-fellow, Roman, typhus had serious consequences, for he had an inflammation of the middle ear. It led to his being hard of hearing. It was difficult to talk to a deaf man.

In the afternoon Marian Tolinski visited me. He reminded me that I was due to write a letter home. As always he wrote the letter for me. I did not even have to dictate it to him, for he had read every letter I had received from home during the last few weeks and was perfectly well aware of what he must write. All I had to do was to sign it.

In the evening Gienek brought me a few apples. It was pleasant to find that my mates had not forgotten me. Now, after the crisis, my appetite was excellent. I felt myself getting better and growing stronger by the hour. On the following day I was walking round the room, and in the afternoon I sat at the window and watched the prisoners strolling about after roll call. In the crowd I noticed Edek Galinski, who signaled that he had brought me something to eat. This turned out to be a giant cucumber, which Edek had wheedled out of *Kommandant* [SS officer, in charge of the entire camp] Hoess's gardener. I decided to eat this delicacy at night in order not to have to share it with anyone.

Someone suggested that we ought to go outside to the hospital yard instead of sitting indoors amid the stink and the stuffy air. Holding on tightly to the banister I walked downstairs all by myself. On a bench outside Block 21 sat a few close acquaintances who were engaged in animated conversation. We sat down with them. It was fun. Only Czesiek S., who as a rule was full of jokes, sat silent and depressed.

"What's the matter with you, Czesiu? Are you ill or something?" someone asked him at last. Czesiek heaved a deep sigh and finally said the words that had been on the tip of his tongue, but which he had kept back because he did not want to be a spoilsport.

"Here you are, fooling about, and you don't know that a great delousing has been announced for tomorrow. All who are ill, without exception, are to be transferred to Birkenau, and we all know what that means. Already today no patient is allowed to be discharged into the camp," he concluded, looking significantly in my direction. A heavy silence ensued. Realizing the terrible impact his ill tidings had created, Czesiek tried to comfort us, but it was obvious that he was doing it without conviction. "Perhaps we can still manage to do something—at least for a few . . ."

Completely shattered by the horrifying prospect of tomorrow's selection, I crept back to my block. I had been so glad to have survived this beastly typhus. I had one last hope: perhaps it wasn't true. I consulted the doctor who had treated me throughout my illness. "Doctor," I asked him quite candidly, "do you know anything about a selection tomorrow?"

"Mm, there'll be something—the usual thing, you know," he said, trying to put me off. "You know the seriously ill are fetched every day for injections. It doesn't concern you any longer. You've got over your crisis. You can relax." And still it seemed to me that he spoke without much conviction. I was sure he wanted to keep the truth from me in order not to make me unhappy.

If it was really true, then there was nothing to be done about it anyway. All night I sat by the window unable to go to sleep. I ate the cucumber, which I had thought I would enjoy so much, without any appetite, simply because I did not want it to go bad. In a state of uneasiness I waited for the dawn.

Next morning the first disquieting sign was the imposition of a strict camp curfew, confirming my worst fears. Without doubt they intended to implement what I had awaited so fearfully throughout this sleepless night: a selection.

CHAPTER 36

THE FIRST ominous indication of an imminent selection was the assembly of all patients on the steps leading into the yard. Waiting there were Dr. Entress and SDG Klehr, together with block senior Fred Stessel, who held in his hand a list from which he read out the numbers of sick prisoners.

Two hundred and ninety. I was read out as the third or fourth. Entress scarcely glanced at me, while the block senior ordered me to stand on the right side of the yard together with those whose numbers had been read out before mine. After a few dozen numbers I realized that the group in which I found myself was the larger. By the wall of the block, standing a little apart, was a comparatively small group of prisoners consisting of the hospital staff. There was thus no longer any doubt that I was among those who were to be taken to the so-called convalescent block in Birkenau—in other words, to the gas chamber. Roman, an old and experienced prisoner, although still a little hard of hearing after his bout of typhus, also sensed danger. We kept together and tried to sidle closer to Block 21 in the hope of joining the group of nursing orderlies assembled there.

The trucks arrived. Camp senior Bock opened the block gate, where Klehr and someone from the orderly room immediately took up positions. They began calling out the numbers in the same sequence as the block senior had done earlier. Roman and I did not answer. They called our numbers a few times, but since no one answered they carried on. We moved slowly, always in that desirable direction, until finally we arrived under the windows of the orderly room of Block 21, where there was a manhole covered by a concrete slab. We had got to our goal. With great effort we succeeded in pushing the heavy slab to one side. The dark and rancid interior of the sewer did not look in the least inviting. But it represented our sole salvation.

Meanwhile the first truck was loaded with sick patients. There was no time for hesitation. At any moment they might repeat their search for the missing numbers. Steadying himself against the walls of the sewer with his elbows, Roman slipped into the narrow opening. When at long last, after much groping, he had found a support with his feet, he stood securely and encouraged me to follow his example. But I still wavered because at the back of my mind was the hope that I might manage somehow to get to the group of nursing orderlies where Julek and Marian were deliberately creating a commotion in order to make it easier for me to get to them. For that reason I confined myself to pushing the heavy concrete slab back into its proper place, the poor wretched patients giving me a hand, little knowing what fate awaited them.

By now the second truck was being loaded. But in the yard the number of sick people did not decrease because Dr. Entress kept sending more and more of them outside. At last I reached the group of nursing orderlies. Marian flung me a pair of their uniform trousers, which I put on at once. Now I looked very much like a prisoner member of the hospital staff. Before long the second truck moved off, taking the selected prisoners to Birkenau. At that moment, the danger was averted. List in hand, Klehr made his way to the orderly room, apparently wanting to find out what had happened to the missing numbers. Once the SDG had left, everybody in the yard began milling about. I used the confusion to speak to the head clerk, asking him to cross me off the list.

"Nothing I can do just now," he said, spreading his arms in a helpless gesture. "Neither Entress nor Klehr will let go of the list. Perhaps I'll manage to do something later," he added when he saw that I was shaking with agitation. Finally he gave me a piece of good advice, clearly with the intention of comforting me a little: "When your number is called out again, be sure not to answer; perhaps we'll somehow manage to smuggle you through."

Slender hopes and dubious advice indeed! Particularly now that SDG Klehr had returned and was herding the sick away from the hospital staff. He succeeded in restoring a certain amount of order; and now he scrutinized the nursing orderlies in case someone had hidden among them. He recognized me at once.

"What's your number?" he asked sharply, since he recalled that I had been dismissed on his initiative. "You're not a nursing orderly." And then, very angry now, he repeated: "What's your number?" Petrified with fear, almost inaudibly, I whispered my number. Klehr stared at me with his penetrating gaze, like a snake hypnotizing its victim.

"I'm healthy, Herr *Oberscharführer* [Platoon Sergeant]." Suddenly I found my tongue again. "I can work, I didn't want to go to the convalescent block." With my poor German I tried to soften Klehr. However, without much ado he caught me by the scruff of the neck and dragged me, still cursing under his breath, to the empty wall of the block, where he ordered me to wait by myself for the arrival of the truck. I was lost. Already I could hear the sound of the trucks returning empty from Birkenau, ready to take back another load of prisoners. I knew I would now be one of the first, so much was certain. The gate was open. Klehr did not let me out of his sight.

"Doctor, doctor," I screamed desperately, no longer caring about anything, as I caught sight of Dehring, who was walking towards Dr. Entress. "Save me! I want to live!"

Dr. Dehring made a helpless gesture. But when he heard Klehr calling out my number he shouted at me urgently in spite of Klehr's impatient demand for him to stop. "Don't move, I'll try a last chance. I'll speak to Dr. Entress."

Meanwhile Klehr was dragging me forcibly to the truck. Just in time, at the very last minute, Dehring came running up and reported to Klehr. The SDG was so furious that I thought he was going to hit him. He would, after all, have to leave me behind because Dr. Dehring reported that Entress had asked him to take me to him.

"Wiesiu," Dehring said quickly, red with agitation, "run as fast as your legs will carry you and report to Dr. Entress. It's on his express orders."

A spark of hope gave me strength. Entress stood in the center of the yard, next to him Fred Stessel, a noncommittal expression on his face, and Klehr standing at attention, listening eagerly to what the officer was telling him with raised voice. When he had finished, Klehr marched off without glancing at me, while I, in my turn, reported to Entress. I tried to create as good an impression as possible. My attempts must have looked odd, since he regarded me scornfully and asked, somewhat incredulous: "Are you quite recovered?"

"I am, Herr Oberscharführer." I tried to make my voice sound strong and healthy.

"So you used to be a nursing orderly. Didn't you?"

I nodded my head in affirmation. I could no longer utter a single sound because I sensed that the matter was taking a favorable turn. Even Stessel, who so far had remained passive, now nodded eagerly and explained something to Entress with conviction. I waited for the verdict.

Entress pondered for a while, then he said severely: "You've got to work well now. Understood?" And, turning to Fred, he ordered: "Dismiss into camp at once. Start with peeling potatoes," he added much more gently.

I came out with a "Thank you very much, Doctor," as I simply could not contain myself any longer.

Entress waved me away with an impatient movement of his hand, as though shooing away an importunate fly. "Be off with you! Dismissed!"

Never before had I been so happy in the camp as at that moment. With a feeling of ineffable relief, I went to the farthest corner of the yard, as far away as I could from the entrance gate. The incensed Klehr was venting his rage, while loading the sick and the convalescent who were not as lucky as I into the trucks. Drunk with my happy fate, I forgot the others. I only came down to earth after all the sick had been taken away. During roll call, when something did not tally, I suddenly remembered Roman. Where was he?

"Roman is hidden in the sewer," I confided to the prisoner standing next to me. After a while Roman was led out from the typhoid block. It turned out that he had not heard the signal for roll call and had been lying under the bed where one of the nursing orderlies from Block 20 had hidden him.

Immediately after roll call I was dismissed from the hospital into the camp.

CHAPTER 37

THE NEXT morning Otto took me to the potato room. Spudbashing was easy work. The cooks who remembered me as a member of the hospital staff fed me extra grub. After a few days I felt so much better that I thought about returning to Buna. But I never went back there. The Buna Kommando was dissolved as a result of the typhoid epidemic, which had not abated after the famous "delousing." I did not intend to return to the hospital, for there lurked death. The best thing would be if one could get into an outside Kommando, far away from the hospital, from selections, from the camp.

Impressed by tales from another prisoner, who told wonderful stories about work in Harmensee, I decided that this Kommando, far away from the main camp, was for me. Prisoners there worked in connection with fish and chicken farming. In my imagination I saw myself eating plump chickens and succulent fish. For days I plagued Otto to get me transferred to this promising Kommando. At last he brought me the news. Good old Otto! Tomorrow I was to be transferred to Harmensee. I was beside myself with joy.

I ran into the hospital to tell everybody the good news. To everyone I promised impossibly big fish, and for Dr. Dehring—to whom I owed a debt I could never repay for saving my life—there would be such a chicken! How happy I was that day.

The green Kapo greeted me coolly. So low a number and yet such a Mussulman? Who was this? Otto had sent him? The Kapo was not pleased. Having inspected me from all sides—in spite of a few days recovering with the potato Kommando and additional feeding by the kindly cooks, I was not much to look at—the disappointed Kapo announced that I would be given a light job until I had recovered. Well, that's not too bad, I thought. In the yard next to a large brick building which looked like a grain store a prisoner was busy slaking lime. That was where the Kapo took me.

"For the time being you'll help him, and later we'll see," he said. Having given the prisoner some instructions, he departed. We were alone.

"Well, what's up, pal? Why are you so scared?" the prisoner asked when he saw my anxious face. "Wait and I'll show you what you have to do."

I found the work arduous; beads of sweat were on my forehead; after a while I was worn out. Slaking lime was far from being light work. Meanwhile my fellow worker mixed the lime effortlessly. He was stripped to the waist. The muscles stood out clearly on his strong body.

It is easy to work with muscles like that, I thought and leaned on my pole, trying to get a rest.

"Don't stand there like a whore at a wedding," he said deliberately, casting a glance at me without interrupting what he was doing. I began to mix the accursed viscous lime.

"Ah well, I can see you're weak," he remarked with a pitying note in his voice. "Do your mixing at the very top, then you won't find it so strenuous," he suggested after a while. "Don't worry, I'll wangle it for you. Only watch out for the Kapo, he's a real shit."

A decent fellow, I thought, and followed his valuable suggestions. And yet he looks like a villain with that flat nose. He was very garrulous, pumping me about everything. I had to tell him where I came from, why the Gestapo had arrested me, where I had worked, and so on and so forth. I told him that I had got over a bout of typhus only a few days ago, in an attempt to explain why I was so lacking in strength.

"No illness gets anywhere near me, mate, not no typhus neither. I'm as healthy as a bull!" He hit his chest a resounding blow with the flat of his hand.

"The only thing is, there's not enough food, damn and blast it," he sighed heavily. "There were times, good times. Now everything's lousy," he concluded furiously. Then he spat in his hands, rubbed him vigorously so that his finger joints cracked alarmingly and energetically resumed his lime-mixing.

I asked him the meaning of *Harmensee-Schule,* the title of our team, and where the rest of the prisoners were working. Apart from him and the Kapo, I had seen no one. And where was this poultry and fish breeding farm of which I had such high hopes?

"Forget it, mate. There'll be no fish nor chickens for you to eat here. Our Kommando hasn't much to do with that. Anyway, the ponds are worked by a different Kommando. And even they have a job to organize anything. Perhaps now, in the autumn, when they're cleaning the ponds of fish, we might organize something. The poultry are looked after by women only. We men just build the chicken coops. That's bricklayer's work, friend. And that lime, you can't get your teeth into that," he said regretfully. "You'll be lucky if you get a full bowl of camp grub. I usually get seconds because the Kapo knows my brother was a famous boxer. By the way, I've done some boxing, too. He likes me because as a rule the Kapos respect only the healthy and strong ones. Well, now you know who I am. Kolka. Brother of Kolczynski. There, pal, and now we'd better get back to mixing this bloody lime," he added resignedly.

I certainly was lucky with. boxers. More than two years ago, when someone had stolen my bread and had wanted to beat me on top of it, the famous "Teddy," Tadek Pietrzykowski, had stood up in my defense. And now here was the brother of the famous Kolczynski doing the heavy work for me.

"Anyway, it isn't all that bad here," he went on, winking at me. "You'll be okay with me. We'll find something to organize. Cheer up."

A truck and trailer piled high with sacks drew up. It stopped by the granary not far from us. The Kapo, having leapt down from the driver's cab, shouted in our direction: "Get on with it, unload."

I shambled after Kolczynski, who stepped forward self-confidently, rubbing his hands as though he wanted to demonstrate in front of the Kapo how much he was looking forward to this work. The Kapo gave him a friendly slap on his broad shoulders. It was obvious that he was impressed by this flat-nosed athlete. After he had positioned himself a little to one side, the Kapo leaned on a stick, while with his free hand he massaged his back, grimacing and groaning all the while.

"Hell and damnation," he lamented, "today I've got lumbago again."

Meanwhile Kolczynski expertly flung the first bag across his shoulders and waited for me to do likewise. I did not know what was in the sacks and how heavy they were. Seeing the ease with which Kolczynski handled his sack, I thought that they might be quite light. I wanted to make a good impression on the Kapo. So, imitating my mate, I reached with one hand for the tie while with the other, holding the sack from underneath, I laid it across my shoulders. When I felt I had placed it securely I moved away from the truck. All at once a diabolical weight forced me to the ground, my knees buckled and the sack shot over my head. There was a crunching sound somewhere in the region of my neck. The Kapo, who had been watching me, cursed and was going to attack me with his stick. But Kolczynski held him back and tried to explain to him in German: "Mr. Kapo, he had typhus. The doctor will work well. But now he is still too weak. Now I will help him." The Kapo seemed to understand some of this gibberish, and the mere fact that Kolczynski called me doctor made a great impression on him.

"Who's a doctor?" he asked in surprise. "That Mussulman? You?" He turned to me, doubtful, but already in a more gentle tone. I had no time for a denial, and Kolczynski was giving me desperate signs not to. Therefore I stammered, "Yes, yes, I look after the sick."

"And what, may I ask, are you, Doctor, doing here in my Kommando?" the Kapo asked suspiciously, viciously narrowing his watery little eyes. And once again Kolczynski leapt to my rescue: "Typhus—great delousation—discharged from sick bay into camp."

The Kapo pondered for a while and muttered slowly: "Oh well, let's see." He made a face again, because apparently he had another twinge of lumbago. Suddenly he gave me a quick look as if he was seeing me for the first time. Then turning his ginger-haired head to one side he repeated thoughtfully: "Nursing the sick, eh? Let's see, let's see."

From the driver's cab the impatient SS man stuck out his head. "You talk too much, Kapo," he said. "Get on with your work."

"Quick, unload, quick, I said," the Kapo yelled at us.

CHAPTER 38

KOLCZYNSKI HELPED me load the sack across my back; then he threw another bag across his shoulders and we walked towards the granary door. I only just carried my sack to the bottom of the iron spiral suitcase which led to the granary loft. I put the sack down, infinitely tired and breathing heavily, and propped it against the banister. But Kolczynski, who had already taken his sack upstairs, now returned to busy himself with mine. Without a load I climbed the stairs to the loft with ease.

"Tell you what. You'll untie the sacks and empty them into this wooden box. That won't tire you too much, will it? I'll do all the carrying. Just see that you finish in time," he said cheerfully. "Wasn't it great, the way I let him have it about the doctor, eh? The Kapo suffers something cruel with his rheumatics, so pretend you're a doctor and give him the works. You must have picked up something at this hospital," he added, smiling, as he went on his way to fetch the next sack.

I was grateful and lost in admiration for Kolczynski.

The afternoon passed quickly. When we had finished work, the whole team lined up and was counted. The SS guards returned from wherever they had spent the day. We went over dams between the numerous ponds and later through a deserted village to our quarters, guarded by our SS men.

All this time the Kapo was unusually quiet. Obviously his lumbago troubled him, for he was limping and groaning gently. After a march lasting half an hour we halted outside a single-story brick building which looked like a village school. A barbed-wire fence ran round it; at all four corners were watchtowers indicating to what use the former school was put now. There was a brief roll call taken by the Kommandoführer, and then the guards took up their places on the watchtowers. Behind the house was a little garden with a few fruit trees lacking any fruit. No doubt the prisoners who used the latrine in the garden had picked it before it was ripe.

Inside the house conditions were cramped. For the prisoners there were only two small rooms where the three-tiered bunk beds and a small iron stove left hardly any space to move. In the room occupied by the Kapo and his underlings there stood, in addition to the bunk beds, a large table and several stools. All windows were barred, of course. Prisoners were allowed outside only at certain times, and then only in order to relieve themselves.

After supper had been doled out, our time was our own. However, what earthly use was that for by that time it was dark, and there was only one solitary little lamp casting its dim light on this stuffy, cramped, dark place. I was assigned a bunk on the "third floor," almost directly under the ceiling. I was about to make up my bed when I heard the Kapo's voice, from the next room, calling me. He sounded as if he were in pain.

"Come here, orderly."

He lay on his pallet, undressed, moaning and cursing his lumbago. Now it was incumbent upon me to demonstrate my medical knowledge. There were no drugs here. If one could at least have given him a pill, but there was nothing. Not a thing. I knew that a massage helped when one was afflicted with lumbago. I had never actually massaged anyone, but I had watched the trained masseurs in the sick bay. Without betraying any lack of self-confidence I set to work, trying to create the impression of one who knows what he is doing. I felt the place where it hurt most and began to massage that very spot, gently at first, and gradually with more vigor.

115

To begin with the Kapo lay still and suffered with patience. But as I concentrated on the most painful places he could stand it no more. He yelled, squealed and cursed. Nevertheless he continued to submit to my treatment. I interrupted my activities for a breather, for I was getting tired. The Kapo used the time to do a few exercises in order to find out whether he could move more easily. As he thought he detected an improvement, he encouraged me to go on massaging him.

"Carry on, orderly, it is already much better."

I had no alternative but to continue massaging him. I improvised, slapping, pounding and rocking him until at long last I succeeded in the Kapo declaring piteously: "Enough."

I had passed the first test of my new profession as "miracle doctor" with flying colors. For presently the contented Kapo declared, "As from now, you are our Kommando nursing orderly."

He was in a good mood and I suggested to him the idea of a small store of drugs—to be shared with the women's Kommando. He took the bait more readily than I expected. Of course, the Kapo was all for it. Just what we needed. However, A moment later he was beset by doubts. "But where will you get the drugs from?"

"From Auschwitz," I said. "From the sick bay."

"Yes, you're right," he replied thoughtfully, adding in a peremptory tone: "At once. Tomorrow the under-Kapo will take you back to the main camp, where you will collect a supply of drugs. Understood?"

"Yes, sir," I confirmed enthusiastically. Everything seemed to be going the way I had planned.

Thus fortune smiled on me on my first day with the Harmensee-Schule Kommando. For having worked well, the Kapo gave me an extra bread ration and a promise of second helpings at every meal. It was with a feeling of great relief that I lay on my not very comfortable bunk, and I hid my extra bread ration under my head. It was to be for tomorrow's breakfast. However, before I went to sleep, I felt myself being bitten all over. At first I thought it was fleas until I managed to catch one in the dark. Holding it between thumb and forefinger, I felt that this something was too big to be a flea. I squashed it with repugnance and was horrified to discover from the offensive smell that it was a bedbug. Whole armies of bedbugs had attached themselves to me, a fresh blood donor. I was used to lice and fleas, but I had never yet come across bugs in the camp. Damn and blast them!

I did not go to sleep until it was almost morning, determined that between the bugs and me it was to be war to the bitter end. And to the list of drugs I was to collect in a few hours' time I added an insecticide.

CHAPTER 39

ESCORTED BY a guard and the foreman, I drove to Auschwitz in a cart. It was early in the morning; the sun had hardly yet penetrated through the milky, damp mist. On the way we passed many women's work teams who were making their way from the women's concentration camp to work at Harmensee. Each woman was carrying at least two bricks intended for the building of henhouses. Our guard gave a cheerful wave to the wardresses he knew; they were accompanied by trained guard dogs. Amid yells and blows female Kapos goaded the emaciated women prisoners, who bent low under the weight of the bricks they had carried for several miles.

After we had passed through the deserted village we came into open country. Here the mist had begun to lift and from afar one could now discern the many looming watchtowers as well as the flat-roofed blocks of Birkenau camp. Immediately beyond the railway crossing, a few hundred feet to the right, were the buildings of a market garden. Once we had passed them, we were not far from the main camp of Auschwitz, a fact which was illustrated by the thousands of prisoners who were marching to work with a song on their lips. We left the cart in a yard and proceeded, without a guard—because we were now inside the outer cordon—to the Blockführers' office from where, having duly reported, we entered the camp. I arranged with the foreman that he was to collect me from the sick bay at midday and help me carry the drugs. I myself went to camp senior Bock and requested an allocation of drugs for the Kommando. Bock ordered me to go to the loft of Block 28, where at present an operation was in progress to sort all drugs which had been brought into the camp by the huge numbers of prisoners arriving daily. My well-meaning friends packed two large suitcases with all sorts of drugs, giving me at the same time strict instructions as to their use, since they knew well that I was only a "Kommando miracle doctor."

From the diet kitchen I managed to get some groceries, such as semolina, sugar, cereal and white bread, which were meant for people with gastric trouble, but which, as I knew already now, would be impounded by one of the female Kapos. In addition I was given a supply of drops that smelled of alcohol, like valerian drops. I took no hypodermic syringes because I did not know how to handle them. Besides, they were too valuable because there were never enough of them to meet the demand of the sick bay. Somebody flung in a few bottles of a liquid smelling of menthol. They were to be used as a mouthwash and supposedly had some alcohol content. I remembered the taste of this "liniment"—as it was called in the camp—from the time of my stay there, when someone suddenly discovered this liquid bore some resemblance to schnapps; I had tried it and paid dearly for my curiosity.

My keenest expectations were by far surpassed. I was in possession of sufficient drugs to supply the needs of a large Kommando for a considerable time. Surely as soon as the Kapo saw the contents of the two large suitcases, I would rise in his esteem and strengthen his conviction that I was indispensable as a nursing orderly in his Kommando. While Bock was getting me a permit to take the drugs out of the camp and I was waiting for my foreman, I visited my old pals for a chat.

In the sick bay things were far from happy. Entress carried out frequent selections, which meant that huge numbers of seriously ill people were injected. SDG Klehr, my special friend, himself administered a few dozen phenol injections daily. For some time now the Political Department had taken an interest in the activities of the hospital; they were particularly struck by the demise

118

of several camp stool pigeons who had been sent to the sick bay as Funktionshäftlinge or as patients. There had also been the sudden deaths of a few Kapos who had been conspicuous for their exceptional zeal in murdering and maltreating prisoners. Hence the tense and nervous atmosphere. It was not enough that the majority of prisoners hated the hospital—because it was generally a place of liquidation—but it acquired additionally a bad reputation in the eyes of the camp élite, who believed they were entitled to VIP treatment. Following the loss of the old stool pigeons, the Political Department sent new ones to the hospital; this time however—having grown wise after the event—they kept a special eye on them, thus in many cases saving their lives, although at the same time enabling us to find out who they were. Because of constant friction among the staff, Bock's position as hospital camp senior was weakened; some wanted to get rid of him, reproaching him on the one hand for not knowing his job and on the other for favoring a group of young men who were useless as hospital staff and whom he had been instrumental in turning into homosexuals. The Political Department, however, regarded him as champion of the Poles, who formed the majority of the hospital staff. There was trouble brewing.

Gienek Obojski, who was generally popular and known to be calm and even-tempered, got into arguments with a few block seniors and fought an unequal fight against them which later was openly discussed in the camp. During his daily rounds collecting the dead in the blocks—they were, alas, there at all times—he reproached a block senior. This particular man was notorious for killing prisoners in order to get their bread rations and for concealing corpses from the corpse bearers while listing them as alive. At the same time, he complicated the work of the corpse bearers and muddled up the "book of the dead" they kept. This book had to be in order, otherwise the numbers would not be right during roll call. Obojski was well aware of the sinister doings of certain block seniors and tolerated them until he could take it no longer. At first there had been a quarrel and then a fight. The block senior struck the first blow, and Obojski was not slow to give him back as good as he got. Screaming at the top of his voice, and streaming

119

with blood, the block senior ran to fetch reinforcements. A gang of murderers flung themselves on Gienek, who, being no slouch, faced his attackers bravely. He got hold of one of his assailants and flung him round and round, taking swipes at the rest of them with this live weapon. Unable to get the better of the enraged Obojski, the block seniors ran to the block leaders' office and reported to the SS men that there was a "revolt" of the Poles in the camp.

Palitzsch was first to arrive in order to subdue the rioters, no doubt hoping to give full vent to one of his towering rages. But when he saw no one but Obojski, all alone, defending himself bravely against a horde of toughs and villains, and, what was more, knocking them out one after the other, he got angry, too, and began hitting the block seniors because of their weakness. The outcome of all this was that Obojski was rewarded for being a valiant fighter, while the block seniors had to do long periods of sport on Palitzsch's orders to improve their condition.

My friends related the course of this dramatic and significant incident to me in the presence of Gienek who, smiling, reproached them for their exaggeration. However, he did not deny that he had, in his own defense, given the block seniors a sharp lesson without being worse off himself.

At midday the foreman turned up. I said good-bye to the boys, promising each of them one of the chickens or fishes which, be it noted, I had so far failed to even see in Harmensee. We picked up the suitcases with the drugs—I gave the heavier one to the foreman to carry, taking the lighter one myself—and walked towards the camp gate. Having been informed in advance by the SDG, the Blockführer did not spend long rummaging in the suitcases since he knew what was inside them, so before very long we got back to where we had left the cart. The suitcases were stowed on the cart, and we waited for the guard to arrive.

The SS man, who was eaten up with curiosity as to the contents of the cases, waited until we had reached the open field. Then he opened them. Supposedly out of curiosity he examined everything and removed a few bits and pieces. Truthfully I was curious myself to see what the various small boxes contained; I opened them one by one, hoping I might strike it lucky, as I knew that some of these drugs had not yet been sorted. I was sure that our guard had heard, too, that when sorting drugs and medicines confiscated from newly arrived prisoners, one would occasionally find quite a few valuable objects because in their naïvety prisoners believed that, while everything else might be taken from them, they would be allowed to keep their drugs. For this reason they hid these valuables among their pills. I was not lucky enough to find anything.

"Well, what did you organize, nursing orderly?" the Kapo greeted us as soon as we had arrived. With pride I pointed at the two large suitcases on the cart. The Kapo whistled appreciatively. Having examined the contents of the cases, he ordered me to establish a first-aid box with some of the drugs I had brought. This first-aid box was to be stored in our quarters; the rest was to be kept in the main building and be also at the disposal of the women. The "liniment," having been recognized as potential alcoholic refreshment, was reserved for the exclusive use of the Kapo. As I was checking once more through the boxes, I happened to open one that contained cotton wool. To my surprise and dismay—for the Kapo was all the time looking over my shoulder—a gentleman's gold watch slipped out from under the cotton wool. Needless to say, it was immediately confiscated by the Kapo.

That evening I had to massage the Kapo again for he was racked with pain. It was easier to treat him now because I rubbed camphorated ointment on his back. He did not mention the watch; besides, he was drunk. He stank of alcohol, camphor and, above all, menthol.

Staggering through the dark, the Kapo knocked against every corner as he tried to find a bucket. He had to vomit. It served him right.

Next morning the Kapo really did look ill. Being a "miracle doctor," I realized, of course, that such were the consequences of poisoning with alcohol, which contained several harmful substances. The smell of alcohol and camphor had gone, but he still reeked of menthol. He must have had a few mouthfuls of the mouthwash on the previous day. Eyeing me askance he muttered angrily: "Liniment, liniment." Did *I* ask him to drink it?

121

CHAPTER 40

THE JOB of Kommando nursing orderly was unfortunately not as splendid as I had imagined. The Kapo never gave me any less heavy work. I went on slaking lime or emptying the pits under the henhouses, which later I had to build. I was just a bricklayer, and my post as a nursing orderly was regarded by the Kapo as an additional occupation, for he used my free time mainly for his own needs and purposes. The greater my popularity as the one and only nursing orderly—an arrangement I was no longer in a position to back out of—the more I actually came to be a real "miracle doctor." The people needed help. Things were not so bad if it was merely a matter of putting on a dressing. It was much worse, however, if somebody was really ill. Then I had to "do magic," as Kolczynski, the only one in the know, would say. I gave the patient some pill or other, mostly aspirin, which could do him no harm and sometimes even helped. If they were really seriously ill, I sent them to the hospital in the main camp, at times with the approval of the Kapo. Time seemed to be racing. We were now in late autumn and with it came hopeless days of gray weather and of cold. The early mornings were very chilly and turned the dew into frost. More and more often I recalled the good times in the sick bay, where I had worked under cover.

One autumn morning, as I was busy cleaning bricks from the demolition site, I saw a never-ending column of women coming from the direction of Birkenau. Each of them carried two or three bricks, which they dropped in a certain spot with a sigh of relief. Then they turned back, reappearing a few hours later with another load. The women walked barefoot, clad in threadbare summer dresses through which their bare skin could be seen. They were all young, suntanned and with traces of beauty which had not yet been wiped out by the camp. They were Jewesses from a Dutch transport. The SS women set their dogs on them, and the Kapos outdid each other in ill-treating the young women, who were almost demented with fear. This sad procession came twice or three times a day. Each day there were fewer of them, and after only one week those still alive looked like worn-out old hags, in whom it was difficult to recognize those girls of a few days ago. A few more days passed, and then they did not come any more. No doubt they had been liquidated because they were no longer fit for work. Our Kommandoführer did not get in a state about it: there were more than enough bricks, and the henhouses were almost completed.

The thought of winter approaching appalled me. How was I going to stand life in this wretched Kommando when I was already now feeling cold and poorly? Moreover, the Kapo had changed his behavior and had begun pestering me. He continued to suffer from rheumatism and lumbago of which I could not cure him. Every labor brings its own reward. Bearing this wise motto in mind, I discontinued my massage sessions with the Kapo, which I hated and which humiliated me in the eyes of my friends. I worked in the Kommando like the others, and I was quite willing to work as Kommando nursing orderly, but I had no intention to go on being "personal physician" to the honorable Mr. Kapo. To hell with him! He had his store of drugs; let him swallow pain-killers and wash them down with "liniment." He had taken to drinking "liniment" again after he had exhausted his supply of the hard stuff, which he had acquired from an SS man in exchange for the gents' gold watch. Although my massages had not cured him, they had given him relief. One evening he came to me demanding that I should massage him.

"Pills not good," he said grimacing. "Massage me," he added peremptorily.

The hell I'll massage you, I cursed inwardly while trying to compose a polite but evasive reply.

"It so happens, Herr Kapo, that I am ill myself today. I've got lumbago." To demonstrate this I made a pained face and put my hand on my back with a gesture I had learned from watching the Kapo. I seemed to have exaggerated the miming because he shouted "What?" barely restraining himself from flying off the handle.

The blood was rushing to his head, and he grew quite red in the face, but he managed to keep his temper.

123

"Very well, very well," he hissed. "Get lost."

He called for his boy: "Block orderly, fetch the camphor ointment!"

The block orderly brought the tube of ointment and handed it to his master. The Kapo personally rubbed the ointment onto the painful spots and, talking half to himself and half to the lad, but so that I was bound to hear it, said, "That's it, now I have to do this myself; our nursing orderly is very ill today." And in a raised voice he added nastily, "He's got lumbago, just fancy that, lumbago."

This did not bode well. I had overdone it. Next morning the Kapo rose, resilient but in a foul temper. He was full of bounce and had to get rid of this surplus energy in some way. He herded us into the yard through the narrow door, screaming and pushing as though we could all go through the door at once. Since I was supposed to have lumbago, I decided to be consistent and continue with my play-acting. I did not push and brought up the rear, struggling along. As I stood in the door, I received unexpectedly an almighty kick which within seconds propelled me into the yard, where I landed on all fours. I got up immediately but felt that I must have twisted my back. The pain spread quickly, and I could no longer stand up straight. The Kapo, who had by now simmered down, tried to pretend that the unfortunate kick was meant as a joke. He gave me a friendly slap on the shoulder and said, trying to sound humorous, "You know, nursing orderly, this is the best massage for lumbago." And he accompanied his words with a light push of his knee into my already rather painful backside.

During the march to work, when he noticed that I was walking hunched up, he tried to be chummy.

"You'll have to organize a few more drugs—and some 'liniment' too, eh!" He laughed, winking meaningfully.

Just you wait, I'll give you liniment. It'll be phenol more likely, you son of a bitch, I thought. But out loud I expressed my willingness to get lots of drugs and more of his beloved liniment from Auschwitz. I decided to take this opportunity if at all possible, of finding refuge in the sick bay and not returning to this crazy Kapo and the Kommando. I had had enough, and besides winter was approaching.

A sudden temperature which I got due to a bad cold hastened my decision. I did not let on to the Kapo that I had a temperature and thus qualified for admission to the hospital. He might have smelled a rat and forbidden my trip to Auschwitz, suspecting that I did not intend ever to return to Harmensee.

CHAPTER 41

IT WAS during the first days of October that I was once again traveling to Auschwitz in a cart sent by the Kapo. I was firmly determined to stay in the sick bay.

Traveling with me was a prisoner from the fish-breeding Kommando, who had been ordered to report to the Political Department. It was easy to guess that this was his last journey. No doubt they intended to liquidate him. It seemed that the prisoner was well aware of the fate awaiting him, for he sat, sad and lost in his own thoughts, not speaking to anyone. I took the seat next to him. Behind me sat the carter, another prisoner, who was clicking his tongue and talking affectionately to the horse, which was lazily trotting along the deeply rutted road. Opposite us lounged the SS man, our only guard. He was an older, good-natured man, who was content to sit here quietly instead of standing for hours somewhere along the cordon with his carbine cocked and ready.

Once we had left Harmensee behind, we were surrounded by a fallow field, still a long way from Birkenau and still farther away from the main camp. Everything around us was silent and empty; it seemed that the mist, swathing everything in a dense veil, had delayed the departure of the columns to their daily labors. This was the long-awaited chance to escape. I glanced anxiously at the fellow prisoner next to me. What would happen if suddenly the urge to escape were to overcome him? Strictly speaking, this was the only chance left to him. Would he seize it? What would then happen to us? To me? I was unable to move. With this temperature and my black and blue backside I should not get very far. For some time now, I had been watching the guard, who was vainly trying to light a cigarette. It did not work; his matches kept going out.

"Shit!" he cursed, leaning his carbine against the side of the cart, which jumped up and down on the bumpy country road. He was completely absorbed with lighting his cigarette. And as if there was a jinx on them, the matches kept going out. Meanwhile the carbine slid, inch by inch, farther in the direction of my fellow prisoner, until at last the barrel lay across his knees. Suddenly the prisoner seemed to have woken from his thoughts; he looked at the SS man who was messing about with his matches, and slowly he grasped the barrel in his hands, which were red and chapped from the cold.

A flame flashed; at last the match worked. The guard inhaled his first draught and exhaled the smoke contentedly. With his free hand he felt for the spot where, briefly, he had put down his carbine. Only at that moment did he realize that the prisoner held it in his hands. The SS man froze. He sat as if hypnotized, the slowly burning cigarette dangling from his half-open lips. The prisoner, who was still holding the weapon in his trembling hands, seemed undecided: ought he to shoot, hit the German between the eyes with the butt, or simply hand it back? The carter, with not an inkling of what was going on behind his back, continued to whistle cheerfully. The cart wheels crunched as they cracked the ice of frozen puddles in the field track.

Time was standing still. Why in heaven's name didn't he do what had to be done? I was drenched with sweat and felt my shirt clinging to my damp skin. We traveled, without stirring, for what seemed to be a long time. From the early morning mist the first towers of Birkenau emerged. The cigarette between the lips of the deathly pale SS man was burning down. The carter turned round. Perhaps he had suddenly felt my trembling back against his own. In a flash he grasped the situation and was petrified. All at once the SS man smiled a relaxed smile. He took the butt out of his mouth, but the cigarette paper stuck to his lips. He tried to get rid of it by spitting and managed it at last. He reached in his pocket, pulled out a pack, then he held out his hand to the prisoner with the carbine and offered him a cigarette as if nothing had happened. This gesture was well calculated. The guard had realized that the prisoner had missed the right moment for action. With a simple, natural movement he broke the tension. The prisoner took a cigarette with one hand and returned the carbine to the guard with the other, just as naturally as the guard had offered him the cigarette.

After that the SS man gave the prisoner his matches. This time, too, the matches would not light. Then he gave him his butt, which was still glowing, for him to use to light his cigarette. Now the prisoner inhaled deeply and after a while blew out the bluish smoke, which quickly disappeared in the morning haze. The whole scene had taken place in complete silence, although it seemed as if the German whispered "Thanks." But perhaps I misheard.

That same day the cart returned to Harmensee with only two passengers. They were the SS man and the carter-prisoner. I remained in the sick bay. The prisoner who had been summoned to the Political Department was shot at the Black Wall of the yard in Block 11.

CHAPTER 42

I was admitted to the hospital as a patient. My temperature was rather high. Whatever it was seemed to turn into a protracted illness. However, after three days the temperature went down, and I was, strictly speaking, well again. My buddies took me to a room on the first floor of Block 28. Conditions there were almost luxurious because we had single beds with sheets and blankets. The ward was for the exclusive use of the camp élite; there were not more than about a dozen patients there. The ward orderly was a good friend of mine named Andrzej. Although I had already recovered, he pretended I was still ill and faked the temperature chart above my bed.

127

SDG Klehr did not often look in—there were no "patients" for him here—and Dr. Entress came even less often. As I was afraid of being recognized by Klehr, Andrzej or his brother would warn me every time his arrival was imminent, and I would leave the ward and hide either in the toilet or in the washroom.

It was already autumn, with rain and snow and the wind whistling somberly through the branches of the nearby poplar trees. I lay cosily in a warm bed, protected and with extra food provided by my kindly friends. Sometimes I even went so far as to venture into the camp for a visit to my old pals. One day Edek Galinski took me to Block 4 to meet Jewish prisoners who worked in the Kommando which was generally called Canada, where the belongings of deported Jews were stored. There I ran across David. He was in excellent health. Canada was different from Buna. David was stuffed to the gills, looked very well and was in the best of spirits. He informed us that on the following day they were expecting a large transport from Holland. There would be plenty of stuff for Canada. He gave me a tin of sardines and some chocolate.

One afternoon when I lay in bed dozing, Obojski burst into the room excitedly. "Wiesiek, come downstairs this minute. I'll show you something. You'll be pleased."

Gienek led me into the cellar where the mortuary was. On the concrete, as always, lay a heap of corpses. Next to it the large body of a giant covered with a tarpaulin. With a flourish Gienek pulled away the cover and with an elegant bow announced to me with delight, "Look, here at your feet, your best bosom friend."

"Leo," I cried, utterly surprised.

One must respect death even if it is your worst enemy's. But I practically glowed with joy. I was so happy that I performed a mad dance, again and again leaping across the huge body which was no longer dangerous, touching the already limp and once brawny arms which had inflicted so much suffering on me, aping him and mocking this giant of whom the whole camp had been terrified, I most of all.

"I've survived you, you villain. You didn't finish me off. Instead the lice got to you," I triumphed.

Gienek had told me all the details of his death. He died of typhus. It was said that every effort was made to keep him alive. As camp senior of Birkenau, he had access to any drug he required in order to protect himself against typhus and its consequences. They filled him with pills and injections. The nursing orderlies never left him alone for a second. For all that, this strong and healthy organism did not pull through. For all that? Later it was rumored that someone helped him to die. In other words, he had been murdered. Allegedly it was known who had done it. Well, whatever the truth, the camp had lost another villain and I another enemy. That's always a relief. That evening I prayed fervently, thanking God for having taken unto Himself one of the worst murderers of Auschwitz. My heart was filled with hope. Perhaps I might survive this camp after all, I thought, for the first time allowing myself the faintest glimmer of hope that such a thing might be in the realm of the possible.

Unfortunately, there were still others who were even more wicked than Leo Wietschorek. Klehr, for instance. I avoided him whenever I could, but in the end he caught me. I was just coming out of the nursing orderlies' room where they gave me extra food, when I ran straight into him. Of course, he recognized me at once.

"What are you doing here?" he demanded, giving me a searching look.

"I am ill," I replied promptly but not very convincingly. I looked the picture of health, and there was nothing whatsoever which would suggest that I was a sick man.

"So you're ill, are you? Don't make me laugh. Which ward are you in, eh? Block senior! Camp senior!" He yelled so furiously that I hardly dared breathe. I was in for it now, no mistake about it.

He gave orders that I was to be discharged into the camp forthwith. He would make the report personally. He threatened the block senior with the bunker; he hurled abuse at Bock, and as for me, he obviously considered me as one who had had it. Once I had managed to get away, but this was the end. Towards midday Bock summoned me to his room in Block 21. I went as though to my own execution.

129

Bock narrowed his little eyes and regarded me silently. The corners of his mouth trembled, his narrow face, lined with wrinkles, grimaced, as was his wont in moments of great agitation or when he was in a good mood. At last he said, "You're in luck, you little bugger."

He is in a good mood, I noticed with much relief and not a little satisfaction. That's a good sign.

"SDG Klehr wants you finished off." He accompanied the last words with an expressive gesture in order to illustrate how he would do it. "But the joke is going to be on him, do you understand?" He tried to express himself as simply as he could to make sure I understood him because he knew that I did not speak German. Bock, then, had decided to save me from Klehr by removing me altogether from his field of vision. He took advantage of the fact that, at that very moment, Klehr was busy with injections in the consulting room of Block 20 and that, by a happy coincidence, an ambulance was about to leave for Birkenau. Therefore he not only removed me from the sick bay but also from the main camp by transferring me to Birkenau. If Klehr were to ask him for me, he intended showing him my transfer card to Birkenau where, as everyone knew, the penal company was, and it was there Klehr planned to send me. Klehr would be satisfied that his orders had been carried out. But I, instead of going to the SK, was to join the nursing orderlies who were temporarily working in the women's camp sick bay, where another SS doctor as well as another SDG were in charge; in other words, a department where Klehr had no business. Presently I sat in the ambulance which was taking me to Birkenau, where a new stage in my camp life was to begin.

CHAPTER 43

AFTER A journey lasting only a few minutes, the van bearing the sign of the Red Cross stopped outside the gate of the women's camp. One after another, the nosy wardresses peeped inside until a young Blockführer allowed us to enter the camp. When we had reached the hospital grounds, the ambulance stopped in front of a little wooden hut. SDG Scherpe opened the ambulance door and ordered me to get out and take the parcels of drugs and medicines into the hut.

Suddenly I was in another world. In an instant I was surrounded by a swarm of chattering young women. How greatly they differed from the ones I had last seen in Harmensee. Above all, they had hair on their heads—normal, long hair, carefully brushed and covered by clean headscarves. They wore neat, striped dresses, stockings and shoes. There was nothing about them to remind one of the ragged, dirty, beaten, starving and hunted women from the outside Kommando. It was still obvious that they were prisoners and, like all prisoners, without rights, but they were treated more gently than the others. The SDG even knew their first names. He treated them kindly and they, in their turn, approached him with a certain informality. When the sick bay Kapo, a good-looking woman, a "political" with a nice face and wearing a red triangle, came in accompanied by SS officer Dr. Rhode, the girls scampered back to their office work. The medical supplies were checked, and while this was going on, Dr. Zbozien entered the office. Everybody seemed to be very satisfied with what I had brought, even Dr. Rhode, a tall and portly SS doctor with a face scarred from traditional German student union duels. He appeared to be a human being with human feelings. I stood alone, near the red-hot little iron stove, and observed the scene with interest. Only after a while Dr. Rhode noticed me. When he saw a strange face he asked, surprised, "What's he doing here?"

I stood to attention and began to reel off the formula I knew by heart. I did not finish it, because he interrupted me in mid-sentence and turned with a questioning gesture to the SDG.

Scherpe briefly explained my presence. "Camp senior Bock has sent us another joiner, Herr *Obersturmbannführer* [Major]."

Zbozien gave me a quick look out of the corner of his eye, apparently surprised about my new trade. From my sick bay days he remembered me as an orderly and corpse bearer; now I reverted to my first occupation in the camp. Dr. Rhode looked me up and down with a critical eye—it would appear that he was favorably impressed because I was in quite good shape—and said absentmindedly: "Good, very good. We have a lot of work here." After that he turned to the woman Kapo and settled down to a conversation with her. Dr. Zbozien explained to me what my work would consist of. Since Bock had sent me here as a joiner, I was to assist Staszek Paduch, who was a genuine joiner, working in this Kommando.

"Staszek is working in one of the hospital blocks. Off you go and find him. I shall have to go on my rounds directly."

On my search for Staszek I came to Block 24, where I ran across Julek K., whom Dr. Zbozien had put in charge of the block to look after the entire women's quarters.

With the words "Ma, meet our new nursing orderly," he introduced me to a fat, elderly German woman who wore a white overall and the armband of a block senior. I quickly glanced at her triangle: black.

Ma held out her plump hand to me and began to talk in a hoarse voice to a stout blonde standing next to her: "Have you heard, Anni?" She turned to me and explained: "Anni is my deputy."

I shook the soft smooth hand of the block senior's deputy. Anni smiled quite pleasantly, without taking her eyes off me. A clean white blouse clung tightly to her ample bosom. Another black triangle. I stood there, a little timid, not knowing what to talk to them about. Fortunately, a new figure appeared in the open door. This one was a pretty young Polish girl whom I had already noticed at the office. At once Julek livened up remarkably.

"Come and meet my friend Halina. He's to stay in our Kommando here and help Staszek in the joinery."

We began to talk, forgetting the two German women, who left after a while with a prisoner who had come to call for them. It was not hard to notice in the course of the conversation that between Julek and Halina, who was the clerk of this block, there existed a close relationship. They gave the impression of being a pair of lovers, which contrasted strangely with the surroundings. I withdrew, pretending to be looking for Staszek, because I saw that they wanted to be alone.

I found him in Block 23, where he was busy repairing the big

132

entrance door. "Well, there you are at last, Mr. Joiner." He greeted me cheerfully. "I've already been told that I am to have an assistant," he said without interrupting his work. "This door needs weather-stripping for the women here; there's a terrible draft. The poor things might freeze to death otherwise. Just look how many of them there are in here." He took me inside the hut. On three-tiered bunks, crowded close together down the two walls of the long hut, lay hundreds of emaciated figures, scarcely differing from skeletons. Some of the women were squatting on their bunks searching for lice.

Others tried determinedly to catch the lice in blankets that were more like rags. Again others were moving naked between the beds, trying to get as close as possible to the one and only stove, which took up the center section of the hut, with the forlorn hope of getting at least a little warmth. The floor was covered with filth for which a muckheap would have been a better place; and when they stepped on it their bare feet made a squelching sound. Living skeletons with pendulous breasts, their bodies wasted, dirty, festering. The mortuary in Block 28 was better to look at. I had seen thousands of corpses, countless numbers of Mussulmen; I had managed to get used to the sight of them, but these sick, starving, filthy, dying creatures made a fearful impression on me. To look at them was appalling.

Staszek noticed that I was trying to avoid looking inside the hut. He took me by the arm and led me to the exit.

"It won't be long, and you'll be used to this sight. However, perhaps things will soon change for the better. Why else have we been brought here? We try to do what we can. And now, come along, I'll take you to my workshop."

Since early that morning snow had been falling gently, covering the lightly frozen mud with a thin blanket. Lying near the block was a heap of corpses, consisting of a dozen naked female bodies that had been carelessly flung one on top of the other. Large rats were already scavenging among them. The rats only scurried away when two women approached dragging the corpse of an old woman behind them; she had obviously died only a short while ago, as her thin body was still slack.

133

"Fresh food for the rats," remarked Staszek as he shunted me to Block 24, where the temporary joinery was.

"Our midday meal will be presently," he said as he noticed the girls bending under the weight of the soup buckets. "You'll see how they look after us here."

CHAPTER 44

THE WORKSHOP was behind a wooden partition in front of the hut opposite the block senior's room. Strictly speaking it was the nurses' room, a very cramped room with three or four rectangular bunks, a little iron stove and a carpenter's bench at the one window, which looked out onto the open space outside the hut. A fire roared in the stove. Someone with almost-red hair was bending over the stove and throwing pieces of wood into it.

Staszek gave her a hard slap on the backside. She straightened up angrily. Threatening him with a piece of wood which she held in her hand, she hissed:

"Stop fooling around, you . . . ." She was looking for the right word and found it. "You lecher."

Staszek put his arms around her and squeezed her so tightly that she screamed with pain and dropped the piece of wood with which she had meant to hit him. Thereupon Staszek loosened his embrace, but kept holding her in his arms, a motion which Fanny interpreted as a caress. Slowly her rage abated and her vulgar and freckled face blossomed into a timid smile, displaying a set of ugly and rotting teeth, while her cunning little eyes squinted lasciviously. Giving me a conspiratorial wink Staszek introduced her.

"Here's Fanny, the beauty queen of the Reeperbahn and—" He wanted to introduce me to Fanny, but she interrupted him impatiently. "I know. Anni's already told me."

She flirted with Staszek, pointing her finger first at him, then at herself and explaining this mime with one word: love. Staszek was falling about laughing, but I was flabbergasted as I listened to

134

further familiar remarks, this time referring to me and Anni, the deputy block senior.

"Anni and you also love. Is lovely, no?" she asked in broken German.

Staszek took advantage of the commotion in the corridor, caused by the arrival of the buckets with the midday meal, in order to push the loquacious and romantic Fanny outside.

"Phew." He breathed a sigh of relief. "I have to put on an act with that repulsive female—for the bread. You, old son, will have to be patient with Anni. It's best to be on good terms with them. Almost the entire staff in this block are German broads like those two, and they have VD as well. Ma, the block senior, is their guardian, a real madam. What a lot of shit!"

"Shit, shit," a woman's voice mimicking Staszek rang out from the upper bunk. From under the blanket peeped a pretty little head with an oval face and raven-black hair, which hid her large blue eyes. Her face was heavily made up and covered with a thick layer of powder. With the expression of a spoiled child, she asked in a childish little voice: "Staszek, dear, do bring me something to eat. I'm so ill."

"All right, all right, but I haven't any time just now, Lisa." Staszek put her off and began planing boards; I busied myself with the straightening of nails in order to do at least something. Lisa said "Shit" and slumped back onto her bunk, while Staszek enlightened me about conditions in the women's sick bay.

"Lisa is another whore, but quiet and clean. For days on end she lies here, sleeping or looking at herself in the mirror and making up her face. Apart from that she's not interested in anything. She's found a pad here like the rest of the Germans whom Ma has made her special favorites. The situation is similar in the other blocks. They rule here, don't look after the sick, steal things from them. But slowly we'll establish some order. Our Kommando is very much appreciated by the women and even by some of the camp authorities, headed by camp Dr. Rhode. Rhode supports our efforts, and above all he supports Dr. Zbozien, whom he considers to be a capable doctor. Things like the temporary control of the typhoid epidemic, the improvement of hygienic condi-

135

tions, the gradual replacement of staff by experts, and, altogether, the organization of medical supplies and hypodermic syringes from the men's camp for treatment—it's all thanks to Dr. Zbozien and a few nursing orderlies from Auschwitz who have been assigned here and who take their samaritan's job seriously. But it's also thanks to all these prisoners—plumbers, roofers, sewage workers, chimney sweeps, electricians, and so on—who manage to get into the women's camp under all sorts of pretexts, who smuggle food, medical supplies, stiffs, linen, sanitary towels, cigarettes; in other words, anything they can lay their hands on that the women lack.

"In return the women give their trust, their gratitude, and at times even their love. Almost every man who comes has a girl friend, a member of his family, or his wife here. Every woman longs for a protector; it is knowing that there is someone who cares for them that gives them the strength to survive under conditions which animals would not stand. With the exception of rats, of course, thousands of these bloody rats, which gnaw the corpses and sometimes actually attack the seriously ill who are not strong enough to chase them away . . . Just look at Julek and little Halina cuddling at the window over there."

They noticed that we were watching them and drew apart.

"They love each other," Staszek went on. "They've got to get something out of this bloody life. Julek has spilled his guts out in this block, and one can see the results. His block is considered one of the best in spite of this staff of whores."

"Whore, whore," Lisa echoed again. Obviously she either found it easy to pick up this kind of word or she remembered it from her days as a streetwalker.

"Staszek, I'm hungry," she wailed.

Into the room came Fanny carrying a bowl of steaming food. She placed it on the workbench in front of Staszek and said, "Hope you'll enjoy your dinner."

She gazed into his eyes like a faithful servant waiting for a word of praise from her lord and master. Staszek wiped his hands on his trousers. He pushed his spoon into the thick soup but did not begin to eat.

136

"And what about his food?" he asked severely, pointing at me.

"Anni's bringing it," she replied huffily, shrugging her shoulders in order to demonstrate that I was absolutely of no concern to her. I was Anni's department. "Why don't you eat, dear?" she said ingratiatingly.

After a while Anni came in and put a full bowl in front of me.

"Enjoy your dinner, lad." Her piping voice invited me to eat.

We were both hungry, so we needed no invitation to get on with our food. Fanny and Anni stood to one side watching us attack the soup without taking the slightest notice of Lisa's entreaties.

"Anni! Fanny!" She pestered first one, then the other, her voice monotonous. Without success, though; the two turned a deaf ear. In the end, Lisa got angry.

"You lazy bitches! You fucking whores! Whores, whores." She decided, at last, to get down from her bed, displaying long, slim legs as she did so. Viciously eyeing her two unhelpful colleagues she flung open the door so violently that the wall shook. Anni and Fanny laughed. Staszek pushed away the empty dishes, cleaned the table with wood shavings and silently resumed work. I did the same. Anni—without receiving a word of thanks—stacked the dishes and left the room. Outside, a few emaciated women fought for the empty soup bucket. In a rage, Fanny ran up to the fighting Mussulman women. The women fled, leaving the bucket unscraped. I remembered the good meal we had just enjoyed and wondered how many of the patients had had to go without food. Lisa returned smoking a cigarette. She inhaled greedily. Then she climbed back on to her bunk. She really did have fantastic legs.

In the room it was pleasantly warm, the fire roaring in the iron stove. Outside it was still snowing; the women who came to collect the empty soup buckets were covered with a layer of wet, quickly melting snowflakes. Lisa was hot. She turned over onto her stomach. Then she flung off her blanket and lay motionless on her back, looking at the ceiling and blowing smoke rings. We worked until late in the evening. The Germans did not look in again on us. Only Dr. Zbozien paid us a visit and talked with Julek for a long time. Afterwards he made a sketch for Staszek of some shelves he wanted made for the outpatients' department. Accom-

137

panied by the SDG, who took us up to the guardhouse, we returned to the men's camp rather late. My first day of working in Birkenau, the camp with the worst possible reputation among the Auschwitz prisoners, had come to an end.

CHAPTER 45

ALTHOUGH I had now been living in the men's camp for a few days, I still did not know it. We left for work early in the morning, when it was still dark, and returned at night. In the women's hospital, on the other hand, I felt quite at home. There was, it is true, a lot of work, but I did not work my fingers to the bone. Staszek did not have a great deal of confidence in my abilities as a joiner. He did everything himself and only gave me things to repair which I could not spoil. Therefore, I repaired tables, stools and bunks, weather-stripped windows and doors, and even carried out some small jobs as a fitter. Occasionally, I would stop somewhere for a chat or sit down or even have a quick snack.

We were told that a bunk in Block 23 was falling apart. I went there to repair it. Actually, I took quite a long time doing the job because in the next bed, head to foot, lay two young girls with whom I started to talk. Halina and Jadzia had recovered from an attack of typhus and were slowly convalescing. Once I had made their acquaintance I often dropped in to say hello. Before long I discovered that I was not the only one to visit them. That meant they already had protectors. Perhaps that was why they were making such a rapid recovery.

Halina was cheerful and witty. I liked her. I knew that she smoked clandestinely. In order to please her I organized some cigarettes for her.

One day, when I was completely engrossed in talking to Halina and gazing at her, I failed to notice that chief wardress Mandel had entered the block. This delightful SS woman hit me over the head with her whip and, worse still, did this in the presence of the girl whose affections I was trying to gain. It is very humiliating for

138

a man to be struck by a woman. After that I avoided this venomous female. Halina was quite well again soon afterwards, and as she spoke German she found a good job in the sick bay office where I went only seldom.

Block 28 was part of the sick bay although it was outside the hospital area. It was one of the first brick barracks which had been built at a so-called convalescent block. Nearby was Block 25, a dumping ground for corpses and dying Mussulman women, who were left there helpless with only one avenue of escape: the gas chamber.

Nicet Wlodarski, who was in charge of the convalescent block, tried as best he could to introduce at least a minimum of medical treatment. Industrious and modest, he was completely dedicated to his work of compassion. He was courageously helped by Berta Ungar, the block senior, a Slovak Jewess who was an energetic and resourceful woman. In contrast to the murky reputation the block senior enjoyed in those days and also in contrast to her appearance—for Berta was a woman with a rather masculine figure and a deep, penetrating voice, strong and clever—she had a soft heart and motherly feelings for the block and the unfortunate women who dwelled there. It is therefore not surprising that in the course of her constant collaboration with Nicet, with whom she helped those who most needed it, there sprang up a friendship and perhaps even something deeper.

For some time I had been a frequent visitor in Berta's block. The indefatigable block senior constantly thought up new jobs. I carried these out myself, for Staszek was now busy furnishing the outpatients' department. My work was not exactly of the made-to-measure kind, but it was usable. In Berta's block I did not have the comforts of Block 24, where it was warm and where the German women made a fuss over me. Nevertheless I felt more at ease here; in fact, it was simply that I was among my own kind.

Possibly it had something to do with the presence of Sylvia, a seventeen-year-old girl of irresistible loveliness. Sylvia was pretty, indeed even beautiful, full of charm and innocence, without forebodings about the fate which awaited her.

I spent almost every free minute talking to her. Our conversations were perhaps naïve, too naïve for two prisoners in a concentration camp: happy childhood days, home, outings, sport, the cinema, first dates. In a word, we talked about everything that made up the happy years of our youth. We held hands, gazed into each other's eyes and forgot the world around us—the suffering, hunger, cold, diet and vermin, violence, injections and gassings, selections and mass murders—and our own eventual extermination. We were so perfectly absorbed in each other, so drunk with the happiness which this pure, platonic love gave us, a love which was platonic because we did not yet know the other, physical love.

At times Berta watched us surreptitiously to make sure that we were not up to anything naughty. Impossible! In spite of her already womanly shape, Sylvia was still a child, while I was too shy and sexually too inexperienced.

One winter's day I found that Berta had obviously been crying. Briefly, interrupting her story with sobs, she told me what had happened on the previous day. Sylvia, together with many other young, pretty, healthy girls, had been ordered to the outpatients' department. Some drunken SS men had arranged an orgy there. Virgins were not wanted in Block 10. In the morning she had been sent to the experimental block in Auschwitz, at the disposal of Professor Clauberg.

I never saw Sylvia again. But later I learned that she was alive and a member of the staff which looked after that wretched block.

CHAPTER 46

THE RAPPORTFÜHRER of the men's camp was called Schillinger; he was stocky, broad-shouldered, with long arms and the face of an ape, a reprobate and the scourge of the prisoners. He came often, too often, to the women's hospital. Rumor had it that he had a mistress here. She was supposed to be the block senior of Block 23, a German with a black triangle.

You could not call little Anni ugly, even though she had gaps in her front teeth. She was quite well built but frightfully vulgar and vicious, as depraved as her protector. Oberscharführer Schillinger was continuously drunk and ill-treated the prisoners at every opportunity, particularly those who, under a variety of pretexts, tried to get into the women's concentration camp. He could not stand our Kommando. What annoyed him most of all were our contacts with the women and the freedom with which we moved about in the women's sick bay, since we were working there with the approval of the camp authorities. On the other hand he—an SS man, a Rapportführer—was forced to smuggle himself secretly into Block 23 for a kiss and a cuddle with Anni, something which he had to keep secret at all costs because his superiors must not get to know about it. After one such escapade, Dr. Rhode—suitably primed beforehand by Dr. Zbozien—forbade Schillinger, who had yet again hit a nursing orderly, and other SS men who did not work in the hospital, to enter the sick bay area, because they could be carrying typhus into the SS barracks. Naturally we welcomed this order, but it also increased Schillinger's hatred of us. Now he made a point of harassing us when we returned to the men's camp at night.

However, he found it hard to manage without Anni. Therefore he would occasionally take advantage of Rhode's absence in order to sneak into Block 23 unobserved. Intimidated, we said nothing. After the sudden and tragic transfer of Sylvia to Block 10 in Auschwitz, I tried to finish my work in Berta's block quickly and returned to Staszek and his workshop. Good-natured Anni welcomed me back cordially but with restraint, like a lost son, whereas Fanny just smirked. They knew only too well why I had not turned up in their block for such a long time.

One day when Fanny was alone with me in the room, she took advantage of the opportunity. Mentioning the name of Sylvia, she drew me towards her bed, indicating quite unequivocally that she fancied doing what I was supposed to have done with Sylvia. I was absolutely outraged and slapped her face hard. She ran out of the room at once. I came to my senses and grew frightened of the witch's revenge. A giggle coming from the top bunk, where Lisa reclined as usual, helped to reassure me. She laughed so much that the whole three-tiered structure shook.

141

"My God! You did that beautifully! Ha, ha, beautifully!"

Much to my surprise Fanny did not take her revenge but actually began to avoid me. Lisa forgot the incident immediately and was once more completely absorbed in gazing at her reflection, which she would do for hours on end.

In Ma's room, where Halina worked, the electric light was out of order. As I was fiddling about with a screw and the rusty socket, I got an electric shock. Sparks were flying, and for a time I was unable to remove my hand. Finally I got another, more severe shock which made me fall off the ladder, luckily straight onto the block senior's bed. Before I had quite come to, I found myself in the embrace of the horrified Anni, who was pressing my shorn head to her ample bosom.

"Darling. Are you still alive, dear boy?"

I was alive all right. All I'd done was to burn the fingers on my left hand slightly. Actually, it was quite pleasant to lie like that, with my head reposing on her plump chest, which smelled of carnations.

Anni used perfume. Now she was stroking my face with her soft cat's paw. "My baby!" She was overflowing with maternal instincts, and her bosom was heaving. Shaking with laughter, Halina turned away. Ma came into the room, surveyed the idyllic scene with dismay and began hurriedly to bring the completely besotted Anni to her senses.

"Anni, you're mad. The camp doctor will be here in a moment. And you, boy, get lost!"

I managed to finish my repairs on the electric lights before they came. Ma conducted the doctors into the block. Anni glided behind us. She turned round and bestowed upon me an innocent, modest, affectionate smile.

Despite everything, Anni's nice, I thought, as I took away the ladder. Pity she's a prostitute. Perhaps there are some among them who are gentle, sensitive and good-hearted. Probably Anni's not a bad girl.

One day the runner from Block 23 arrived with the message that block senior Anni was calling for the carpenter. He was to come and bring his tools in order to repair something. As was his

142

wont, Staszek, who was busy with a serious job in the outpatients' department, sent me. Ever since my adventure with the Mandel woman I was not very keen to go to Block 23, the more so since I might meet Rapportführer Schillinger there who, nothwithstanding Rhode's ban, still visited the block from time to time. The runner took me to the block senior's room and asked me to wait; the block senior would come presently. She was tidying up the block, cursing her staff, the patients and the whole world with choice swearwords.

While I waited for Anni, I took a look round her room. In contrast to the mess, the dirt and the slovenliness in the hut where the sick lay, Anni's room was most tidy. The two-tiered bed was nicely made; there were Kelim rugs on the walls making a colorful splash, shelves concealed behind cotton curtains, a clean sheet on the table and sheer curtains made from the bandaging gauze which was so noticeably lacking in the sick bay. In the corner of the room stood a wooden washstand with a mirror and all the paraphernalia absolutely necessary to keep one's body clean. In a word: comfort. Anni came into the room all worked up and went, without taking any notice of me, to her washstand where she took off her headscarf and began to brush her hair. In order to remind her of my presence I said, "Good morning, Anni."

"Morning," she drawled without turning round. "Where's your boss?" she asked after a while, keeping on brushing her hair. I thought she was displeased that I had come when she had expected the boss, the real expert; therefore I explained to her that Staszek was very busy just now.

"Yes, yes, I know," she said with conviction. "But you're a good carpenter, too, aren't you?" she asked, not without a certain scepticism in her voice.

Pointing at the bed, Anni explained what she wanted me to do. I had to cut through the uprights at each end in order to make the double bunk into two single beds. Child's play! It only took a few minutes to complete the job. Anni helped me to lift the top bunk to the floor, and I helped her to rearrange her room. When that was done, Anni sat on one of the beds to try out which was the more comfortable. I sat on the second bed, bouncing up and

143

down, thus demonstrating its good quality while thinking of the comfort to which Schillinger could now look forward. Similar thoughts must have gone through Anni's mind, because she suddenly started to laugh.

"Many thanks," she said cheerfully. "And what do I owe you?" she joked, pointing at my work.

I collected my tools and shrugging my shoulders turned to leave.

"No, no, that won't do." Anni sprang to the door and turned the key in the lock. Hiding it behind her back she began teasing me, saying over and over again: "I've got to pay for it. I've got to pay for it." She gave me a promising smile.

She was mischievous and nimble as a cat. The key kept slipping from my hand. She hid it in so ingenious a manner that as I searched for the key my hands wandered involuntarily over the folds of her dress. This pleased her but, quite against my will, excited me. This game of hide-and-seek went on for some time, with Anni, all aroused, growing steadily more aggressive; it was perfectly clear what she had in mind. At the same time, I remembered Fanny and Sylvia. That sobered me somewhat. I could have taken the key by force, but I was afraid of getting on the bad side of the block senior who had so mighty and dangerous a protector as Schillinger. At any time, on any pretext, Anni could incite the Rapportführer against me. I was in a very difficult situation, particularly since Anni was no longer able to contain herself. Apparently she had not slept with anyone for some time.

At long last she believed that I was as aroused as she was and no longer prevented me from reaching down for the key in her brassiere. As soon as I had managed to extricate the key, I rushed to the door. In my hurry I was clumsy and could not open it. Meanwhile Anni, taken by surprise, came down to earth. Furious, she looked around frantically for something heavy. Not finding anything suitable she reached for a bucket of water which was standing under the washstand.

Suddenly the door opened. I just managed to grab my toolbox and take one leap, but the cold shower still caught me in the open door. The water ran down my back like a waterfall and, at the same time, drenched the SS man who was approaching Anni's door at that moment. I ran like mad away from the block; in my ears rang the block senior's cry of horror and the curses of the German. Quite out of breath I burst into the workroom, wet and frightened, expecting at any moment a visit from my fellow sufferer, the SS man. No sooner had I fixed myself up a little than Staszek came in and told me that he had seen Schillinger inside the sick bay area. My legs gave way under me with agitation. So, it was he whom I had run into outside Anni's door. However, there were no consequences. It seemed that the SS man had failed to recognize me because he had a bucketful of water in his eyes. Besides, Anni would no doubt have found ways of appeasing him. When we met again after this incident she was not in the least cross. On the contrary, she laughed wholeheartedly, thus proving that she had at least one good trait of character: a sense of humor.

CHAPTER 47

AT LONG last Staszek gave me a serious piece of independent carpentry to do. I was to build a medicine cabinet with a large number of divisions and shelves. Since our workshop was definitely too small for this job, I transferred my activities to the rear part of Block 22 where, for the time being, there was a store of bunks which represented our sole supply of materials for the making of simple furniture ordered by the women's hospital.

I was just about to finish this cabinet, and was whistling a tune which I had heard somewhere, when I felt someone standing behind me. It was Roman G., a frequent visitor in Block 22 in these days. He was dressed up, smoothly shaven, fragrant, wearing dazzlingly polished officers' boots, clad in breeches. He stood, his head to one side, regarding the medicine cabinet as a connoisseur at an exhibition of paintings would admire a masterpiece.

"Not bad, not bad at all, Wiesiu"; he praised me, which he did only rarely. "Did you make that yourself?" he asked incredulously. I nodded and went on whistling in order to let him know that his remarks were a matter of complete indifference to me. That annoyed him, of course. Therefore he considered it necessary to react accordingly. "Who'd have thought it? It's simply inconceivable. I always thought that you couldn't make anything with your own hands," he emphasized the words, "you lazy bastard."

I went on whistling, ignoring his catty remarks. Ever since I had known him, he was always getting back at me.

"However, you don't know that melody very well, do you? How can you whistle such a beautiful melody so out of tune? Listen, old son, listen carefully. This is how it goes."

Roman cleared his throat for some time. Then he decided to hum the piece I had whistled out of tune. He did not manage to do it very well and proceeded to make excuses for himself. "Bronchitis, dammit." He put his hand on his throat and felt it gingerly, then with an airy wave of his hand he declared: "I'm losing my voice in this fucking camp."

He cleared his throat again and resumed his singing; this time he didn't sing at all badly. "And do you at least know where this comes from?" he asked, cleverly interrupting his recital at exactly the right place—where he could not reach the top note, his high C being choked off by hoarseness. "That's a bit from the *Bolero* by Ravel. Ravel, you fool."

I smiled, remembering an incident at the beginning of our stay in the camp. Roman was taken out of the line-up because they knew that he was a singer (something, incidentally, with which he tried to impress us at all times), and they ordered him to teach us to sing "Here in Auschwitz I must stay." It was his Auschwitz debut which had helped him in his camp career.

Meanwhile Roman began to recall his former glory. "Ah, yes, those were the days! Italy, La Scala . . ." He broke off suddenly when he noticed my ironic smile. With a resigned wave of his hand he quoted a saying which was addressed to all who failed to understand art, that art which he, Roman G., represented in this camp.

"What's the use, why cast my pearls before swine?"

He smoothed his jacket, straightened his cap and pulled a small parcel from his pocket. Then he pointed at the wooden partition separating us from the large TB ward and asked in a natural voice, "Is it all right to step inside? None of our slave drivers in there?"

"You can go in by all means. Rhode isn't there, and Dr. Zbozien is busy in outpatients." I threw a glance at the parcel and could not restrain myself from making a snide remark: "Bella's waiting anxiously." Roman's hand, which was holding the parcel, twitched nervously. Silently he swallowed the allusion, which he could not have failed to understand. Once more he carefully checked his appearance, put on a dignified expression and walked into the ward in step with "Here in Auschwitz," whistled by me.

Bella was a girl of tender years, a Southern European beauty. Taken from Hamburg together with other prostitutes, she had finished up in Auschwitz, where she was given a number, a black triangle, a job and an entry on her index card in the form of three small crosses. Everything about Bella was "super." Even her syphilis test was positive, as Roman would say in his unfeeling but not unwitty way. The fact that Bella had VD did not prevent him from visiting her. He brought her delicacies an ordinary prisoner would not even dare dream of. But then he had power, connections and an orderly who could procure anything he desired. True, these transactions took place in exchange for the gold teeth of the dead, but who would have given a thought to such paltry matters?

Bella tried as best she could to show this generous protector her gratitude for his care, his gifts, his concern. But what could she offer him in return?

Confined to her bed, all she could give was her body because she possessed nothing else; Roman knew about her illness and was, consequently, not particularly keen to sleep with her. It was enough for him just to see her, perhaps at times to touch her feverish body, her body which was hot with fever because, in addition to syphilis, she had tuberculosis. Roman, an aesthete, an artist, a man with—doubtless—great imagination, feasted his eyes on her exquisitely beautiful figure, her delicate suntanned skin, which had not yet been attacked by the destructive disease. With the tips of his trembling fingers he explored her splendid young

147

breasts, supposedly examining their physical condition. Did not the patients address him as "doctor?" In the beds next to Bella, the starved, dirty, stinking skeletons were dying, young and old, all of the same horrifying appearance, pitiable women, consumptives. Compared to them Bella seemed to be more beautiful still. It is doubtful, by the way, that Roman saw anyone other than Bella, who lay on a clean sheet, so striking side by side with the pus-soaked bunks on which the other women died. Why should he spoil his aesthetic enjoyment by looking around the disgusting room full of suffering, pain and death?

I turned away from the gap in the door through which I was watching them. I would catch myself at times, preferring to look at nude Bella rather than at the emaciated, forsaken and helpless sick women, who were only waiting for death.

Bella fell asleep. Roman tiptoed out of the ward. The fearfully gaunt, filth-blackened hands of the sick were held out to him, imploring aid. Roman seemed not to see them. Quietly he closed the door behind him.

CHAPTER 48

AT LAST my first product, the cupboard, was completed. According to Staszek, I did not make a bad job of it. We took it to the outpatients' department. Almost simultaneously a truck from Auschwitz drew up outside the hut. The people from Auschwitz brought boxes of medical supplies and a few surgical instruments. The nurses passed them round from hand to hand, while Ena, a pretty Slovak Jewess who was chief doctor in the women's hospital, decided where they were to be put in the large cupboard I had made. Dr. Zbozien seemed to be satisfied. There were far more medicines and drugs than the official allocations permitted. Engrossed in conversation with Bock and Orla, the woman sick bay Kapo, about development plans for the women's hospital, Zbozien never noticed the secret longing glances of admiration from Basia S., who was head over heels in love with the young and energetic doctor. SDG Scherpe sat straddling the table and did not join in the conversation. He did not seem to care whether the medical supplies were for the treatment of the sick or whether it was phenol, which he used to kill the newly born and the seriously ill with injections. Incidentally, he did not do this with the same enthusiasm and zeal as his colleague in this field, SDG Klehr.

Block senior Bock greeted me with a smile and one of his little jokes: "How are you, carpenter? How many women have you had so far?"

I blushed since his remark was overheard by Halina's colleagues, and I was a little in love with her just then. Bock played the funny man, but I heard that he was in serious difficulties. The Political Department continued to suspect an organized conspiracy in the men's sick bay. They started interrogating several members of the hospital staff. Shortly afterwards many doctors and male nurses were put into the bunker. Once again Bock was accused of collaborating with the Polish intelligence in the sick bay. After a while some of the prisoners were released from the bunker, but others remained incarcerated, among them Gienek Obojski, Georg Zemanek and Fred Stessel. These three were charged with being in contact with the women's camp and with the civilian population outside the camp in order to pass on information from the camp and prepare their escape. Their fate was uncertain; they might be shot at any time. This was not very encouraging news. Here in Birkenau things were a little more tranquil, at least in this respect. The Political Department—so it seemed at least for the time being—did not display great activity. Unfortunately, it was the calm before the storm. In the first days of June 1943 the Political Department came for a young woman on whom a letter written by Gienek Obojski was found. The affair was spreading farther and farther afield. One could guess how it would end.

January came, and with it a severe frost. As I had no coat, I always felt very cold on my way to the women's concentration camp. I did have a woolen sweater which they had sent me from home, but that was definitely not enough to keep out the cold. A woman who worked in the clothing depot gave me a thick warm jersey. I did not enjoy wearing it for long.

On the evening of the very same day, as we returned from work, we were stopped by two Blockführers and taken to the

149

guardhouse where Rapportführer Schillinger was already waiting for us. Anyone who had anything hot tried to get rid of it before the search. Not everyone succeeded. On Julek they found a cigarette lighter; Nicet had an ampoule of some sort of drug; I wore two sweaters, one on top of the other, which was not allowed. Explanations were of no avail. At last Schillinger had caught us on his beat. For a long time now he had been lying in wait for just such a chance. In the women's camp, where our immediate superior, Dr. Rhode, was favorably disposed towards us, he could not harm us. But here in the men's camp he, Schillinger, was the arbiter of life and death. He took down our numbers, gave each of us a few kicks and hustled us back into the camp on the double, pausing on the way to make us do sport as a punishment. After morning roll call we were to report for punishment to Rapportführer Palitzsch, who was now in Birkenau, and to Lagerführer Schwarzhuber, whom we hardly knew at all.

Dejected, we lay down to sleep without exchanging a word. Each one of us was preoccupied with his own thoughts; under the circumstances they were not exactly cheerful. The silence was interrupted by Roman's cracked voice.

"I've always suspected that your carryings-on in the women's camp would end like this," he said, sounding not in the least upset about it at all. "We'll have to fill the free places, won't we, George? There's no telling how long they'll be staying in the SK." George merely shrugged his shoulders. What business of his was it? They were Bock's lot. Let him worry about them.

Dr. Zbozien gave us a glimmer of hope. He promised that he would speak to Rhode in the morning; perhaps something could be achieved that way.

The next morning we reported for punishment. As Roman had predicted, we were sentenced to detention in the penal company. However, on account of Dr. Rhode's intervention and his assertion that we were irreplaceable as workers in the women's camp, our detention was changed to *Stehbunker* [confinement in a cell where the prisoner is forced to stand up all the time, literally "standing-up bunker"]. We were to serve our sentence at night while working normally during the day. I had received the most severe sentence, three weeks continuous Stehbunker, which was tantamount to a slow death. This sentence was, at the intervention of the camp doctor, changed to six weeks, so that I was to go to work normally and stand in the bunker every other night. As far as I was concerned, Schillinger had obtained full satisfaction.

That same evening I had to report at seven o'clock at the main office in Block 2. From there the Blockführer on duty was to take me to one of the brick-built blocks where the Stehbunker cells were situated.

CHAPTER 49

I WAS there punctually at 5:00 P.M., waiting for the SS man in the anteroom of the office. I was alone. My friends served their sentences at other times. After a while the SS man came in; he was tall and somber-looking, one of those who had searched us yesterday together with Schillinger. Carrying in his hand a bunch of keys which he rattled continuously, he led me to the block immediately next to the penal company. He turned the key in the padlock on the thick, iron-mounted wooden door, lifted the bolt, slid back the iron bars, and allowed me to enter a very narrow passage, dimly lit by a single bulb hanging from the ceiling. From the frost-covered ceiling the light was reflected in a thousand glittering sparks. Along the inner wall of the bunker, directly above the concrete floor, were three small doors, about a yard apart; they were furnished with wide bars from which hung padlocks.

With his heavy boots the SS man kicked the first door and demanded in a sharp voice: "Anybody in there?"

From behind the concrete wall a weak, half-choked voice replied: "Here, Herr Blockführer."

"How many?" the SS man asked briefly.

"Three," came the feeble reply.

"Get in there." The SS man turned to me and opened the small door from behind which the voice of the prisoner had come. "Come on, you cunt!"

On all fours, for I could not have squeezed myself inside, I crawled into the black mouth of the standing-up cell. The Block-führer helped me in my clumsy attempts to get inside the narrow room, which reeked of excrement, by giving me a hefty kick in the backside.

"Get a move on, you bastard," he snarled impatiently.

It was not easy to squeeze oneself in between three men who stood crowded together in so small a space. At last! The SS man shut the door behind me; I heard him turn the key in the padlock. Through an air vent high up on the cell wall I saw the light go out in the passage. It grew totally dark and still. The peace was only interrupted by the main entrance door banging shut. The heavy steps of the departing SS man died down in the distance. Only now did the bunker return to life. In the impenetrable darkness, I felt on my face the stale breath of my three fellow sufferers. One of them was breathing with great difficulty, and from time to time he whimpered; "Water, food, water!" Now he hung onto me with his full weight, seeking support and warmth. I felt his wasted body tremble with cold and exhaustion. He stank abominably.

The other two were holding up to some extent. From them I learned that they had been standing in this cell for two days with-out food or drink. They had been sentenced to Stehbunker for an alleged attempt to escape from the camp. At the time when they were pushed into this cell, there were already two prisoners in it. One of them died shortly afterwards. It was with great relief that they had removed his corpse yesterday.

It was easier to stand up when there were just three. They com-plained as I now had to come into their cell. There was only one hope, namely that this third man here would be dead by morning. That way we would only be three again.

From the concrete floor, damp cold came creeping up. With my back I leaned against the icy wall. Under my shoulder blades I felt a stabbing pain which was getting worse. The pain in my legs was increasing steadily. How was I going to endure it in here till morn-ing? And what about the other three? Surely they will never get out of here alive. As if they could read my thoughts they began to wail: "My God, I can't go on. They've left us to croak here." An alien sound intruded in between these moans and groans. That was the gong. Has the night passed? I shifted uneasily.

"Lights-out," someone sighed with regret.

And there was I thinking morning had come. How slowly time was passing. So I had another ten hours in front of me. The whimperer on my left slid down lower and lower; his moans were growing weaker. The prisoner standing at the opposite wall leaned his head against my arm. I leaned mine against his. This way it actually felt warmer.

I must have slept for a while because I started up when one of the prisoners yelled: "You're crapping again, you fucking idiot." This was addressed to the whimperer who kept on his feet with his last ounce of strength. He muttered something unintelligible and dirtied his pants. The stench, which was already intolerable, grew even more offensive. The man kept sliding down and pressed on my legs with his full weight. As my hands were free, I raised him up into a standing position again. Now he leaned limply against my body, his head on my shoulder. Tiredness was overwhelming. In the camp over there, I thought, they're lying in their bunks in reasonable comfort. If at least these damn walls had some sort of indentations or protruberances, but there was nothing, only a smooth, frozen, slippery, frost-covered surface. I went back to sleep again. I was awoken by the terrible cold, which seemed to have penetrated to my very marrow. I was completely stiff. The pain in my back felt as though someone was plunging a sharp knife between my shoulder blades. The man to the left of me stood as before, leaning on me with his whole weight. I changed my uncomfortable position, and at that moment his body slid to the ground, completely slack. I tried pulling him up but could not. My hand accidentally touched his unshaven face. It was ice cold. While I was asleep he had died.

"Has he dropped dead?" asked the one who, not long ago, had called him a fucking idiot, fearfully.

"Poor kid. They'll kill all of us, I'm sure. Oh God, have mercy on us," he sobbed without restraint. The second man began to pray loudly. His voice trembled; he was shaking as if he had an attack of malaria.

And this was how time passed. Slowly, oh, so slowly, one second and another second, waiting for the inexorable death which would overtake the two starving prisoners who were still alive. I was so much better off than they. I was waiting for the morning gong and the SS man who would take me out of here so that I could go to work. My heart beat violently when I heard the gong, whose sound barely penetrated into this small, dark cell, isolated as it was from the camp by thick walls.

Outside the bunker door the frozen snow crunched under the feet of the SS man, who was again rattling his keys. In the passage he started cursing and said in disgust: "What a stink! Yuk! Anyone alive in here?"

In reply there came the whimpering voices of prisoners locked in the cells.

"Shut up!" he shouted, and they all fell silent at once.

When he opened the door to our cell, he turned to me and said peremptorily: "Well, nursing orderly, get out of here."

Clumsily, on all fours, I crawled through the dark opening, dragging behind me the body of the man who had died. Rigor mortis was already setting in.

"Only one?" the Blockführer asked in surprise.

"The other two are still alive," I explained, rising ponderously from my knees.

I dragged the corpse out into the snow, while the SS man once more locked and barred the bunker, accompanied by the desperate cries of the captives. It was still dark outside; only the brightly lit windows of the camp kitchen threw a light on the snow-covered ground. A severe frost burned my cheeks. The SS man let me go, but not before he had struck me across the shoulders with his bunch of keys.

"Fuck off, you stinking pig."

My stiff legs could barely carry me, but still I ran in the direction of my block as if I had been given my freedom.

Rested and refreshed, the nursing orderlies were getting up. In the little stove the fire was crackling. Sympathetically and with a yawn Roman inquired: "Did you have a bad dream, my boy? You don't look as if you'd slept well."

No one laughed at this not very funny joke. He must have thought it rather fatuous himself, for he changed his tune immediately, trying to be kind to me and snapping at the room orderly instead.

"Wacek, where are you, you so-and-so? Can't you see that there's someone here frozen to the marrow? Get him some hot coffee at once. And with sugar."

Putting on a warm, woolen vest he muttered indignantly to himself: "He can thank that son-of-a-bitch Schillinger for this—the beast." However, he could not maintain the pose of a compassionate fellow prisoner for long, and proceeded to ask me an offensively personal question: "I suppose that's for Anni, eh?"

The coffee was hot and sweet. I forgave Roman his silly taunts. When I arrived in our workroom at the women's concentration camp Staszek at once ordered me to go to bed. I climbed onto the upper bunk next to Lisa.

She thought I had come to sleep with her.

"Stop messing about, Wiesiu," she giggled, patting her hair into place.

I lay down on the bed next to hers, covered myself with several blankets and fell asleep immediately. I woke because someone was tugging at my hand. It was Lisa.

"Get up," she said, looking down. "Food's here."

Down there stood Anni with a steaming bowl of soup.

On the following night I went back into the bunker in order to serve another of the twenty nights of punishment that were waiting for me.

CHAPTER 50

I DECIDED to follow the advice of my experienced colleagues. I must, above all, find out which of the Blockführers was on duty on the day I had to go into the Stehbunker to serve another night of my punishment. Much was to depend on his attitude, kindly or harsh. In the main office I was told that on this day Blockführer Schneider was on duty. This meant that one might be able to circumvent the strict regulations because Schneider was known to be neither particularly strict nor assiduous in the execution of his duties.

I put on a warm Canada underwear, insulated my back with

paper from a cement bag, and slipped on two shirts. Round my feet I wrapped paper bandages. Over my woolen socks I put foot cloths, and only then did I get into my striped prisoners' garb, as well as two jerseys and a scarf. In place of leather shoes, I wore wooden clogs that were several sizes too large. Dressed like this I looked huge. In accordance with my appearance, I moved in a clumsy way, much to the amusement of my fellow prisoners, who had been watching my preparations. I checked the contents of my pockets: cigarettes, matches, a slice of bread and margarine, a candle.

Thus equipped I squeezed myself through the outpatients' department, which at this time was crowded with patients. The Mussulmen got out of my way with alacrity. My huge frame aroused respect in them, unlike Roman, who at the sight of me shook his head. "Crazy, you've gone completely crazy. Lunatic! If Schillinger catches you, you'll have had it!"

"Come on, Roman, Schillinger won't poke his nose outside the guardroom in this frost. And Schneider is on duty. I've made sure," I said and walked past Peter who was standing silently at the exit of the outpatients' department. "Wait a minute," Roman held me back, "did you say Schneider?"

He reached into his pocket and pulled out a packet of luxury cigarettes. "Give these to Schneider and tell him they're from the sick bay block senior. He'll treat you more kindly. And tell him also to drop in on us later. Okay, Peter?"

Peter nodded assent.

"All right, be off with you then and close the gate behind you. There's a terrible draft here."

The frost must have been severe, for the moisture froze in my nose and my ears were quite stiff. It was not far to the office. A few minutes later I opened the gate of Block 2. It was five o'clock. There was nobody about. After a few minutes I heard voices outside and approaching steps. First came Schneider, behind him Camp Senior Siwy and Arbeitsdienst Victor, who was gesticulating wildly. I reported to Schneider, and disregarding the presence of the other two, I handed him the cigarettes and repeated what Roman had told me to say. For a while the Blockführer looked at his present, then he whistled appreciatively and slipped it into his coat pocket. Meanwhile Victor opened his door and urged Siwy to come in with Schneider. But first Schneider had to take me to the bunker.

"What a frost," said Siwy, rubbing his hands. "You'll be very cold in there."

"Come on, come on." The SS man hustled me along towards the exit, since he wanted to rid himself as quickly as possible of his unpleasant task. After all, he had two calls to make, one at the Arbeitsdienst's office and the other at the sick bay. Outside, on the way to the bunker, he asked me in broken Polish: "Why are you being punished? What have you been up to, eh?"

"Well, nothing, really," I replied. "I was wearing two jerseys, and Rapportführer . . ." Schneider interrupted me with a laugh.

"And how many have you got on now? Five, from the looks of it. You look quite bulky."

In the bunker all was silent. It was empty. Apparently my fellow sufferers from the night before had died, and their bodies had been removed during the day.

I chose the last cell in order to be as far away from the door where there was a draft.

"Herr Blockführer," I summoned up my courage, "may I take the chamberpot from the unoccupied cell?"

"Take as many as you like, but be quick about it."

Presently I had four chamberpots in my cell. Surprised but amused, Schneider remarked: "You must have the runs."

He locked the cell door behind me, turned off the light and, a little later, turned the key in the main bunker door. I was left alone in the impenetrable darkness and complete silence. I could hear the beating of my heart. I even heard the rustling of the paper I had wrapped round my shoulders.

In a corner of my cell I put the four chamberpots one on top of the other. Now I was able to sit on them in comfort. That was why I had fetched them from the other cells. Schneider thought I had diarrhea I recalled, not without satisfaction.

I waited for the evening gong sitting down. That evening it could be heard particularly clearly. I waited for rather a long time, listening for any unauthorized persons. Silence. Now I could light my candle. At once it grew warmer and more pleasant. The thick, frost-covered walls of my cell glittered with a thousand icy sparks. I lit a cigarette. I actually enjoyed it.

What a good thing it is that I'm alone in this cell, I thought aloud. When I heard the sound of my voice I did not feel quite so alone. This silence stirs me up. Whenever my legs go to sleep I can get up, jump about or sing if I want to. I began to sing, I stamped my wooden clogs; in a word, I began making a lot of noise if only to chase away this damned silence which fills me—I don't know why—with fear. The wooden clogs were ideal to insulate one's feet from the cold which came creeping up from the concrete floor. My hands were cold, but I had the candle to warm them by. Next time I must bring a few more of them. They're useful to warm yourself and also to read by. In the sick bay a well-thumbed book, *The Leper Woman,* was in circulation. It didn't matter what sort of a book it was, as long as it helped to pass the time inside the Stehbunker more quickly.

The candle was burning down, and I put it out. Despite the warm clothing it grew colder immediately. In order to warm myself I began to hop around, dancing a fantasy dance to the accompaniment of whistled tunes. However, how long can one go on whistling and stamping the floor in one's wooden clogs? At last it made me tired. I sat on my chamberpot throne and fell asleep.

I did not know how long I had been asleep. At any rate, I suddenly awoke from a terrible crashing and clattering; it was my chamberpot edifice collapsing. Drowsy with sleep, I did not at once grasp where I was and what had happened. I leapt up, banged my head against the bunker wall and came back to reality with a bump.

I piled up the chamberpots again, ate a piece of bread and, to save my candle, burned my many paper bandages one by one. They were burning well without ashes or smoke, and for a brief moment made a huge fire and provided much heat, so that after a while the melting frost began to drop in lumps from the bunker walls. I sat down and fell asleep right away. I awoke from the noise of the bunker door being opened.

"Hey, you there. You're not frozen to death, are you? Where are you? Come out." It would seem that Schneider had forgotten in which cell he had locked me up last night. He must have hit the bottle with a vengeance, for he looked rather the worse for wear.

In the end I got quite used to my nights in the Stehbunker, and the SS men got used to me. As I was, so to speak, a regular customer, they did not treat me too badly. They did not search me nor did they beat me, whereas they often ill-treated newcomers. Particularly Blockführer Perschel, or "Horseface," the Kommandoführer of the penal company. I noticed that my low camp number filled them with a certain degree of respect, as did the length of my punishment in the Stehbunker, a stay which I bore with courage since I recuperated during the day in the women's camp. Thus it was that I reached the last day, or rather the last night, after which my punishment was to end, without major difficulties.

It was the end of February, and although there was no longer any snow, the evening was exceptionally cold. While, as usual, I was waiting for the Blockführer in the anteroom of the office, I felt terribly cold. I wanted to get into the bunker as quickly as possible, for in there I would know how to make myself comfortable. Blockführer Baretzki arrived on his bicycle. Without taking any notice of my report, he took a bulging bag from the frame of his bike and went into the camp senior's office. After about an hour he emerged from the office, asked me to wheel up his bicycle and was off without my having had a chance to say a word. A few minutes later he returned with another bulging bag from which came the mysterious sound of clinking glass. At about ten o'clock they came out. Victor led the bicycle with the empty bag which dangled from the frame. Baretzki looked stoned out of his mind. I stood in his path, intending in this way to demonstrate my presence. He pushed me aside and muttered: "What are you doing here? Go away. Run along, damn you."

"Or he might change his mind," whispered Siwy and pushed me beyond the block gate. From afar I could hear the Blockführer's voice dying away in the night: "Everything's fucking awful."

CHAPTER 51

FOR SOME time now there had been a slight improvement in conditions inside the women's sick bay. To a large extent this was due to Dr. Zbozien and his group of nursing orderlies, who did everything possible to alleviate the fate of these unfortunate women.

The "suppliers" from the main camp at Auschwitz worked efficiently, despite the intensified checks and investigations which the Political Department introduced in the late autumn, in spite of the shooting of a few members of the main camp's hospital staff towards the end of January 1943.

Among those who perished was Gienek Obojski, who was shot by his employer, Palitzsch, in person. Gienek's fate was shared by Teofil Banasiuk, who was killed by Klehr by means of an injection on the orders of the Political Department. In this way they disposed of eyewitnesses to all the murders which were committed mainly in the yard of Block 11. Neither did Georg Zemanek and Fred Stessel ever get out of the bunker. They were shot. Bock was relieved of his post as camp senior of the prisoners' hospital. He joined a Kommando far away from the main camp. Some of his protégés, who thus no longer had anyone to support them, went to seek their fortune elsewhere.

Even though in the women's sick bay some sort of order had been achieved, conditions in the camp continued to be appalling. Dirt and hunger took their toll among the women who were already wasted away by camp life. Lack of water encouraged the spread of a typhoid epidemic, and under the circumstances it was impossible to contain it. The camp authorities used the same radical means to put an end to this epidemic as they had done in the men's camp a year earlier: they carried out selections. On a single day several thousand women were sent into the gas chamber. In one fell swoop the camp physician, Dr. Rhode, reversed his image by taking a very active part in the selections. It would seem that he had capitulated. Dr. Zbozien's group was dissolved. Some of the doctors and nursing orderlies returned to Auschwitz, others remained in Birkenau for good, myself among them.

I became sick bay clerk in Block 12. The office was in a small room on the right-hand side of the corridor leading to the outpatients' department. There were three of us working here. Karol, the eldest, was our chief; Zygmunt, my fellow countryman and the same age as I, who had come with the same transport from Tarnov, was his deputy. My work consisted of writing out death certificates. The description of the illness from which the prisoner had died also applied to those who had been murdered in the camp. Shot, killed by injection, gas chamber. Each one had to have his case history—a fictitious one, of course. That was what the camp authorities demanded, and that was what I was ordered to do. I must admit that, to begin with, I wrote "heart failure" in the case of prisoners who I knew had been shot. Later, though, I decided that there had been too many of these heart failures, and that it might end badly for me if the Political Department were to notice; consequently, I wrote the death certificates as they wanted them. In the case of a man who had been shot, for instance, I wrote diarrhea; and in another case, in which someone had died of diarrhea, I wrote heart failure; and again for a prisoner who had been killed by injection, "inflammation of the kidneys," and so on. In brief, it was nothing but a barefaced falsification of the death records, an obliteration of all traces of mass murders that had been committed on defenseless prisoners.

During the first half of March, large transports of prisoners began to leave Auschwitz and Birkenau for other camps. It was mainly the Poles who were sent away. On one of the transport lists was the majority of staff from our hospital, myself among them. The next morning we had to march out to Auschwitz from where supposedly we were to be taken to Neuengamme camp.

My last night in Birkenau. I stepped outside the block in order to get a breath of fresh air. The whole camp was already fast asleep. Leaning against the wooden boards of the hut, I inhaled the smoke of my cigarette. I had taken to smoking and was slowly becoming an inveterate smoker. I hoped that in this new camp there'd be something to smoke.

From the distance came the barking of dogs. From the watchtower next to the guardhouse came the voice of the SS man reporting: "Guard number 3, nothing to report." It appeared that some high-ranking officer was checking to see that the guards were not asleep on duty. From the small woods a heavy, sickly sweet smoke wafted across, slowly hiding the endless line of electric bulbs along the electrified barbed-wire fence. I shuddered because suddenly it was turning cold. Time to go to bed. No regrets for Birkenau. Who knows, things might be better in another camp, after all. They were just then starting on the construction of giant crematoria, and that did not bode well.

However, in the end I did not leave with this transport. Together with a few nursing orderlies, I was called back as an essential worker, and began work as a carpenter in the hospital in Block 8. Working in our block were a few doctors, mainly Jews, who were quite content with their fate, which allowed them to work far away from Block 12, or, in other words, at a safe distance from Head Physician Dr. Zengteller.

The carpenters' workshop was in the yard in a wooden shed, the wall of which also separated the yard from the camp street. On the other side the yard abutted upon the spot where the outpatients' department was, which later would be used by the SDGs to administer phenol injections.

The carpenter was a lean little Jew from near Vilna, an industrious and excellent craftsman. Since my training at the hands of Staszek Paduch, I considered myself a good carpenter, and began work without supervision, with more confidence than skill. The real master quickly recognized my lack of qualifications, but he did not wish to hurt me. And so, from time to time, he would let me do some small and not very important job, which afterwards he would praise immoderately thinking that this would be sure to please me, since I had tried so hard to earn his praise.

I had managed to establish myself quite well in this carpenters' workshop. The little iron stove which we used to melt our carpenters' glue was our kitchen; on it we fried potatoes which we organized from the camp kitchen. Our modest menu was enriched by delicacies like lard, streaky bacon or onions sent to me from home (at that time we were already permitted to receive small parcels). We tended to find the camp kitchen's offerings of soup of rotten or frozen turnips less and less to our taste.

The carpenter was on friendly terms with two tattooists, one of whom came from the same town as he. The other was a young Slovak Jew. On account of their jobs, they had contacts with the new arrivals. Therefore they could gather what they wanted from the newly arrived transports. In return for the potato pancakes with which we would liberally furnish them, they supplied us with figs, dates, raisins and maize cakes, which had been brought by Greek Jews, huge numbers of whom were liquidated in the gas chambers in those days. Only a small proportion of them ever

162

reached the camp after they had had their numbers tattooed on their left forearms. Not used to heavy work or to camp conditions, they quickly became Mussulmen. It was they who formed the majority of patients in Blocks 7 and 8.

CHAPTER 52

SPRING CAME, a typical Birkenau spring. The snow melted; the sticky clay soil did not allow the water to run away. Large puddles formed everywhere. The mud was so terrible that it was only with difficulty that one managed to lift one's feet out of the sticky mess. Our camp senior, "Pa" Biernacik, once he had completed the necessary repairs in the block, began tidying up the yard between the huts. For this work he employed the Greeks, who crept through the camp, forlorn and trying to hide from the camp Kapo, who delighted in pouncing on them and treating them most cruelly. They much preferred to work under Pa's vigilant eyes, who was admittedly demanding but who never made use of the stick he carried around at all times. Before long it was possible to cross the yard without sinking into the mud up to one's ankles. And by the wall something was being created which a little later was to be called a small garden.

One morning we noticed the slim figure of Dr. Kitt, accompanied by the SDG and Dr. Zengteller, enter Victor's block. That meant only one thing: selection for Block 7. Meanwhile Pa had just returned with some sod for his beloved garden.

"Pa, Dr. Kitt has gone to Seven," Waldeck, his deputy, reported. "They've been in there for some time. It seems to be a big selection."

"Okay, okay, I'll go," Pa replied. "Let me just tell them quickly what they have to do with the sod."

At last they emerged from the block. For a while they stood in consultation. In his hand Victor held a large pile of patients' record cards, while the SDG carried another bunch of cards. Everybody knew that they were the cards of those who had been selected for the gas chamber. For a long time Dr. Kitt was explaining something to Victor, who clicked his heels every few minutes, nodding and crying energetically, "Very good, Herr Obersturmführer."

On Victor's orders the block orderlies began to conduct the patients out of the block. Meanwhile Drs. Kitt and Zengteller, led by Pa, entered our block. Was there to be a selection here, too? That did not happen very often. Slowly the yard filled with patients. Those still able to stand formed a tight group in one corner of the yard. Many sat or simply lay on the damp ground, completely indifferent to what was going on around them. And new patients kept coming out of the block.

There was to be no selection in our block just yet. Having given his SDG an order, Dr. Kitt walked quickly towards the gate; bringing up the rear was Dr. Zengteller, who, with his short little legs, could barely keep up with him.

A few hundred patients had now emerged from Block 7, and there was no end to be seen. The SDG counted his cards carefully and then went back to Block 8 from where he did not return for some considerable time, which led us to believe that he was injecting and killing the very seriously ill. The carpenter was very agitated—the selection as such no longer affected us very much; it was the order of the day, something that had to be, irrespective of whether or not it shocked us—but for some time now he seemed greatly perturbed. When he heard the noise of trucks arriving at the gate, he ran like one demented into the yard, searching for someone among the patients, but withdrew at once as soon as he noticed the SDG returning from Block 8. We locked ourselves in our hut, and through gaps in the boarded wall watched what went on in the yard. The first rows of waiting patients disappeared through the gate. We could hear them being loaded on the trucks. The carpenter, who could not take his eyes off the gap in the wall, was trembling all over and muttered something in Yiddish which sounded like a prayer. Suddenly he turned to me and, speaking in elegant Polish, uttered a few sentences which were continuously interrupted by deep inner emotion: "He is still there. They haven't yet taken him away. There he stands. There, by the wall.

164

Do you see him? He's perfectly healthy and now he's going to the gas chamber. My God. And the Scharführer keeps going back and forth, and I can't help him. If I show myself he'll take me as well."

"What's his number?" I asked, guessing what he wanted me to do. If it had been SDG Klehr I would most certainly not have dared to go outside. But I was not particularly afraid of this one, for I remembered him from the women's camp. He was tolerable. I grabbed the first handy tool and a piece of batten and walked out into the overcrowded yard. I cornered Waldeck and told him what I had on my mind. He was on his way to find Pa in order to ask him to save the lives of two patients on behalf of the tattooists. Two or three, what was the difference?

After we had conveyed our urgent business to Pa, he gave a resigned wave of his hand.

"That'll do, that'll do. I've got a few myself whom the doctors asked me to save. Everybody has somebody whom he kept hidden and I'm supposed to get them out. The SDG is holding on to all the cards," Pa complained, drawing some mysterious hieroglyphics in the sand with his stick, a sign that he was thinking quite intensively. Suddenly he turned to Waldeck: "Fatso. Run quickly to the block and bring me the cards of the ones who have already been injected. But get a move on it. Perhaps we can work something out."

Waldeck raced to the block while Pa started a lively conversation with the SDG in order to divert his attention from what was going on behind his back. The staff of Block 7 took advantage of the SDG's inattention in order to snatch friends and relatives away from the yard and lead them back into the block, having first given their numbers to Victor. Victor, who was quite boldly rummaging around among the cards the SS man held in his hand while being distracted by his conversation with Pa, quickly exchanged the cards of patients who had just been taken back into the block for the cards Waldeck had slipped to him. In this way he exchanged men sentenced to the gas chamber for those who were already dead, that is to say, for those whom perhaps less than an hour ago the SDG had murdered with phenol injections. Victor carried on in this way for quite some time, but at long last the

165

angry SDG shouted: "What are you doing, Victor, have you gone crazy?"

For a moment, Victor froze, taken by surprise, but he managed to compose himself. Snatching the whole bunch of patients' record cards out of the hands of the SS man, who was dumbfounded, he ran to his nursing orderlies and started berating them, waving the record cards under their noses:

"What's this fucking mess you're making here, you fucking cunts. Is this the way to look after the sick in the block, you stupid Jews? Get these Mussulmen out of my sight this minute and stop them from running all over the place, can't you, you Jewish swine."

Victor was beside himself; he raged, he cursed using foul language, he even struck someone, but he achieved what mattered to him most. He held in his hand the patients' record cards and without them it would have been useless to hide patients in the block who were due to go to the gas chamber. Each card in the SDG's hand was a death sentence. Meanwhile Pa drew the German up to our hut and kept talking to him reassuringly: "Somebody will have to get things sorted out around here. Block Senior Victor will see to it, don't fear."

"Yes, yes, I daresay," the SS man replied, a little less irate. "But mind you, everything must tally."

In fact, Victor had taken care of everything. Seven hundred patients, that is to say, as many as the camp doctor had selected, were put on the trucks and taken to the gas chamber. The numbers had to tally because the SDG kept an eye on that. Here there was nothing to be done. "Everything must tally." All one could do was to exchange the sick for the dead, and in that Pa and Victor succeeded completely. Through their fuss, they eased the SDG's vigilance. In the presence of Kitt they would not have dared to put on such a performance. A handful of patients had been saved, but for how long? In two or three days there would be another selection.

The SDG was possibly not as stupid as all that and perfectly aware that behind his back some shenanigans were going on with the patients. Let them! Sooner or later, no one would get out of here, anyway.

He cast a glance at the corpse-strewn yard, where the corpse bearers were already busily running backwards and forwards, and walked slowly towards the gate where an ambulance bearing the sign of the Red Cross was waiting for him.

CHAPTER 53

ONE SUNDAY afternoon I had a "date" with Halina. As I had a little time to spare I decided to drop in on Edek S. in his block. It turned out that he, too, was busy preparing for a meeting with his girl friend, who worked in the women's kitchen. He washed, brushed his clothes, shaved—he had very little stubble—and he preened as if he had a proper date.

At last Edek had finished. The camp street was as crowded as the main street of a large city. Everybody was hurrying to a concert by the camp kitchen, which was being held near the barbed wire separating the men's camp from the women's camp. The women's camp was arranged exactly like ours; on the left was the kitchen, on the right the sauna, one of whose wings screened off the guardhouse. It was at this screened-off place that all those who had a "date" would congregate. The camp orchestra played gay waltzes. With my eyes I sought Halina who was somewhere in the crowd of gesticulating women. There was, however, no chance for conversation because the distance was too great and the orchestra drowned out everything.

There she is! Tall, slim, long blond hair which moves slightly in the wind. I thought she saw me because she tried to say something in sign language; it looked as if she was thanking me for the cigarettes I had sent her through Edek Galinski. Gestures, facial expressions, that was the whole conversation. But at least it was very pleasant to look at her.

Everybody waved his hands, everybody expressed with his gestures something that only the other could understand. Standing over there were mothers, wives, daughters, girl friends, acquaintances.

Edek grew lively and nudged me in the ribs. "Do you see, that's my girl? There, she's standing outside the kitchen."

I pretended to be interested but could not take my eyes off Halina's lovely appearance.

"But can't you see?" Edek was getting excited. "It's the one who has come forward just now," he explained. I had to look; I noticed her at once.

"But she's a German," I exclaimed, astonished. "Kapo! Got an armband."

"So what, you dope," he replied, outraged. "With our girls there's nothing but trouble. But with one like her it's the whole thing, without great fuss and introductions. She'll give you a cube of margarine, too, to keep you strong and vigorous." Edek laughed roguishly.

"You only live once. Tomorrow you may be dead without ever having tried it, you stupid git."

Suddenly the women started to move. They ran in all directions as fast as their feet would carry them. I gave a sign to Halina to flee, but she was so busy trying to puzzle out my incomprehensible miming that she never noticed Rapportführer Drechsler on her bicycle, racing straight at her along the camp street.

"Run, Halina, run, quickly!"

In vain I tried to drown out the orchestra. The horrid Drechsler, with her horse teeth, had already reached Halina. Flinging her bicycle on the ground she struck Halina with her bony hands on her head, back and chest. Halina, who had been taken completely by surprise, did not shield herself from the blows, nor could she tear herself away because Drechsler held her by her hair and was slapping her face like a madwoman. We watched this scene helplessly. I closed my eyes because I could no longer bear the sight.

"She's let her go, the old witch." I heard a voice, filled with hatred. I opened my eyes. Poor ill-treated Halina was staggering behind the sauna building. Drechsler, triumphant, got on her bicycle at the very moment when a runner coming from the guardhouse began to call out: "Camp seniors, camp seniors, forward!"

After a while a camp curfew was announced. A large transport was said to have arrived. We were hustled back to our blocks.

Only the *Sonderkommando* [literally, special squad, Jews who were forced by the SS to work in the crematoria] marched out to its daily work in the crematorium. "Left, left and left," the Kapo set the pace. "A song!" Behind them moved the Canada team, accompanied by a few excited Blockführers. A large transport. A rich transport. And this time it wasn't poor Greeks who arrived; this transport came from France. "Faster, faster, come on," the SS men goaded their team nervously.

There'll be Canada galore!

In the evening a fiery glow reddened the sunset. The heavy sickly smoke of burned bodies floated across from the little wood, a sign that the Sonderkommando had not been idle.

That night I slept well in spite of everything.

CHAPTER 54

WEEKS PASSED, no different from the weeks which had already passed. Transports arrived and were, as a rule, immediately liquidated in the crematoria. Then there were selections; typhus, malaria and dysentery further decimated the prisoners. The Political Department created havoc, for the bunkers were overcrowded, and shootings were an everyday occurrence in Auschwitz. From time to time someone tried to escape, but the end was usually tragic.

In time the camp grew; new sectors sprang up all the time beyond the ramp where the numerous transports from all over Europe were unloaded. One of these sectors, Sector E, was occupied by gypsies. Prisoners from our camp had already been transferred to Sector D. A part of Sector C had not yet been completed, to be just like B, where soon the establishment of a family camp was planned. Sector A was the Quarantine. The prison hospital had a special block assigned to it, Block F, in close proximity to crematoria 3 and 4, which were on the point of completion.

Prior to the new transfer, there took place a great delousing

169

drive and another selection. The sector the men had occupied up till then was taken over by the women.

Sector F, the prison hospital, was then only in the process of being built and organized. There were already about a dozen barracks, four of them typical Birkenau barracks, big wooden stables where up to a thousand patients could be accommodated, as well as eleven small barracks with windows, capable of housing one hundred twenty patients each. Also under construction was a separate bath-hut, one of Pa's pet projects; for he now held the responsible post of prison hospital camp Kapo.

Hans continued as camp senior, but he was now completely kept under by power-hungry Dr. Zengteller.

I settled in the block of Bock, who had been transferred here. Bock was finished; his lungs were being ravaged by TB. Morphine, with which he secretly injected himself, revived him for a while, but as soon as its effect wore off, one would see a man who was at the end of his strength, helpless, lacking willpower, an utter ruin. I felt sorry for him, but I could not help him. He was completely dependent on the drug. Shortly afterwards he was once again sent to join a Kommando, where he died after injecting himself with an overdose of morphine.

I was one of the oldest prisoners in the sick bay. I regarded this as sufficient reason for doing nothing or almost nothing. I hid whenever I could. During my three-year stay in a concentration camp I had mastered this art so well that camp senior Hans was quite convinced that I held an important post in the prison hospital, which was why he treated me kindly. But while I was able to hoodwink old Hans, Dr. Zengteller was not so easily deceived. He was now chief physician in charge of the entire prison hospital. He knew me well and knew also that I had no intention of overworking. In his presence I pretended to be busy. He was quite obviously out to catch me doing nothing.

I sometimes helped Pa with his tidying-up jobs, of which there were a great many in the newly erected prison hospital, mostly on occasions when camp doctor Helmerson was present in the sick bay. Pa quickly got my number.

"You just wait, you young so-and-so," he threatened when he

170

saw me disappear as soon as Helmerson left. Then he shrugged resignedly and muttered to himself: "A shit, that's what he is, a real shit. But you wait, I'll set Zengteller on you."

Of course he never did. Pa did not really like Zengteller either, although the doctor appreciated Pa's unremitting energy and his eagerness for work.

Edek Galinski came more and more often to visit me, the reason being that here in the sick bay there was a great deal of work for the fitters, in connection with the new bath block. Usually he brought some booze, which both of us came to like more and more because it liberated in our youthful minds thoughts which, when sober, we should not have dared to voice: we were planning to escape from the camp. This thought was uppermost in our minds, so much so that we no longer needed the stimulation of alcohol in order to work out in detail several versions of our escape, theoretical for the time being, until Edek could have a chance of transferring to Birkenau permanently. During the next few weeks he would step up his efforts to bring this about. According to our plans the escape was to take place the next spring unless circumstances should force us to put the date forward.

The first step was to establish contact with someone outside the camp, with someone on whom we could rely, who would never betray us, but rather give us his help. Presently an opportunity presented itself. But even before that I was appointed block senior. Any requests or explanations on my part stating that I was not in the least interested in this post were of no avail. Pa remarked succinctly: "It'll be you, and that's that. You've done enough bumming. And if you don't want the job, off you go, into the camp."

Now, at the beginning of autumn, the prospect of more camp life was not at all enticing. There would be none of the comforts I had enjoyed in the sick bay. On the other hand, the post of block senior—for some time now there had been the tendency to fill the important posts in the camp with Poles—was irksome, not only because of the responsibility, but also because of its link with the dreadful tradition dating back to the time when the block senior was the controller of life and death. And Pa had his own policy,

171

which he implemented consistently. Within a short time, then, he had filled almost every important post in the prison hospital with Poles. The Germans did not have much say here. It was the Jews, who formed the majority of the medical staff, who were given a chance to speak up.

In addition we acquired a new camp doctor in the person of young Dr. Helmerson who, it was rumored, had been transferred here directly from the eastern front thanks to some string-pulling on the part of his father, who was something very high up in the police and who wanted to protect his darling son from the dangers of war. Dr. Helmerson very quickly grasped what was expected of him. If at the beginning of his reign he still dared to halt a selection, soon after appropriate instructions by the camp authorities as to his duties and the way in which he was expected to carry them out, there began a veritable reign of terror. Almost daily, he could be seen prowling in the blocks, selecting patients for injection or for liquidation in the gas chambers. Most frequently he would go to the isolation wards, where his behavior was worst of all.

I became the new block senior in these two blocks, which were reserved mainly for typhoid and malaria patients. So as not to be transferred into the camp forthwith, I was forced to take on the post, but I did not wear the block senior's armband. As Dr. Helmerson had not yet met me, I always sent my deputy, a congenial Jew from Cracov named Gang, who spoke German fluently. After a few visits to the isolation ward, Dr. Helmerson was convinced that it was Gang who was block senior, while I would make myself scarce under some pretext or other. Dr. Zengteller was furious with me, although he kept his mouth quiet. So did camp senior Hans, because by now he was afraid to produce the real block senior, who was never in the block whenever the camp doctor paid a visit, a fact which the latter might interpret as lack of respect for his person. Later Hans took me to task, Zengteller raged and threatened, but I invariably used the same excuse, namely that I could not speak German. Pa always backed me up, because he wanted to keep me in this job as block senior at any price.

172

Due to Pa's determined attitude Zengteller could do nothing. I went on being block senior, while for Helmerson's benefit, my part was played by Gang. Obviously this kind of *status quo* could not last, but nevertheless it did endure for a little longer.

CHAPTER 55

I ARRANGED with Edek that we would speak to Szymlak in order to find out whether he might be a suitable person to help us in the event of our escape from the camp. I was to sound him out cautiously, but not tell him of our intentions until I had made absolutely sure that we could count on him.

Szymlak was one of the few civilians who worked inside the camp, and, what was more, he worked unsupervised. The authorities trusted him; the best proof of this was the fact that he had been working inside the camp since its inception (that is to say, since the summer of 1940), without ever having any quarrels with them. This, surely, must be taken as proof of his skill and discretion because among the prisoners it was generally known that, on occasion, he would do them small favors without ever getting caught. Old Szymlak was highly regarded as a tiler and as such he worked in our prison hospital during the installation of the bathhouse. I had already known the old man three years earlier in Auschwitz, where he carried out similar work in the SS sick bay, the headquarters and in the prison hospital. This made it a great deal easier to start a conversation with him.

Szymlak recognized me at once and greeted me cordially. He pulled out a tin of tobacco, rolled himself a cigarette and offered me one. Then we sat on a low wall and began to talk.

"You're keeping well," the old man remarked. "It's three years since last we met. Actually, you look better now."

"One scrapes along somehow, you know," I replied honestly. "I get the odd food parcel from home, and over there in Canada it's possible to organize something now and then." I pointed in the

173

direction of the crematorium in order to direct the conversation onto the right track.

"So many people perish here." The old man nodded his head with compassion. "The people know everything that goes on here. One can see the smoke from a long way off. But, God willing, everything will soon be over." Szymlak was growing talkative. "They are being defeated in the East, and the West is stirring, too. They're bombing as often as they can."

Suddenly he changed the subject. He seemed to think that he had already said too much.

"Everything is in the hand of God. Somehow it'll all work out. We must keep a stiff upper lip."

The conversation was getting us nowhere. I did not need to enlighten Szymlak as to what was happening in the camp. He knew the camp inside out, and had done so for years. He saw everything, he knew about everything. One had to approach him from another angle. Both of us were beating about the bush, neither daring to speak openly. It was obvious that, in spite of everything, we did not trust one another.

How was I to begin? I scratched my head as if that might help.

"Are you worried about something?" the old man inquired. "Perhaps I can help somehow?" Szymlak led me to understand quite plainly that he was inclined to help me. If I don't start now, I thought, we'll never get together. I'll ask him for a small favor to begin with, and afterwards we'll see.

"Herr Josef, I'd like to send a letter to my folks," I said quickly, watching out of the corner of my eye the impression these words had made on the old man.

Szymlak twirled his thick moustache and pondered for a while; then he looked me straight in the eye and said with a sigh of relief: "Why didn't you say so before, son. I'll do it for you. You write what you want to say on a small piece of paper so that I won't have any difficulties concealing it. My daughter'll copy it and send it to the address you're going to tell me now, and that's it."

Up until then he had addressed me formally. Since that time the old man called me by my first name. He took the note.

"But not a word to anyone," he admonished before he left.

The ice was broken. All we had to do now was to draw the old man cautiously and systematically into cooperating more seriously with us.

CHAPTER 56

AND NOW transports kept coming thick and fast. Not only from the ghettos of Sosnowiec and Bedzin; they were liquidating ghettos in all the large towns of occupied Poland. As a special treat, transports arrived from France. At the same time, mass selection in the camp increased steadily. The sick were no longer the only ones liquidated. From the men's camp D as well as from Quarantine (Sector A), a few thousand Jews were selected who were considered incapable of doing heavy work. They were gassed and their places taken by Jews from newly arrived transports who had been selected as able to work. The crematoria worked nonstop. The smoke, nauseating, heavy and sickly sweet, crept quite low between the huts, penetrating everywhere; there was virtually no air to breathe. In addition, autumn was here, with its damp and rainy days, dull and hopeless.

Even the greatest optimists among us, who had believed in an early end to the war, now lost hope. We must all perish here. Now they are finishing off the Jews. There can't be many of them left; soon they'll start on us. Our only comfort was the thought that we would not allow ourselves to be driven into the gas chambers without offering resistance. Meanwhile we watched thousands of people start on their last walk into the little woods from where there was no return. All that remained of them was this nauseating, suffocating smoke which enveloped, like a veil of mourning, hundreds of low-built huts where several thousand prisoners lived, who, enslaved by a handful of armed and ruthless "supermen," waited for their turn to come.

The SS carried out "clean" work only. It merely did the killing. The rest, the "dirty" work, was attended to by the Sonderkommando, which consisted of a few hundred young and strong Jews

175

who, at the price of cremating their daughters, wives and parents, were allowed to stay alive. They were witnesses, but that was not all. Under duress they took an active part in the cruellest possible crimes humanity had ever invented. In the room where the new arrivals undressed, members of the Sonderkommando handed them soap and towels, telling them that they were going to have a bath. Then they led them into the gas chambers from where, after a while, all that could be heard were the terror-stricken moans and cries of the dying. The members of the Sonderkommando had ceased to be human beings. All human feelings had been taken away from them, burned to ashes together with those they held nearest and dearest to their hearts. Now they were inured to human suffering. The death of others no longer made an impression on them. They knew that the fat ones burned better than the lean ones, that there was less trouble with transports coming from the West, who simply believed in these towels and soap, than with local ones. The members of the Sonderkommando knew very well that they would stay alive as long as there was something for them to burn because they were still needed to do the work. Of all the feelings the one left to them was the fear of their own death, a fear which swelled as they became more intimately aware of the whole bestial machinery of murder. They knew well the price they would have to pay for their lives; that was why every one of them abandoned himself to the delusion that he would stay alive if he worked well, if he did everything he was ordered to do. But somewhere, deep in their hearts, in the core of their hearts, there flickered the flame of hatred, subdued for now through fear for their very lives.

Thus they lay in wait, assiduously carrying out every command in order not to attract attention on any account, in order to survive because fate might have chosen them of all people to be the avengers.

With foresight, the Germans would, at intervals, liquidate them secretly. Suddenly, in moments when their vigilance had been lulled by good treatment, they would disappear. New ones took their place, and the sequence was repeated. In the camp the Sonderkommando were nevertheless regarded as some of the better

176

off. They had plenty to eat, were well dressed and bore themselves well; they were taken notice of because they smuggled out the valuables of people who had been gassed, the valuables which became the trading currency of the camp. The situation was similar in Canada, a Kommando which handled the belongings of the dead, the difference being that the Sonderkommando had nothing to do with the corpses and thus there was no need for them to be liquidated. The property depot, or Canada, was the last sector immediately behind our sick bay, in between crematoria 3 and 4, from which it was separated only by a nonelectrified fence. This meant that from Canada as well as from the sick bay anything happening in crematorium 4 and the sparse pine woods which surrounded it was fully exposed to the view of everybody. True, they put up something like a screen about three yards high, which hid the entrance to the gas chamber and the cremation pits; nevertheless the impenetrable pseudo-hedge, with its wilted leaves dropping, permitted one to see precisely what it was meant to conceal. The best place from which to see everything was Block 15, as yet unoccupied, and situated opposite crematorium 4, some seventy yards away. If one opened a dormer window at the gable end of the roof a little, one could, standing on an empty bed, comfortably observe the whole process in every detail.

For members of the Sonderkommando, who were used to seeing scenes of this kind every day, this was something quite normal. But for us, although we had experienced a great deal during our more than three years in the camp, it was still a shock so great that one lost one's belief in everything, even in God. If He existed—and it is in this belief that I was brought up—how could He allow these murders of helpless human beings, carried out by other human beings whose soldiers wore on the buckle of their belts the words "God with us"? Bathed in cold sweat, I watched these Dantesque scenes, holding tightly the damp hand of Edek or Waldeck who, like me, were convinced that there was no God. At least not here on this small plot of earth, which apparently was outside His control.

Something extraordinary happened. One night during the liquidation of one of the numerous transports, Oberscharführer Schillinger, the Rapportführer of the men's camp in Birkenau, one of the most hated and cruel SS men, was shot dead. The news spread through the camp like wildfire and was greeted everywhere with rejoicing.

"The hand of God," some said. "Fate has punished the criminal," asserted others. In the course of a few hours, every detail of this incident was, more or less credibly, known. It was a fact that it had been a woman who had killed him. He had, after all, always had a weakness for women; that was his undoing.

This is what was supposed to have happened: Schillinger, eager as always, was assisting that night on the ramp during the reception of a new transport of Jews, in the company of his crony Hauptscharführer Emmerich. Both of them, slightly drunk, accompanied the transport to the crematorium. They even entered the changing room, guided either by thoughts of a little stealing or in anticipation of the sadistic enjoyment of watching the timid, defenseless, undressed women who moments later were to die a painful death in the gas chamber.

The latter version seemed to me to be the more likely, if one considered Schillinger's predilections, particularly when he was drunk. His attention was drawn to a young and reputedly beautiful woman who refused to undress in the presence of the SS men. Incensed, Schillinger went up to the woman and tried to pull down her brassiere. In the struggle she managed to snatch his pistol, with which she shot Schillinger dead and injured Emmerich, who had come to Schillinger's aid, in the leg. Simultaneously, the other Jews tried to lock the doors from the inside. Upon hearing shots, the SS men who had been standing outside rushed into the changing room and, realizing what had happened, began to massacre everybody. Of this group of Jews, none died in the gas chamber; the enraged SS men shot them all.

The incident passed on from mouth to mouth and embellished in various ways grew into a legend. Without doubt this heroic deed by a weak woman, in the face of certain death, gave moral support to every prisoner. We realized all at once that if we dared raise a hand against them, that hand might kill; they were mortal, too.

Because they feared the consequences of this significant deed, the SS men tried to terrorize the camp. That very day discipline was tightened up, and bullets whistled on the camp street. But that did not alter the facts. Rapportführer Schillinger died in the crematorium, in the very place where he had sent thousands of human beings to their deaths in the name of Nazi ideology. Reaction came swiftly; prisoners straightened up, hope grew once more. A spontaneous, although still weak, campaign of self-defense was born.

On the afternoon of that same day, some people lined up in the little woods next to crematorium 4 and took to active resistance. When I heard the sound of vigorous gunfire I ran with Waldeck to our stand in Block 15. Strictly speaking, by the time we got there it was all over. Here and there single shots could be heard. The little woods were strewn with corpses, mainly men. They were still dressed.

As a rule, if the transport was very large, there was not enough room for everyone in the changing room; therefore they were ordered to undress in the little woods. This situation was similar. It would appear that women and children undressed first and then lined up in a long row directly behind the screen, from where they gradually disappeared through the door of the changing room. Now, terrified by the gunfire, crazed with fear, they crowded into the "shelter" of the changing room, clutching their bundles of clothing in their arms and trampling on each other. There arose the shrieks of lost children, the heartrending cries of the women, the groans of the people trodden underfoot and above all this the dull thuds of blows from SS rifle butts on heads, shoulders and backs of the half-undressed men, some of whom joined the crowd jostling inside the crematorium. Threats, shouts and blows did their work. As soon as the last ones had been squeezed into the changing room and the door shut behind them, there was complete silence. After a few minutes, a group of members of the Sonderkommando emerged from the side door of the crematorium. Exhorted by the SS men to hurry, some of them stripped the men who had been shot, while others piled the corpses in a heap in the crematorium yard. From a distance, the dull screams from hundreds of throats rose from the interior of the gas chambers despite the thick walls. Cyclon B was taking effect.

179

CHAPTER 57

IN ADDITION to its close proximity to the crematorium and to Canada, our prison hospital also bordered on the gypsy camp, separated from it merely by a ditch and some barbed wire, which was not electrified in the daytime. The gypsy hospital was looked after by doctors and nursing orderlies mostly from the main camp, in addition to some women from the women's camp sick bay. Making contact with them was easy. One needed only to ask one of the children who were always scampering about near the wires, and the child would fetch whoever was wanted. The children liked doing this, since they had already learned that they would be rewarded. They were hungry little waifs, unbelievably dirty and ragged, as were their parents, who would sit for hours outside their huts looking for lice in their tattered clothes. But there were also well-dressed gypsies, especially the young and beautiful girls. There was no need for them to come to the wires begging for a piece of bread or a cigarette. They sat in the block seniors' rooms, in private quarters where the music played, the girls danced, intoxicating liquor flowed and sex was freely available. The matter of racial inferiority tended to become blurred in the course of orgies and drinking bouts, in which the entire high society took part including SS men, led by Rapportführer Plagge, who was almost unrecognizably changed, benign, almost amicable. He, too, had a mistress here; besides which he drank hard and filled his pockets with easily grabbed jewelry. I knew what went on with the gypsies because I was so close a neighbor. Sometimes I managed to get inside the gypsy camp under a pretext, such as taking twins or some other patients to the hospital's special block.

The block was at the exclusive disposal of the anthropologist Dr. Mengele, who was also camp doctor of Sector B, an exceedingly elegant and good-looking SS officer who, thanks to his attractive appearance and his good manners, conveyed the impression of a gentle and cultured man who had nothing whatever to do with selections, phenol and Cyclon B. What he was like in reality was something we were to learn soon enough. We were attracted by the gay life which was so different from our own.

180

We secretly envied some people. Thus it was not in the least surprising that after evening roll call we would stand by the fence of the gypsy camp watching the "free life" of the gypsies. Young gypsy women, those of the second kind, that is to say, unnoticed by the influential élite and not hired for their harems, would show off for us, dancing for a few cigarettes, which were thrown to them through the wires as tribute and in appreciation of their talent.

There was one such girl at the fence, who did her dance in a particularly titillating manner, and for this her generous and aroused audience rewarded her with the lion's share of cigarettes. The appearance of this vivacious little gypsy girl ended unfortunately in tragedy. One of the cigarettes bounced off the wires and fell between them, but on the gypsies' side. Without giving the matter much thought, the girl leapt across the forbidden zone and tried, squatting, to retrieve the cigarette. Her shoulders, however, touched the wires which were already electrified for the night. She was dry, and that was possibly why she was not immediately killed. Her burned body sizzled in the places where the wires were touching it. They penetrated deeper and deeper into the hands and chest of the victim, who twitched convulsively. Everybody was petrified with horror.

There was, however, one quick-witted young gypsy who earlier had encouraged the girl to dance and then had taken from her the cigarettes she had "earned." Throwing his jacket over her hands, he grabbed a corner of the girl's dress and began to tug with all his might. The wires would not yield. Another gypsy used a pole to unhook her hand, which had gotten caught. The guard in his tower gesticulated from afar, but mercifully he did not shoot. The girl, unconscious and burned, was carried to the sick bay by the gypsies. She did not die. I saw her a few days later, still wearing bandages, but once again prettily dressed and well groomed. I bet that when she was in the sick bay one of the VIPs noticed her beauty as well as her hidden assets. She did come back to the block where she had nearly lost her life. Probably her family lived there. At the sight of her people would throw cigarettes, but although they fell well away from the fence she never again bent down to pick one up.

Sometimes Jurek Z. sauntered past the wires in the company of beautiful women. He had been a nursing orderly since the start of the camp. He helped with dressings in the outpatients' department in Block 28. After the establishment of the gypsy camp, Jurek and a friend who came from the same town were appointed canteen managers. Considering conditions elsewhere in the camp, this particular canteen was quite well provided, and business in the gypsy camp flourished. The gypsies were allowed to keep all their personal property. The authorities permitted this and thereby created the illusion of a normal, albeit regimented, life. The canteen did not do badly. On sale were specialities like snails, beetroot, slightly stale salads, as well as combs, toilet paper and the like. These things were for sale to those who could pay for them. The gypsies had already spent all they possessed. It was known that some of them owned gold and jewels. These were not acceptable in the canteen, but the manager had money, and one could make a deal with him. What was the use of all these pieces of jewelry when the children were crying for food, and when one might at least buy some slightly stale salads? Camp rations just were not enough to fill their bellies.

There was plenty of money outside the gypsy camp that the prisoners received officially from home. Canada, too, supplied large amounts of money which, outside the gypsy camp, was not viewed with much favor. If, therefore, one was shrewd, one might do good business. Jurek, as it turned out, was shrewd, very shrewd indeed. The canteen prospered and business flourished. But it was also necessary to do something with this accumulation of baubles, to use them as bartering counters. And so barter trading across the wires came into being. Although neither the men's camp next to the gypsy camp nor our own sick bay was in the market for gypsy gold, because they had their own gold from Canada; what they were interested in were cigarettes, which the civilians trading with prisoners did not supply in sufficient quantities (because the merchandise was comparatively cheap and thus not sufficiently lucrative). It was easier to get alcohol because of its high price. This was why whole boxes of cigarettes from the gypsy canteen went across the wire into Sectors D and F, and in exchange all kinds of liquor flowed from these camps into the hands of the enterprising canteen managers.

However, the requirements of the gypsy camp were enormous. Food was supplied by the kitchen; not turnip or nettle soup, that was for ordinary mortals. In the kitchen store cupboards there were foodstuffs taken from transports that had gone to the gas chambers: sardines, chocolate, oranges, tins. These were additional provisions for the SS, not for ordinary mortals. For officers and their families. The enterprising cooks sold some of these foodstuffs for gold and dollars to trustworthy prisoners who were shrewd. They, incidentally, also took part in the feasts. In this way they profited twice; what they sold they also ate. Since there would always be a shortage of booze, they supplied that as well— not for nothing, naturally.

The Rapportführer had smelled a rat. Therefore his palm had to be greased. After all, the gypsy camp was no concentration camp, more a family camp. There were Funktionshäftlinge here, too. But without them there would not be so many comforts here, either. They were shrewd and—most important—they were discreet. They would not squeal because they would themselves be caught. In for a penny, in for a pound, as the saying goes. It was worth the risk. Three years ago, Plagge would have cold-bloodedly ill-treated so insignificant a prisoner as Jurek. Now he sat at the same table, boozing and fondling the girl who had already slept with Jurek.

Jurek had a firm grip on them all. He satisfied them and in return had a free hand. Trade was doing very well thank you. He was a little afraid of Bogdan Komarnicki, who was always snooping around in the gypsy camp. Everybody knew that he had been sent by the Political Department, and he was known to be a spy. What else could have brought black-eyed Bogdan here? Perhaps he meant to denounce a secret organization? In the gypsy camp? Not on your life! No one here was interested in such things. So, what now? But of course! That's it! To start with, a little booze. Bogdan drank, but he could hold his liquor. A gypsy girl, maybe? He was young, handsome. So, why not? The girl wanted to get something out of it, didn't she? Okay, a pretty ring, a diamond. However, that alone was not enough for Bogdan. If the whole thing were to blow up, he might try to hush up his part. How about a little blackmail, then? If the old man were to hear about it, he might liquidate him just like that. The boss's wife, Frau Boger, liked bangles and baubles, like any woman. She might be useful one day. She had influence with her husband, and it was important to have such an intermediary with the chief of the Political Department.

A flame leapt from a crematorium chimney. The smoke, this characteristic sickly smoke, once more crept across from the little woods, fouling the air. As long as they burned, there would be enough gold and jewels. All one had to do was to sell them at a profit, and then everything would be fine. All one needed was to be shrewd, and Jurek was that, without doubt. They didn't call him "king of the gypsies" for nothing!

CHAPTER 58

EDEK HAD not been to see me for a few days now. I had got so used to his presence that I felt an emptiness if I did not see him for some time. Of late we had had long conversations and arrived at a certain concrete conclusion: we must escape from the camp. We did not yet know how and when, but in any case we knew we had to begin preparing for it slowly. It could not be done in a hurry. Too many people had already paid for such haste with their lives, and not only with their own. We intended to work it out in such a way that no one else would be at risk to reprisals on the part of the SS. Our acquaintance with Szymlak might be very useful. In a short while Edek's Kommando was to be permanently transferred to Birkenau. It was easier to escape from Birkenau. That suited us well. As soon as they had been transferred, I would try to get into his Kommando so that we might be together. The Kommando was convenient because it afforded the opportunity of moving about the whole area inside the big outer cordon. This was not unimportant. We'd think of something. We had sworn each other to silence. Not a word to anyone.

At long last, however, Edek turned up again. He had lost some weight after a few days in the bunker. He was lucky. He had not been liquidated, nor was he sent to the penal company. He was transferred as a fitter to Sector D of the men's camp in Birkenau. His Kommandoführer continued to be Rottenführer Lubusch, who was also in charge of the locksmith's shop in Auschwitz. I remembered Lubusch from 1940, when he was a Blockführer. He was too lenient, that was why he did not keep his post for very long. He even had clashes with the authorities and was consequently sent away for some months, to Breslau or Stutthof, I believe. They wanted to teach him the proper way to handle prisoners in concentration camps in a special penal camp for the SS. The result was, as it turned out, exactly the opposite. Not only had his attitude towards prisoners not changed, but he actually treated them more leniently still. However, now he was more careful and knew how to put on a front.

In our plans we considered him as a man on whom we could count at all times. Especially Edek, since I was rather inclined to expect help from Szymlak, who seemed to me to be safer, even if only because he did not wear an SS uniform.

One morning when I was in the washroom, as usual—I would hide in there whenever Helmerson came to inspect my blocks—I was suddenly summoned by Zengteller and, for the first time, taken before the camp doctor who was himself carrying out a search in my bed. I was convinced that this was Zengteller's work. I was too old a prisoner to hide anything in my bed. Thus I was certain that he would find nothing. I stood to attention before His Majesty and began: "Block senior of 7 and 8 reporting . . ." I did not finish because he interrupted me at once.

"Block senior? Are *you* the block senior?" His voice heavy with irony and suppressed fury, he gave a look of unmistakable rebuke to Hans, the confused camp senior, who was rummaging mercilessly in my pallet in order to hide his alarm rather than in the hope of finding anything.

This might have been the end of the search but for the fact that under the bed they discovered two large food parcels in a cardboard carton. One of the parcels was from my parents, the second I had received only a day earlier from Szymlak's daughter. Hans took everything out of the parcels and put it on the table.

Helmerson was livid with rage. "Our soldiers die of starvation at the front, and scum like this live in the lap of luxury."

185

That was nothing. After all, we were allowed to receive food parcels. Things only really started when they opened the cupboard and out tumbled the silken Canada underwear. I wore silk underwear because the lice did not cling to it as they did to cotton. Getting it was no problem when one lived next door to Canada. Besides, for some time now underwear and civilian clothes from the clothing depot in Birkenau had been distributed quite officially. Therefore I explained quite boldly: "This is underwear from Jews, from the transport," I stumbled on, "from the clothing depot."

Perhaps I might still have wriggled out of it, but lying on a shelf were about twenty cakes of camp soap. This soap was kept in the cupboard; what else was I to do with it? It had been issued to me for patients, for seriously ill patients in the isolation ward who could not wash anyway because there was no washroom in the ward. Patients washed only on being admitted to the hospital and on leaving it. With my poor knowledge of German I was not in a position to explain all this, and Zengteller made no effort to help me because he wanted me to get caught. He fully intended that I should be made to look like a thief. He knew only too well that I did not need these lumps of clay that went by the name of soap, because everybody had good-quality, scented Canada soap, which was not hard to get.

"Camp senior," Helmerson said severely, pointing at me, "dismiss into camp at once to do penal work."

At last they departed. I was just breathing a sigh of relief after this unexpected visit when I was summoned again. Short of breath and frightened, Gang came to fetch me. He had just enough time to tell me that Helmerson had caught little Wladzio. What could he have caught Wladzio doing? I thought as I walked uneasily behing Gang.

Wladzio was a boy of about fifteen who, by some miracle, had remained from a transport, together with some boys of the same age. He was an orphan. His parents were sent to the gas chamber immediately after their arrival in Auschwitz. I had hidden him in the block among the sick, which was not allowed but was general practice if one had to help someone practically. Wladzio helped

186

the nursing orderlies with their cleaning; he looked after my things and my food parcels because he had no one from whom he could have received any. Just then he was busy washing a shirt for me outside the block and was caught committing this crime.

It turned out that he was not a patient but not a nursing orderly either, that he was washing my shirt, a silk shirt at that, using, fortunately, Canada soap. Camp senior Hans tried to shield Wladzio by calling him my Pipel, which Helmerson probably took to mean that he was my servant, because at the word Pipel he looked cross at me and spread his hands in a gesture of despair. Zengteller explained something, talking long and earnestly, pointing now at me, now at the uncomprehending Wladzio. I gathered that he was trying to save him by intentionally pushing me deeper and deeper into trouble. The affair began to take such a bad turn that I started to be seriously worried I might end up in the penal company at least. Fortunately, Dr. Helmerson merely ordered camp senior Hans to dismiss me from the sick bay into the men's camp D immediately after evening roll call, with the order that I was to be employed doing heavy laboring at Königsgraben, where the penal company worked day in, day out. Since this order had been given orally, I got away without having to report for punishment. I was transferred to Sector D in the normal way and was thus committed for labor duties.

CHAPTER 59

THE ARBEITSDIENST was an old prisoner, a Pole from Silesia, called Jozek Mikusz, well known for his extremly lenient attitude towards his fellow prisoners.

"What the hell have you been up to, to be transferred so suddenly?" Jozek asked, amused.

I briefly told him what had happened.

"You're lucky he didn't make a written report. Now, where shall I put you?" he said thoughtfully. "You're not going to work with the shovel, are you?"

"Let him come with us," Edek suggested, happy that now we would be together, which fit in well with our plans.

Perhaps we might have wangled it, but at that moment we were joined by Arbeitsdienst Victor Tkocz, who threw a wrench in the plans.

"You were a clerk over there and block senior as well, so you can be a clerk over here. You're not really a craftsman. We'll put you in Block 8. They've got a clerk there already, but he isn't efficient, and you shall help him."

I thought that this job wouldn't be too bad. Winter was approaching; it was better to be indoors than to be knocking around with the Kommandos, particularly since the women's camp, where I wanted to go, was out of bounds for everybody from other camps, allegedly on account of an epidemic.

As soon as I had settled down in Block 8 I understood at once why Victor had been so keen for me to go there as assistant clerk. The block senior was a German, a political prisoner from Buchenwald, who had only recently been transferred to Birkenau. He was intelligent, disciplined, lenient and soft, not very energetic, and definitely different from the majority of German trusties (although, on account of the less severe regime in the camp, they were no longer quite so bloodthirsty). The Russian prisoners of war, who formed the majority of the block, did not give him any great measure of respect. His culture they took for weakness. As a result, they ignored him completely and did not take him seriously at all.

The clerk was quite a different kind of spirit. Cheerful and natural, an old Auschwitzian from the first transport, No. 537, Jozek Wasko knew how to gain the liking and even the appreciation of the apparently not very disciplined group of Soviet prisoners of war. But this companionable relationship between Jozek and the Russians did not please camp senior Danisz. He did not like the Russians because they were impudent, and as for Wasko, he was hard, too sure of himself, with not enough appreciation of his "lord and master" and his orders. Hence Danisz harassed poor Jozek. He was, however, unable to get rid of him because it would have meant complete anarchy in the block. I realized why Victor, a great friend of Danisz, was so keen to have me in Block 8 as

188

assistant clerk. Sooner or later, as soon as an opportunity of removing him presented itself, I was to replace Jozek. No doubt
they counted on my fully appreciating the "favor" they bestowed
upon me by not sending me to do hard labor and assumed that as
former block senior I would be capable of keeping the "Bolsheviks" on a tight rein.

When I became assistant clerk, I did not have a thing to do.
Once he had ascertained his numbers, Jozek would lapse into
idleness, and together we killed time with endless conversations.
During one of these prolonged chats, we were surprised by Danisz
while we were sitting cosily, enveloped in clouds of cigarette
smoke. When I noticed Danisz approaching I quickly put out my
cigarette. But Jozek inhaled even more deeply than usual and thus
provoked the camp senior, who was furious with him anyway.

At that time no trusty would have dared strike an old prisoner.
But Danisz had a bad temper. If in the end Jozek had not run
away, he might well have killed him. The block senior wisely
stayed in his room. I stood petrified and waited for him to attack
me next. Instead I heard him say: "You are now the clerk here,
understood? Block senior!"

The startled block senior glided from behind the door.

"There's your clerk."

And to me he said in broken Polish: "If I catch you smoking
again I'll break your neck, you motherfucker."

Thus I became Jozek's successor. Fortunately, before very long
we acquired a new block senior. This time he was a Pole, Adam
B., who had come into the camp almost a year before. He was tall,
of sturdy build, elegant, always serious. He wore breeches as well
as officers' boots and looked like a typical officer from pre-war
days. Possibly it was his martial appearance which persuaded
Danisz to make him block senior in this "difficult" block. But
appearances can be deceptive. It turned out that Adam was a real
human being, decent, quite energetic, but fair. He was clever
enough to put on a show in front of Danisz and the Blockführers
by shouting and displaying his eagerness. But basically he was
sentimental, soft, even emotional, a trait which became particularly plain when he received letters from his wife in Cracov,
whom he adored and for whom he longed. I shall never forget the

189

moment when one of the Blockführers ordered him to give a beating to a prisoner who had hidden under his bunk while his Kommando was marching out to work. The Russian stood these five blows easily, but Adam suffered grievously during the beating. One could see it in his face that was flushed and damp with sweat. He was responsible for the block and had to carry out the order; otherwise he would have gotten it himself. To hand out punishment goes with the post of block senior. I would not have liked to be in his position.

Much to his relief, but to the despair of a few dozen Jews from Canada and the clothing depot, who also lived in our block, Danisz accommodated his friend, camp Kapo Jupp, in the room where, up until then, the office had been. Jupp was delighted to deputize for the block senior in this part of his duty. He was an old criminal, short and scraggy, a physical nonentity with the face of a sadist and alcoholic. He was an exceptionally bestial creature, a murderer of Jews and Mussulmen, of anyone who showed signs of weakness. He had respect only for the Russians. As soon as they were in a crowd, he did not attack them because he was afraid. As for me, he looked at me askance, but did not hurt me, just like Danisz, who treated me graciously. They still had not figured me out. The block senior and I did not take long to come to an arrangement. I was responsible merely for keeping the index cards of arrivals and departures, for accompanying patients to the hospital when required and for supervising the room orderlies.

There were three of them, all Jews. The eldest, Jankiel, good-natured and very orthodox, was quiet, self-contained, honest. I felt a liking and trust for him at once. The next—nicknamed The Barber because he plied that trade among others—was quick, nervous, very talkative, deft and not too honest, but he was under the influence of Jankiel. The third was Ici Mayer, a powerfully built redhead, lazy, vicious, with mean little eyes that darted here and there and did not bode well. He had had a dark past in Majdanek, of which I had been warned. They said that he had more than one Jew on his conscience. It was clear that he was a spy, a coward, a rogue and a toadie. Danisz and Jupp treated him very well. I was convinced that he paid for this treatment because he had many friends in the Sonderkommando. The other two room orderlies hated him like poison and wished he would drop dead.

I would have to watch my step with this character and try to find a means of getting rid of him, as he might become dangerous. Edek now spent whole evenings with me, and we spoke almost exclusively about our plans to escape. Ici might eavesdrop on us. He knew that I did not like him, but he did not care. He had strong support from Danisz and Jupp, and consequently did not have to take much notice of me. Even the block senior supported him because he seemed to be afraid of getting on the camp senior's bad side.

The four hundred Russians who lived in the block were a solid crowd of men but, so it seemed, not very disciplined. Later, when I got to know them better, I found to my surprise that they had a discipline of their own, and any transgression against it risked punishment by lynch law. If they found a spy among them they liquidated him immediately. In the prison camp they represented a special caste. They were "prisoners of war," and although at first they were treated like the other prisoners, they succeeded in time, at least in part, to gain the rights of prisoners of war. Perhaps Stalingrad helped them there, although even before that, Lagerführer Schwarzhuber would, at times, display an odd weakness towards them by treating them a little better than the rest of the prisoners. That was why those who remained from the first Russian transport, the ones who had not been killed, had decent posts, especially in the kitchen, in the depots and in some of the blocks.

Most of them, however, worked in the breakers' yards or in the Kommando called Mexico, two huge Kommandos which employed hundreds of prisoners. The breakers' yards dealt with unloading, dismantling and sorting airplanes, Allied as well as German, large quantities of which were taken to the siding alongside the Auschwitz-Dziedzice line, half-way between the main camp in Auschwitz and Birkenau. It was the spot where the Jews had once arrived. Work in the breakers' yard was very hard. Nevertheless the Russians were eager to be in this Kommando for reasons best known to themselves. Later I, too, got to know the magnet which drew them there. Outwardly it seemed that the main attraction was alcohol, which could be found in various parts of the airplane and which was smuggled into the camp in large quantites inside their water bottles, from which they never parted.

There were two kinds of alcohol to be found: ethyl and methyl alcohol, frequently poisonous. They knew all about it, though; they traded in both. They liked drinking the stuff themselves and, interesting to relate, it never did them any harm. As traders they were no less competent than many a Jew from the Sonderkommando or from Canada. I would even go so far as to say that they were more crafty. They needed "merchandise" for further bartering, this time for the civilians who worked in the breakers' yards. They swapped gold and jewelry for tobacco and, above all, for proper alochol, which could be exchanged in the camp for bread, bacon, sausages and other foodstuffs. They needed to supplement their meager camp rations if they wanted to keep themselves in reasonable condition, considering the very heavy work they were forced to do.

CHAPTER 60

AT FIRST I found it hard to make myself understood with these Russians. I could not speak their language, nor did I really have any liking for them; they repaid me in kind by treating me, the successor to the generally popular Jozek, with reserve and undisguised suspicion. They ignored me completely, answering any of my orders with the brief and succinct phrase, "Fuck off."

It was worst on Sundays when we did not work. In the afternoon there was the obligatory louse check, followed by an hour's compulsory rest on our beds. Louse checks did not radically alter hygienic conditions in the camp, but they did force some filthy pigs to wash at least once a week (in cold water, it is true), as well as change their underclothes, although even the fresh ones invariably contained nits. Even the enforced hour's rest on a Sunday afternoon after a week of twelve-hour days was nothing but a kind of harassment, for the authorities deliberately suppressed the urge to move and prevented contact between prisoners in different blocks. Nevertheless, this was an order which camp senior Danisz and the Blockführers observed meticulously. Any noncompliance with this compulsory leisure would give them ground for renewed torments and beatings. I might shout until I was blue in the face; they did not understand me or did not want to understand me. Finally, Jozek came to my aid.

"You don't know how to handle them. Don't get all worked up, don't shout; it's all the same to them anyway."

Jozek leapt onto the stove and adopted a Napoleonic stance. With a wave of his hand he calmed down the shouting and began to launch into a speech in a histrionic voice, trying to speak in Russian: "Comrades, boys, members of the Red Army!"

The Russians were familiar with this solemn introduction. Some were already laughing and starting to take off their shirts.

"Well, come on, strip, what are you standing about for? Do you want the lice to eat you alive?" He turned to a group of prisoners who showed no inclination to have their clothing searched. With joking, teasing, laughing, threatening and cajoling he managed to attain his goal, while I noted the numbers of men who were particularly filthy and louse-ridden; later the room orderlies would take them away for a thorough delousing, something the prisoners liked least of all.

That same evening there was a curfew. The block senior posted me at the door—I was to watch that no one left the block under any circumstances—and removed himself to his office. Kola was one of the Russian prisoners of war left from the very first transport. An old camp inmate, he worked in the kitchen, cared nothing for any orders and now pushed me roughly aside in an attempt to get outside. I explained that he was not to go out of the block because if he was caught by Danisz or one of the Blockführers who were now patrolling the camp, he would be beaten and I would get it in the neck as well. With my body I barred the exit, but Kola shoved me in front of him, and we started to wrestle. Suddenly he broke away; however, I managed to get hold of him by the collar and drag him back into the block. Before I knew

193

where I was, blows began to rain on me thick and fast so that everything went black. Enraged, I went after him and returned the blows.

We battled for what seemed a very long time. Facing each other like two fighting cocks, we were soon surrounded by a circle of spectators, who came running from all over the block. The Russians of course encouraged Kola, while I was cheered on by Edek and a few other prisoners. Everybody was having a wonderful time. But we did have a real fight.

The camp Kapo shrieked with delight at the sight of blood; by now we were both bleeding profusely. The block senior tried to separate us. But seeing how worked up we were and realizing that persuasion was in vain, he had recourse to what in such cases is the only remedy: a bucket of water emptied over the two of us had an immediate effect. The Russians led their protagonist away with a swollen nose and a spendid black eye. I remained behind on the battlefield with a cut lip, which was already quite badly swollen. Jankiel applied a compress. The Barber cleaned up my scratches. Edek complained that I had not given Kola enough of a beating. Kuzak the priest said indignantly: "Heavens, my boy, isn't being in this camp enough for you two?" Ici Mayer disappeared, no doubt intent on reporting the fight to Danisz. Kapo Hans, whom this exhibition appeared to have put in a very good mood, sent his Pipel with a tin of sardines and a bottle of schnapps.

And I, once I had recovered my composure, began to realize that this incident had been in very poor taste. After a while Mischa arrived with "The Professor" for a parley. Both these men commanded great authority among the Russians. No one ever contradicted them. They were just and fair, and everybody had to acknowledge it. One might suspect that there existed a well-concealed, strongly disciplined organization, and that its driving force were these two men, whose minds were head and shoulders above the majority of prisoners of war in Block 9. I was therefore not greatly surprised to see them standing before me now.

I had to listen to their reproaches concerning my conduct and my taking part in a stupid brawl with someone as uncouth as Kola; I was told that this fight was not very much to my credit, that I had set a bad example for every other inmate of this block, for every political prisoner who had been enslaved by our common enemy, the Germans. This was roughly the tenor of The Professor's speech. I had quite enough of his homily, although in my heart I thought he had a point. There had been no need for this. Certainly it had not gained me any popularity with the Russians, with people with whom I was forced to live.

At last Mischa suggested that I should apologize to Kola. This was too much for me, and Edek leapt up from his stool. But what Mischa had in mind was something quite different, and it took The Professor, with Jankiel interpreting, to clear up the business completely. What mattered was that I should make peace with Kola before the eyes of the whole block. I agreed not very readily, for I feared a trap. The Russians were stirred up. If I went into the block—our conversation took place in the bread store—I might possibly not come out alive. On the other hand, I had to believe in the good intentions of Mischa and The Professor because they were well disposed towards me.

Terribly frightened, I went to see Kola. Edek remained standing at the hut door, just in case one might have to call for help. Kola's bunk was somewhere in the center of the hut. Mischa and The Professor walked out of the block and left me to my own devices in front of his bunk. Kola was sitting on the upper bunk alone, putting a cold compress on his painful eye. There was not a sound in the block. Everyone was watching us tensely. We sat side by side, in silence; then he looked at me and I looked at him and we began to laugh. Kola was first to speak: "You fool—me fool! Come let us drink to our reconciliation, clerk," he said, and embraced me. Then from under his blanket he pulled a bottle, knocked out the cork with a deft movement and indicated with his finger the level down to which I was allowed to drink. Handing me the bottle, he said: "Drink, clerk, to our reconciliation."

I was already gagging because I knew that it was vile stuff.

"Drink, go on, drink!"

My eyes were popping out of their sockets, the harsh liquid ran across my mouth, the wound on my lip burnt like fire. With difficulty I reached the level he had indicated; I knew that otherwise the "drink to our reconciliation" would not have been valid. Kola drank his share in one gulp. Once more we shook hands, and only then did the others join us. A drinking bout began. Somebody was always bringing more liquor.

Reassured about my fate, Edek also produced a bottle, the one Hans had given me as a reward for my militant attitude in the fight. The booze did its work; my head was ringing, everything was going round and round and I saw double. In the morning I awoke on my bunk with a terrible headache and a mighty thirst. Next to me sat Edek and Kola. They gave me something to drink, and after that I felt a little better.

After this incident there were no more misunderstandings between the Russians and me. After that time they trusted me.

CHAPTER 61

EDEK SPENT almost every evening with me. I converted the bread store in our block into a comfortable place for our meetings. Often we were joined by Mischa and The Professor. The latter regularly read German newspapers, which Edek brought for him. The Professor asserted that he could read between the lines. Whenever he read a news item about German victories he would clean his spectacles, slap his thighs and say, "Good, good. Everything's going according to plan."

He knew already how the war would end. The Germans would be thoroughly defeated, the Nazis hanged to the last man, all the Slav peoples united in one large commune and so on. As far as victory was concerned, we agreed with The Professor, but we did not quite agree with the rest of his predictions. We had quite a different opinion concerning these matters. As soon as Mischa and The Professor were deep in a lively discussion, we would discreetly take ourselves away, leaving them with Jankiel, with whom they could make themselves understood more easily. We had our own plans; what use was politics? Our plans were daily coming closer to reality.

Blockführer Pestek was a frequent guest of my block senior. He was about thirty, skinny and plain. At first glance he did not look very likable, and his harelip did nothing to enhance his charm. The SS cadres really must be scraping the barrel to have accepted so puny a specimen in their ranks, and what was more, as a Blockführer with the rank of Rottenführer, whose task it was to treat prisoners with a firm hand. I had never seen him strike anybody, nor did he ever raise his voice. He came from somewhere near the Polish-Romanian frontier, from Czernovitz (at least that was what Blockführer Schneider asserted, who also came from that part of the country), spoke excellent Polish and did not distinguish himself by his cruelty. The two shared a predilection for trade. They merely differed in that Schneider liked to haggle, whereas Pestek took anything he was offered. He would even accept ordinary watches, which were quoted most unfavorably on the camp commodity exchange.

Business flourished. I did not even have to run any risks. Without having to leave the camp, I possessed liquor, SS sausage, cigarettes and at times even English chocolate. Pestek would arrive outside the block on his bicycle and hand me a bulging bag; I took out the merchandise and placed the "payment" inside. In the meantime, Pestek went through other blocks, ostensibly on duty. When he returned he took his bag, fastened it to his bicycle and rode away whistling.

Sometimes he came unexpectedly. Then I might not have anything with which to pay him. He would wait patiently until the next time. There was some secret between him and the block senior. I suspected that through him Adam was in touch with his wife in Cracov. Therefore I thought that if Pestek, in addition to carrying on illegal trading, was possibly also a link between the camp and freedom—suggested by the constant whispering going on in the block senior's room—he might in some way be persuaded to help us with our flight plans. We ought to test him. Edek was all for it, for we had already decided that we ought to make contact with an SS man who would sell us two uniforms because we intended to escape disguised as SS men.

One day, when we knew that Pestek was on duty in our block, Edek did not go to work but hid in my block. As the block senior was absent, we sat down in his office and waited impatiently for the Blockführer to turn up. Outside in the corridor stood Jankiel.

197

We had arranged that he would act as lookout during our conversation with Pestek, who was just arriving on his bicycle.

"Attention," shrieked Jankiel, taking hold of the Blockführer's bicycle at the same time.

"Where's everybody?" Pestek asked, glancing into the room on the opposite side of the corridor where camp Kapo Jupp lived. I ran from my room in order to make my report: "Block 8 occupied by . . ."

He interrupted me, took his bag from his bicycle and proceeded to the block senior's room. Edek stood to attention. Surprised, Pestek asked: "Where's the block senior?" He placed the bag on the table next to the card index.

"The block senior has gone to the main office. He'll be back presently," I replied calmly in Polish.

"And who's he, then?" he inquired, also in Polish. He sat down and looked keenly at Edek.

"That's my friend, Herr Blockführer, an old organizer. It's he who supplies me with these various bits and pieces."

"Is he safe?" he asked, reaching for the bag.

"Safer than I."

Edek played with a twenty-dollar coin, throwing it from one hand to the other. Pestek could not help noticing it.

"What have you got there?"

"You're welcome to it," said Edek nonchalantly, handing over the shiny twenty-dollar piece. Pestek rummaged in his bag and produced a bar of chocolate. It was meant for the block senior, but seeing that he was not here . . . He rubbed his hands and went up to the stove, where the fire crackled.

"Winter's coming," he remarked.

Edek knocked the cork out of a bottle.

"What are you doing, you madman? I'm on duty," he added, a little more kindly.

"Just a glass, Herr Blockführer. A little glassful won't hurt you. No one'll notice, because everybody drinks," Edek said cheekily, and poured some liquor into a cup. Pestek drank with us and talked about all sorts of things, but somehow we could not direct the conversation to the subject that interested us most.

"Perhaps you could bring us some more of this English chocolate?" Edek asked, looking for another starting point. He must have hit on the right thing, for Pestek began at once to talk about English prisoners of war, and quite specifically, about an officer whom he had helped to get in touch with a family in the camp at Theresienstadt.

Edek winked at me triumphantly. He was on the right track. If Pestek talked about such things now, we might risk making a suggestion to him.

"I'm fed up with this camp," Edek said suddenly. "If I had an SS uniform, I would go away . . ." He said "go away" quite delicately, but Pestek understood him very well.

"Go away, go away." He laughed. "And where would you go? Winter's coming. There's nothing threatening you here, and by spring many things may have changed."

Nothing doing. Pestek was cleverer than we thought. Why should he take serious risks and start getting involved in our affairs? That was not the same as doing a bit of trading. I thought we had put him off. He came less often and quite obviously avoided conversations with me, confining these strictly to our exchange of goods. But I did not lose hope that one day he might be more amenable.

Winter came. We no longer thought of escaping. Pestek was hardly seen in our block anymore; he was Blockführer in the family camp. I had learnt this from Schneider, a frequent visitor to our block. Schneider also dealt in liquor, but I did not have much confidence in him. He was too chummy with Blockführer Grapatin, and he was one with whom one had to watch one's step.

CHAPTER 62

DESPITE THE arrival of numerous transports destined for the gas chamber and the continued selections among the sick and even the healthy, conditions in the camp improved noticeably. The Auschwitz people ascribed this to Liebehenschel, the new Kommandant and successor of Hoess. The Russians, above all The Professor, thought that it was the result of defeats suffered by the

199

German army on the eastern front. Others maintained—as they received news from "informed sources"—that changes in the camp regime were due to radio reports from London which suggested that the Allies were aware of conditions in the camp. There were still others, mainly old prisoners, who regarded the present time as a period of transition, a result of slackened discipline among the SS men who were busy liquidating Jews and stealing their valuables at every opportunity. This did not leave them much time for what went on in the camp. Times were different from the days when a block senior or Kapo would kill without mercy for the sake of a few portions of margarine or a few slices of bread. Now the Poles received food parcels, the Jews had gold and jewelry, and the Russians offered booze.

At first a Kapo or block senior might try the old methods, but they soon discarded them, because they found that if they used the old methods under the present conditions, they would have to eat bread and marge. Moreover, they would not have been in a position to eliminate people at will, especially since the authorities increasingly treated the prisoners as a work force.

A very small proportion carried on as before, if only from habit, venting their rage on the Mussulmen, but not doing it too often so as not to annoy "influential" prisoners. In recent days it had happened that a Kapo or block senior who had been too eager had been beaten up in some dark corner of the camp, where he had strayed to deal with one of his victims. The "influentials," however, had increasingly more and more say and were to be respected. It was mainly Poles who occupied the important posts in the camp, taking advantage of the favorable situation. The criminals remained at the top, but their hands were already tied. They had no choice but to feign friendship, since they had gotten nowhere with hostility.

Instead they tried with "good treatment" to atone for their old sins. In particular they respected the main office with its unlimited possibilities for entering the names of people one wanted to get rid of on lists of the transports, which were more and more often leaving for other camps.

No one from Birkenau wanted to leave for another, uncertain

200

camp, least of all the old criminals and "deserving" cases because they feared revenge from any who might remember. They all knew of cases where men had perished under mysterious circumstances, transported and locked in a goods wagon together with the gray mass of prisoners.

I decided to rid myself of Ici Mayer. He was forever snooping, spying, eavesdropping. At the last moment, so as to surprise him and give him no time to escape, Ici was placed on a transport. However, he managed to get free. He must have paid Danisz well because not only did he, at the last moment, drag Ici from the line of prisoners waiting to be transported, but he actually took him into his own block as a trusty. Ici Mayer may have suspected that the whole thing had been my doing. I showed my anger only too openly. At any rate he kept out of my way and set camp senior Danisz against me, who became quite clearly less well disposed towards me. He still tolerated me, but I felt that he was only waiting for an opportunity to catch me.

Pestek, on whom I had counted, let me down. He no longer turned up in my block, although I saw him sometimes walking up and down near the Blockführer's office. One day he came unexpectedly, conferred briefly with the block senior and vanished just as quickly. After that I never saw him again.

Until the bombshell burst. Blockführer Pestek fled and allegedly got a Jew out of Theresienstadt. It was rumored that he was in touch with the English intelligence service, according to Schneider, who became talkative after he had drunk some alcohol. But what was certain was that Pestek had disappeared. Edek was not too worried about this interrupted connection. He said he was in the process of working on someone new and that one would have to organize dollars because he was likely to need them at a later date. Therefore I began to save. Until now we had usually spent these savings on food and drink, but now we had a goal. Slowly our somewhat amorphous flight plans were taking on a more concrete shape. We would escape in the summer. By that time Jaroslav was sure to be in Soviet hands, always assuming that the advancing Russians would be able to keep up their pace. There would then no longer be any fear of reprisals against our families. Collective responsibility in the camp was a thing of the past; we should not endanger anyone. We had a great deal of time. All that was necessary was for us to prepare ourselves well.

In mid-February Edek entered into an agreement with Lubusch, his former Kommandoführer. He told him the whole truth. If he was to help us, we must keep no secrets from him. He promised to get us two uniforms in a very short time. He mentioned that he had financial difficulties. We were prepared for this, and his demands were not unreasonable. However, one week, two weeks passed, and there were no uniforms. One evening Edek told me to get him two hundred dollars, and to get it by the next day. Lubusch needed the money. I went to see Karl, a Yugoslav Jew from Canada. He did not have the money readily available, but he tried to get it from his own people, and this he did. He did not ask for anything in return. He did not drink, and he had food in abundance. I gave him a cigarette box which a prisoner of war had made from a part of an aircraft. He was at least as pleased with this trifle as I with my two hundred dollars. Karl was one of comparatively few prisoners working in Canada who was not demoralized by the ease with which he could make a fortune. He would certainly take things into the camp from time to time. But this he did in defiance, lest more goods should fall into the hands of the murderers of his entire family. What he could not bring, he flushed down the toilet. But he had also stashed something away because he counted on coming to an arrangement with someone planning to escape from the camp. As an older man, his physical condition was less than perfect, and he was no partner for such an adventure. Once before he had been deceived by a black marketeer he knew well. This man had positively milked Karl by promising that he would escape taking along Karl and his friend, who was even older than Karl, by way of a fictitious bunker which was supposed to exist in Mexico. He managed to cheat the naïve Jew until the time I opened Karl's eyes. Perhaps this was why he got me the dollars so quickly and unselfishly.

Since the day on which the uniform was to be handed over had not been fixed but was near, I arranged to be on duty every day at the wires by the side of the ramp where the fitters' hut was because it was arranged that Lubusch would leave the parcel with the precious contents there. Tomorrow everything would be ready.

The day was beautiful and quite warm for the end of February. Not a sign of snow. I stood behind the last row of huts, leaning against the wooden wall, which was slightly warmed by the sun. In front of me, a few yards away, was a deep ditch. Right behind it were the wires, then the ramp, empty for once, and to one side of it the fitters' hut. Far away on the horizon the distant mountains, brilliantly white, merged into the blue of the sky. Freedom was there. I glanced briefly at my watch. It was shortly before twelve. According to our arrangements, it was around this time that Lubusch was supposed to arrive on his bicycle and leave the uniform in the hut where Edek was waiting for him.

I saw him from afar. He came from the direction of the main guardhouse, down the path running alongside the railway track. He had strapped to his bicycle frame a bursting bag. When he arrived at the hut on the side facing our camp, so that he could no longer be seen from the Blockführers' office, he unstrapped the bag, leaned the bicycle casually against the boards and went inside. He closed the door behind him so firmly that the whole hut shook and the bike leaning against it fell over. After a while Lubusch emerged. Without glancing round, he got on his bicycle and rode off. He was nervous, or perhaps it only seemed so to me.

Now Edek looked out of the door to make sure nobody was near and ran to the wires; I, too, approached quickly. Camp Kapo Jupp could be heard yelling from afar, but he could not yet be seen. As I took the large parcel from Edek, trying to hurry the job, I got caught on the barbed wire and badly scratched my hands. Edek smiled mockingly.

"Keep calm. These are only clothes. He'll bring the belt and weapon next time. Mind you hide it well."

Jupp's hoarse baritone voice was coming steadily nearer. I leapt across the ditch and walked alongside the wires of the gypsy camp to safety. Without meeting anyone I entered my hut through the side door, heaving a sigh of relief. I was terribly afraid.

Suddenly I realized that I had no idea where to hide this parcel. I considered the bread store, but the room orderlies were there now. On the spur of the moment I climbed onto my bed and hid the uniform in the straw of a mattress. Not mine, of course. I hid the shirt and trousers in the mattress of a prisoner we called The Hunchback. If worst came to worst he would have to explain everything, not I. I did not like him. It was my intention, anyway, to take the uniform from its hiding place as soon as possible and conceal it under the floor of the storage depot.

That evening I went for a walk in the camp with Edek. For some time now we'd been walking away from the block in order to be able to talk at ease.

"You didn't half have the jitters, and don't deny it." Edek laughed. I did not deny it.

"Weren't you scared?" I asked him.

"No," he answered perfectly naturally. "Why be scared? After all, we'll have to risk a great deal more. What is worse is that Lubusch doesn't hold out much hope of getting another uniform. By the way, did you hide it securely?"

"Don't worry," I replied firmly.

Two or three days later we were sitting with Jozek, who had invited us for a drink on the upper bunk, listening to Dino singing. The Hunchback, who lay on the next bunk, intending to buy himself into our party, reached into his straw mattress looking for a bottle which he apparently had hidden there. To everyone's surprise and to my horror he pulled out the SS trousers together with the bottle.

Edek looked at me angrily. Luckily The Hunchback refrained from any further searches inside his mattress. He was firmly convinced that the trousers had gotten there by accident during the exchange of straw mattresses on the occasion of the last delousing drive. It never occurred to anyone that it might be a pair of SS trousers. A little later, the clever Hunchback did notice the similarity, for it was the green color of the cloth which made him catch on. Since he was already a little tight, he bragged loudly that he would sell these trousers to an SS man, and that in this way he would be getting back the drink with which he had entertained us. Thus all we could do was to wait until The Hunchback took the trousers out of the camp. And then we would have to find out to whom he had sold them. At this moment we could under no circumstances afford to show any interest in the wretched trousers, or the crafty Hunchback might have uncovered our plot. As Jozek was clerk in The Hunchback's Kommando, we would have to talk to him about the trousers without letting him in on our plans.

Jozek realized quite quickly what it was all about. He had been watching us for a long time and saw that we were plotting something. He promised not to say anything and to keep an eye on The Hunchback. By the following day we knew who had bought the trousers. The lucky fellow was an SS man who worked as a stoker in the boiler room of the barracks next to Mexico.

By the following day Edek had recovered the trousers. Upon being asked how he had done it, all he would say was "Don't worry."

Edek was right; he had every reason to be outraged with me. I had taken the whole business much too lightly, and I decided to be more careful in future. For the present I hid the uniform properly under the floorboards of the bread store. For safety's sake I pushed a cupboard over the spot.

CHAPTER 63

Two weeks passed and Lubusch had still not come up with the rest of the things. Meanwhile the entire population of Theresienstadt camp was completely gassed. Later the rumor circulated that London had announced the news to the world on the radio. It was hard to say how much truth there was in the rumor because in the camp the smallest rumor simply grew into a legend (as, for instance, the deeds of General Sikorski whose name to us was synonymous with freedom). Despite incessant selections, liquidations and gassings, the first spring breezes helped to bring about a better mood, strengthening the belief in the possibility of surviving the camp, the belief in a better tomorrow. The number of escapes rose rapidly; however, many attempts miscarried. And all the time we waited impatiently for Lubusch and the rest of the things.

It was taking far too long; I stopped watching at the wires. Then one day a little Jew came running into the block with the message that someone was calling from the ramp for me to come to the wires. It could only be Edek. And it meant that Lubusch had kept his word. The day was not very favorable for this kind of smuggling. Camp Kapo Jupp was on the rampage, and as a rule he would take up his position near the wires, where he hunted for small parcels. Just in case I might need it, I slipped a bottle of booze uner my belt. I knew Jupp's weakness for alcohol.

I ran to the wires where Edek was waiting for me. Not very far from where we were standing, Jupp was at that moment confiscating some smuggled goods from a prisoner. He was so busy with the unfortunate prisoner that he paid no attention to us at all. I wanted to wait until Jupp left this area; but Edek, obviously anxious to get rid of the weapon as quickly as possible—there was, on the ramp, the constant danger of a search—sent me to the opposite corner, next to the gypsy camp. Quick as a flash he unbuttoned his jacket, undid the belt and handed it to me through the wires. With equal speed I opened my jacket, buckled on the belt and pushed the pistol holster against my shoulder. We talked for a while in order to allay the vigilance of Jupp, who was in fact already watching us. I went away from the wires without undue haste. I leapt across the deep ditch and found myself face to face with Jupp. He stood with legs wide apart, self-satisfied, holding in one hand the trophies he had captured earlier, and in the other his stick. Smiling roguishly, he looked me over with half-closed eyes, particularly the place on my belly where I had hidden the bottle as bait. Raising his stick a little he poked me a few times in this very place and, feeling something hard, guessed without difficulty what it was I had concealed there.

"Well, clerk, what have you organized?"

I put on my artful dodger face and opened my jacket a little so that he got a glimpse of the neck of the bottle. Jupp smacked his lips contentedly.

"The real stuff?" he asked hopefully. "You go back to the block. I'll come later. I'm very busy today." He laughed and handed me the parcel he had just then taken away from the prisoner. "You might as well take this too, my dear clerk." He rubbed his hands, pleased with himself. "Today the Camp Kapo shall have a feast."

Suddenly he was off, shouting at someone whom he noticed sidling up to the wires. I had to chuckle inwardly, for had I not been cunning, too? I reached the block without further difficulty. Perhaps now Edek will at last soften again.

I hid the belt and weapon immediately in the place where the uniform was. So now we had one complete SS man's uniform. Edek was pleased. So was I. And Jupp, too. He had had a good day, for his pockets were stuffed. That evening he drank himself unconscious.

CHAPTER 64

SOMETIME DURING the second half of March I was again called to the wires. There was no one about; therefore Edek handed me a large parcel without making any attempt to conceal it. At the first moment I was convinced that he had gotten hold of another uniform. But I felt a heavy weight in my hand and looked at Edek in surprise.

"It's meat, fresh meat. Let Jankiel cook it any way he wants to."

Fresh meat here in the camp. That was a special treat. Jankiel maintained that it was game, most likely deer meat. Jasinski, the new block senior, let us have a small stove. Jankiel set to work joyfully. Delicious smells wafted from the block senior's room. They lured Jupp, who kept looking into the pot and smacking his lips loudly. However, after several hours cooking the meat was still tough.

At night Edek told me in strict confidence where the meat had come from. The Drechsler woman had a handsome dog, the terror of all woman prisoners. To everyone's great joy and Drechsler's deep grief, the dog had been found that morning hanging in the wires near the guardhouse, in the proximity of the fitters' hut. After the Kommandos had marched out to work, the electricity was switched off. Drechsler ordered the fitters to remove her dog from the wires and bury him in the ground, which she generously watered with her tears. The dog had been large and young; so they quickly dug it up when Drechsler's back was turned, cut off the best meat and buried the rest again.

We tasted the carcass. It did not taste at all bad, but it was still a little tough. We decided not to tell anyone what kind of meat this was, especially since Jupp was keeping a keen eye on the pot because he assumed that what was cooking inside was venison. There was a lot of meat. We were generous, for we knew that Jupp had invited his good friends Danisz and Bednarek. Let them eat dog meat.

The next day was Edek's name day. We celebrated together with the Jozefs in Block 4. There was more drink than food, and the pooch served as a side dish, particularly as it had by now become more tender. Generally speaking, everybody at the party knew where the meat had come from, but no one minded. We were joined by Jozek M., who was well liked by everyone. Trailing behind him was Arbeitsdienst Victor, who did not enjoy great popularity among prisoners. He threw himself on the meat and simply could not get over the fact that we had so much of it because he had already eaten some of this venison at Jupp's. He ate and drank and at last he cleared off. Unfortunately he returned after a while with two Blockführers, Baretzki and Schneider, who were in a very peaceable, almost friendly mood. They knew they had come for a fight. The atmosphere was not the best, for the company of Victor and the two Germans acted rather as a damper, especially as the whole block was there to see.

We were by then too drunk not to let them feel the hostility, and we did not fear the consequences. But they never noticed. They ate, drank and cracked jokes as if they were pals of ours. All at once, one of the fitters started barking, growling, playing with a bone and generally imitating a dog. After a while we all began acting like barking dogs. At first the SS men were amused by this wild game. However, they knew enough Polish to catch the odd word, in between barking and laughing, which revealed the tragedy of the Drechsler dog. They pretended not to believe this story. They were sure, they said, we had stolen the meat somewhere from the kitchen or the abattoir. In any case, we parted

208

company quickly, because we feared the revenge of the drunken Blockführers.

The story of this dog party soon spread all over the camp. For a few days Danisz, Jupp, Bednarek and Victor were followed by surreptitious barking noises. They were furious but did not show it. Nor did Drechsler ever find out that her beloved dog had been consumed by SS men in the company of prisoners, and washed down with schnapps. They had to keep silent; they could not revenge themselves because it would have shamed them to admit such a thing.

CHAPTER 65

SPRING WAS triumphing quite obviously. Outside it was growing warmer all the time. The puddles were drying up; after evening roll call the camp street was thronged with strollers. The howl of the alarm siren nearby sounded different from usual. From somewhere came the dull rumble of anti-aircraft guns.

Occasionally there came the sound of a brief whistle from a locomotive at the Auschwitz station and something like the gentle, scarcely audible, hum of aircraft engines. We were convinced that these were English and American squadrons on their way to bomb large Silesian towns. There was great excitement and never-ending discussion among prisoners. It was only when sleep overcame us that the nervous whispering ceased.

The next day three Russians from the breakers' yard escaped. It turned out that they came from my block. The siren howled once more. With somber faces the Blockführers counted us over and over again, one after the other, countless times.

Roll call dragged on and on. Blockführers and higher-ranking trusties departed in order to search for the escaped prisoners within the confines of the outer cordon. Before nightfall they returned. Their search had been unsuccessful. Lagerführer Schwarzhuber ordered the end of roll call and simultaneously a camp curfew. As a punishment our block was ordered to remain standing.

209

We stood to attention, rigid, lined up in several rows between our block and Block 6. Blockführers ambled between the silent rows, striking the Russians as they passed. In the dark all one could hear was the dull thud of blows and the cursing of the SS men. The cold grew increasingly distressing. To warm us up they began to make us do sport, but even that bored them quickly. No doubt they were also hungry because they took turns disappearing inside the guardhouse. The last one could not stand it either and departed after he had invested Danisz and the Camp Kapo with authority.

About an hour later Rapportführer Wolf arrived and ordered us to return to our block. There was no evening meal. The whole block was punished. Although the punishment was drastic, especially for the Russians, who received no parcels, they tried not to show it. A few swore loudly, but the others promptly pacified them. They were hungry. But it was obvious that they were trying to demonstrate their solidarity with their fellow countrymen who had escaped. They went to sleep quickly. Soon there was complete silence in the block.

Two days later the siren howled again, announcing yet another escape. Again the escapees were three Russians from our block. They worked in the breakers' yards. Roll call was brief. Only our block had to do Stehappell, lasting as long as the previous ones, inclusive of blows and sport. But this time we were allowed our evening meal.

From now on there were more and more cases of escape, mainly Russians and Poles. Gradually the authorities got used to this state of affairs. In time they even dispensed with Stehappell.

Our flight plans were finally fixed. Since getting a second uniform was out of the question, we decided that Edek, whose German was better than mine, was to be an SS man taking a prisoner—namely me—to an outside Kommando, namely to Raysko, Harmensee or Budy. The date of our escape was to be some time in June because by then the corn would be high and would partly conceal us on our long walk to the wooded mountains near Bielsko. The uniform and weapon were safely hidden. We still had some time in hand.

In May I would get myself transferred to another Kommando

210

which worked outside the camp, preferably to the building works Kommando where Edek worked. For the moment I used my accumulated savings to buy two pairs of high boots which were made a little like German boots and a little like Polish officers' boots. I also procured civilian clothing and two pairs of breeches, of which one pair was meant for Edek, although he never actually wore them. He would need them only on the day of our escape; hence they were hidden in the bread store. I put on the obligatory stripes with red paint, which was easily removed.

When the fine weather came I reminded Edek that he had promised to take me to the women's camp one of these days. I had not been there for some time. I wanted to see Halina again. On the way I planned to inspect the famous Mexico of which I had heard so much from Dino, who bragged of his amatory successes with the Greek Jewesses there.

One day Edek informed Tadek the glazier, who was Kapo of the building works Kommando, that he intended to take me along next day. I also informed Jasinski so as to avoid any sudden surprises. The block senior was cooperative. I covered up for him occasionally when he left the camp with the roofers' Kommando in order to meet his wife, who had come from Silesia to live near Auschwitz especially to see her husband.

On the following day, dressed in dungarees and carrying a toolbox, I joined a large group of about two hundred fifty fitters in Tadek's Kommando and walked out of the camp.

"No funny business now, you two," Tadek warned us, half afraid that we might try to escape, an activity which lately had become so fashionable.

"No fear," Edek reassured him, "if we should do that at any time, we wouldn't endanger you. There are other Kommandos."

CHAPTER 66

THE ORCHESTRA kept playing merry marches while we passed the guardhouse, caps off, in step with the music, and carefully counted by the SS men. When we had gone a few steps we separated from the Kommando and made our way to Mexico. Edek, playing the guide, wanted to show me as much as possible. We turned to the left in the direction of the only partly completed Mexico. We had arranged with Dino on the previous day that we would visit him, intending to do a little bartering with him so as not to go to the women's camp empty-handed. We had difficulty finding him among the dozens of barracks.

As we walked along asking for Kapo Dino, we overtook scores of emaciated women with shaven heads, wearing torn and dirty rags. Most of them were barefoot; only a few wore clogs on their bony feet. Outside one of the blocks lay a few almost naked Greek women on the bare ground. Most of them were young but terribly wasted, dirty, disheveled. Silently and slowly they looked over what was left of their dresses, searching for and killing lice. From them a stench came surging at us which we had not met anywhere, not even in the women's camp. There was, by the way, no water in Mexico. The wells were only then being dug. The stronger women, who were not yet emaciated, probably from the last few transports, were at work. They carried earth on stretchers hastily put together from a few planks. Others were passing bricks or planks, or they laboriously pushed heavy wheelbarrows, constantly getting stuck in sand or mud puddles. Fat, stocky German women Kapos, black triangles on their striped dresses, drove these hardly moving Jewesses to work with shouts and blows.

Some of them still showed traces of southern beauty. There were two who stood out from the others. Better dressed and fed, with seductive youthful curves, they were clearly favorites. It was here that the hunchbacked under-Kapo hung around. When he saw us, he hurried towards us, nonchalantly swatting a Mussulman woman who was barring his way.

"Hello, clerk, come for a fuck? Hahaha," he laughed coarsely. "Let me fix you up." He gave me a cheerful wink. I did not even bother to reply. I would have liked to have given him a good blow. I could not stand this creature. Ignoring the fact that he was being ignored, he continued to play the big shot.

Two women Kapos were standing not far away. He went over and began to banter with them, teasing and haggling, constantly glancing in the direction of the pretty young girls, who were quite obviously only pretending to work. Finally The Hunchback gave a packet of cigarettes to one of the Germans, whereupon the second one put out her free hand—in the other she held her stick—demanding her share. He was generous; he gave her a packet, too. It was worth it. Now he could have one of the Greek girls.

Once more he turned round to us and nodded his head invitingly.

"Well, what about it, think it over," he said, his voice half choked with pent-up passion. "Well?" he repeated without waiting for a reply. "Come along," he said, with a peremptory movement of his head, to the girl, who followed him obediently into the first barrack.

I learned from one of the foremen where Dino was. He showed us a barrack where a tall, well-built Greek Jew was standing in the door. When he saw us coming, he vanished inside, only to reappear immediately, accompanied by Dino.

We went inside. The Greek remained on guard. Although the interior of the block was not yet finished, Dino's room was comfortable. On a stool, propping his arms on the table, sat an elderly bespectacled civilian wearing a yellow armband.

Dino introduced him as the builder and me as the clerk of the Sonderkommando. Whatever made him do that, I wondered; but I fell in with Dino because he was giving me desperate signs behind the builder's back. The builder spoke Polish but liked to intersperse the conversation with German expressions. As for me, he treated me with particular respect, offering me cigarettes and addressing me by my surname. The Pipel, a Greek Jew, was preparing a meat dish on the stove. Dino produced some schnapps, and the civilian kept offering German cigarettes. We struck a bargain: for twenty dollars we bought half a liter of schnapps, for a watch a few packets of cigarettes.

Later Dino took the builder to one side and talked to him insistently. After a while the builder picked up his bag and walked to the exit, greeting us with raised arm and a smart "Heil Hitler."

A *Reichsdeutscher* [German citizen], no less. A queer bird. Dino presented me with his plan. Only now did we understand his incomprehensible behavior. The rapacious builder was determined to amass a fortune here by buying the jewelry of gassed Jews whom he, being a German, hated. During the next few days he intended marrying his daughter to a Nazi in Katowice. As a wedding gift he wanted to give her a beautiful ring with a large diamond. For a handsome stone he would pay with foodstuffs of all kinds as well as alcohol. The fact that Dino had introduced me as clerk in the Sonderkommando was for a good reason; the builder knew very well who in the camp could lay their hands on the largest hoard of jewelry: Jews from Canada or the Sonderkommando. Besides, he thought that as a Jew I would not dare to haggle with him, a German. In fact it would not have occurred to me to cheat him, as had happened on certain occasions with Poles or Russians. Dino had in his possession a ring with a four-carat diamond, and, in addition, an imitation which looked remarkably like the real stone. All he needed to do was to execute a deft exchange of the stones; this, too, he had already worked out. The loot obtained in this manner was to be shared and shared alike. I agreed. Why shouldn't this cunning pig fork out for his Nazi wedding? What was more, this would provide me with another opportunity to get out of the camp, this time with Dino's Kommando. Edek, too, liked Dino's fraudulent plan.

Nobody having stopped us on the road between Sectors D and C, we reached the fitters' hut, the last stage before one got to the women's camp. We left the schnapps with Jurek. At midday he was to hand it across the wires to Jankiel or The Barber, who at that time were supposed to be on lookout nearby. We took the cigarettes along with us.

From the hut we could clearly see that only wardresses were on duty at the guardhouse. Towards men their attitude was, as a rule, more kindly. Edek reported quite properly, announcing the arrival of two fitters for work.

The wardress looked with approval at the handsome prisoner.

"Okay, come in," she said, without taking her eyes off the self-assured Edek. Suddenly, as if in passing, she asked ingratiatingly: "Have you perhaps got some cigarettes?"

Gently but meaningfully she opened the lid of the desk, which

214

served to note the numbers of prisoners going in and coming out. We knew the habits of these gentle Germans. Almost simultaneously we reached under our armpits and took out the cigarettes we had hidden there. Simultaneously two packets of cigarettes dropped into the slightly open desk. As a token of her gratitude she warned us to be careful because chief wardress Mandel and Kramer, the new camp Kommandant of Birkenau, were at present visiting the camp.

In fact, we did notice Kramer's convertible standing next to the main guardhouse. The Kommandant's chauffeur, ever eager, was making a prisoner do sport. He was luckily too far away to be dangerous to us.

As always, at the gate next to the barrier, stood the little Slovak girls. *"Na zdar,"* they greeted us cheerfully. *"Na zdar,"* replied Edek. Then he asked them to tell Mala that she should come to the meeting place they had arranged as soon as the chief wardress had left the camp with Kramer. For safety's sake we thought it better to postpone our visits until later and went instead to the washroom in Sector B where the fitters' Kommando was working.

In order to kill time we began to work. I was sawing up a pipe when someone appeared with the news that Mandel and Kramer were leaving. At once we went to the prison hospital, Edek to the X-ray room, as usual, while I burst into the sick bay office. Halina was not there. From one of her colleagues I learned that she was in bed in the nurses' room, which was in the same barrack as the X-ray room. Halina was pleased at my unexpected visit. Even during her illness she did not lose her high spirits. She was sweet and cheerful. She showed me a photograph of herself taken before she became a prisoner in the women's camp, which her parents had sent her as a postcard. The censor let it pass, probably on account of the innocuous text on the card. I had not been there more than a few minutes when someone came in to warn me of the imminent arrival of the SDG. I had no way of escaping, and there was no time to get away either. I could already hear the sound of his boots in the corridor. On the spur of the moment I squeezed myself under Halina's bed. I had no sooner managed to conceal myself there when the SDG came in.

215

"Well, how are you today, Halina. Ill again?"

Halina was ill rather frequently. This time there was something wrong with her eyes; she even wore dark glasses. It must be something serious because, as I had heard, Dr. Rhode was interested in her case and had, in fact, taken her to the eye hospital in Katowice, a very unusual occurrence in the camp. One had to admit that there were occasions when Dr. Rhode gave proof of his humane attitude where individual patients were concerned. However, this in no way prevented him from carrying out mass selections of women patients to be taken to the gas chamber in the name of the fight against typhus.

The SDG settled himself comfortably, moved his stool up to Halina's bed and began to chat to her. Their conversation seemed to go on for ever. Lying rigid in a thoroughly uncomfortable position I nearly suffocated since I was trying to breathe as little as possible so as not to betray my presence.

My skin began to itch terribly, no doubt from fleas—of which there was an abundance here—that were crawling all over me. I suffered and silently cursed my bad luck. This was the second time that I found myself in such a situation. Meanwhile the SS man was telling jokes, and Halina was laughing. In front of my nose stood the huge boots of the German, so close that I could smell his boot polish. Damn and blast, when *is* he going to leave?

"Hey, you, come on out!" someone shouted. "Quick, get a move on."

Could he have seen me? Oh God, I've been caught again. I continued to lie there, not moving. Then came Halina's voice: "You can come out, he won't harm you. He saw you the minute he came in."

"Come out" was easily said. It was quite an effort to get out from under this wretched bed. I must have looked a sight because the SDG was falling about laughing. Let him laugh. I consoled myself with the thought that had it been Klehr I should have been finished. Halina would have caught it, too. In this instance, all I had done was to make a fool of myself once again.

From outside the window the women were shouting "SDG, SDG," their call echoing from mouth to mouth.

No doubt the camp doctor was coming.

The SDG straightened his belt and rushed outside; we were alone. I was in a foul temper after this silly incident. In order to put me in a better mood, Halina gave me her picture, which was fastened over her bed with drawing pins. As if she sensed that I was not to see her again.

I went to fetch Edek from the X-ray room. Mala was no longer there. Edek was sleeping sweetly on the gynecological table, which was used for the sterilization of patients. We had scarcely managed to leave the X-ray room when we ran across Dr. Mengele, who was explaining something animatedly to Dr. Schumann. Behind them trotted the SDG. As we passed them we took off our caps according to regulations. Schumann, in civilian dress, apparently very absentminded, greeted us with raised arm. The handsome Dr. Mengele did not so much as glance in our direction. The SDG stopped us. In sharp and raised tones he asked whether we had repaired the tap in the washroom.

"Yes, Herr Oberscharführer," we replied with one voice. He was only a *Sturmmann* [Private], but after this ingenious lie he was, in our eyes, promoted.

On our way back we met Wiesiek P., who recently had been block senior in one of the blocks of Sector D. He would invent all sorts of pretexts in order to slip into the women's camp, mainly, as he would announce himself, for amatory purposes.

The camp had spoiled him a little. Young, handsome, rather too plump, self-assured, an old camp inmate, he had fortunately only this one weakness: women. On them he concentrated his whole energy. Apart from that he was, in fact, a good and helpful comrade. He took up the stance of a cynic because it seemed to him that this made him seem more manly. He lied because he wanted to show off, particularly with his conquests.

"I just had a fantastic adventure. There I was, lying on my bunk, not alone, of course, and you know what? Suddenly there is this voice right above me saying: "What are you doing here?" I turn round, and standing over me was Hössler himself. You've had it, my lad, I thought. However, he just looked at me and laughed: "Oh, it's you, is it. Well, carry on." What? You don't believe me? He recognized me, I tell you. He likes old prisoners. But the wardresses love us even more. Do you know Irma Grese, Edek? Pretty, isn't she. The women say she's a lesbian. She's as lesbian as I'm homosexual. I tell you she's so passionate—I see you don't believe me. I swear to God that the two of us . . . So what? The SS men carry on with women prisoners, like that Effinger, for instance. Why should I, an old prisoner, not make love to an SS woman if she wants to herself. One lives only once. Tomorrow I might go up the chimney. Well, I must be off, I promised to drop in on someone, you know. *Heil!*"

During the afternoon Edek met his Mala once more. I stayed with the fitters. I had had enough of these romantic adventures.

CHAPTER 67

ONCE AGAIN three Russians who lived in my block had escaped. There were no reprisals, and roll call took place normally. Next morning, immediately after the Kommandos had marched out to work, there was a major search in Blocks 4 and 6. Among the SS men carrying out the search was Boger, head of the Political Department in Birkenau. This meant that there was something in the camp the Political Department wanted to ferret out. It was only these two blocks that they turned upside down; luckily they did not get to my block.

I was terribly frightened. It was a job to control myself, and my room orderlies noticed it. Jankiel watched me carefully, and as soon as the SS men had left the camp he told me without beating around the bush that he suspected Edek and me of having hidden something in the bread store. Moreover, he had a good guess as to what this something was and advised me to hide it elsewhere as soon as possible. Russians were escaping quite frequently. A strict search of our block was a distinct possibility, and then we would all be in for it.

He was right. I really had to find a good hiding place for the few weeks that were left before our escape. The trouble was I did not know where. It was also alarming that more and more of our fellow prisoners guessed our escape plans. I was sure Jozek Wasko knew. Jankiel and the priest had discovered the hiding place; therefore they knew its dangerous contents. Edek was bound to reproach me again for letting more and more people in on the secret: it was a situation which created the additional risk of accidental discovery of our plans. As for their discretion, I had no doubt whatever about it.

In order to hide our treasure outside our block I was forced to take into my confidence yet another person who might agree to hide both uniform and weapon in his block.

There was only one barrack in the whole camp suitable for this purpose. That was the admissions block, which had no block senior because the block was empty most of the time. The clerk who lived there permanently was called Jurek, a good fellow, his camp number 227.

Jurek agreed unhesitatingly. He, too, was thinking about escaping and would very much have liked to come with us. I promised to talk to Edek, although I knew in advance that I should tell him nothing at all, at least not yet. I had to work on him first because I knew he would be furious when he learned that yet another person was in on our plans.

As I turned the whole business over in my mind, Jurek showed me the place where our dangerous load was to be concealed. That very day we carried it from my block to Jurek's. Now it lay safe, under the roof of the landing, wedged between the double layer of boards which formed the ceiling of the corridor. No one would have considered it possible that here, in this clearly visible spot, something might be hidden. It could only be found if they were to take the entire barrack to pieces, and that had not happened yet, not even during a very strict search. Edek seemed to be so very satisfied that he did not reproach me for having told Jurek about the escape. He knew him very well, by the way.

Jurek was one of the absolutely trustworthy ones. From the moment we had hidden the weapon and the uniform on Jurek's block we were often his guests, especially during the evening when it was less noisy there than in our block. Sometimes the block would fill up, mostly with young Jews who had been picked out from the last few transports. However, they never stayed long, for they were either distributed to different camps or taken to Quarantine, from where they were then sent on elsewhere or placed at the disposal of Dr. Mengele, especially if they were twins. In the course of time, there were a few dozen of these who, at the express wish of the SS doctor, were reserved for him.

CHAPTER 68

ONE DAY I marched with Dino's Kommando to Mexico in order to carry through the diamond transaction. It was early, and the builder had not yet arrived. Dino used this opportunity to instruct me yet again as to how I was to behave during the transaction. He handed me a gold cigarette case and a bundle of banknotes, which had been cunningly prepared in such a way that at the top there were a few dollar notes, whereas underneath, not visible, were German notes, which were of no great value here. However, the bundle looked as if it was all dollars.

I put the ring with the genuine diamond on my little finger, while Dino put the fake one in his pocket. Thus equipped I was to dazzle the diamond-hungry builder with our riches.

When he arrived the builder greeted me garrulously, like an important personality. Casually I drew the gold cigarette case from my pocket and offered him a Gauloise. I saw that this made a profound impression on him. He ran his plump, trembling fingers over this "toy" and weighed it in his hand.

"How heavy it is," he remarked. "You have a lot of this gold in your camp, haven't you?" He handed it back to me, though. "Not enough to eat, is there? Not enough drink either, huh?" he asked, a hopeful note in his voice.

"Ah, it's not too bad," I replied firmly, playing the role Dino had allocated to me. "For this"—here I flashed my diamond before the builder's greedy eyes—"you can get anything. The SS men themselves bring what is needed." Don't let him think that I am all that interested in doing business with him.

"Have you got something to drink, sir?" Dino intervened at the crucial moment. He did not want me to overdo things.

The builder rummaged for a long time in his large bag. He put a bottle and a slice of bread and bacon on the improvised table. It looked as if he was going to offer these delicacies. I reached nonchalantly into my shirt and produced the bundle of prepared notes. I peeled off the first twenty-dollar note from the top; it vanished like a flash in the huge bag of the civilian who was unable to resist this temptation. The German was visibly astonished by my wealth. We had him where we wanted him. Now we could start on the real business.

He took the beautiful ring with the glittering stone and looked it over with his dirty, greedy, plump fingers. Round and round, again and again. Then he suggested that he would take this diamond to Katowice to have it appraised. He had, he said, a friend there who was a jeweler. No, no. By no means. I could not agree to that. When he brought the goods, he could have the ring. Otherwise we were just wasting our breath talking about it. At last the bargain was struck. Tomorrow he would deliver to Mexico a goose, a side of bacon, a few pork sausages and four liters of alcohol. He would then receive the diamond ring from Kapo Dino to whom I would hand the ring. In order to prove this, I handed the ring to Dino. My part had come to an end. I had played it well and without worrying that by ripping off the civilian I had become an ordinary con man.

The wily builder did not keep his word. Although next day he did turn up with his merchandise, it was only half of what we had agreed on as payment for the ring. He promised the second half for later. How he managed to smuggle so large a quantity of goods into an area which was closely guarded by the SS remained his secret, but it certainly proved his skill.

Dino was nevertheless pleased with his bargain when he handed over the diamond—the fake one, of course—to the German. I guessed that the transaction had been completed when at about 10 A.M. I was called to the wires. I took Jankiel and The Barber to help me. Dino and his people were already waiting. In no time at all, the merchandise was unloaded from stretchers and redistributed right behind block senior Danisz's block. If he could

221

have had an inkling of the delicacies that were being smuggled into the camp behind his back!

That night after his return from work Dino took away half of everything, perhaps to Danisz, who knows? There was the remarkable coincidence that no one disturbed us while we were smuggling such a large quantity of stuff. Ah, to hell with him. I had received my share. As for the builder, as soon as he realized that he had been cheated by the Kapo and this black-haired Jew from the Sonderkommando, he would surely have a heart attack. He could not get at Dino, who was, incidentally, pretending to have been himself a victim of my swindle.

CHAPTER 69

LIFE IN the camp continued normally, which meant, as always, that the majority was working hard, constantly exposed to harassments, beatings, selections, gassings, shootings, interrogations by the Political Department, sustained by a bowl of turnip or nettle soup, dependent on the moods of SS men, masters over life and death of thousands of helpless prisoners. No one was certain that he would still be alive the next morning, not even the élite, of whom, after almost four years in the camp, I was one. I was, it is true, not threatened with starvation. I received quite large food parcels from home and also from friends. Besides, I would have managed, even if I had been all alone.

The Political Department was constantly snooping around. One had to be wary of spies, overeager trusties and transports, an increasing number of which were allegedly sent into the interior of the Reich. One never knew whether such a transport might not land somewhere in a gas chamber; and even if that was not the case, our departure from Auschwitz would foil our well-advanced plans for the rapidly approaching day of our escape.

Large transports of Hungarian Jews had arrived. Never before had there been so many. Train after train arrived on the ramp. Out of the trucks tumbled masses of people: men, women, old people, teenagers and children. They brought with them everything they possessed. Huge piles of goods and chattel were unloaded and stacked in heaps which hid the rows of people who walked slowly past a group of SS men. Here, where the selection took place, life hung on a wave of an SS officer's hand, pointing to the left or to the right. Only a small minority came into the camp, mainly young women and young, healthy-looking men. The rest, carrying their hand luggage, went in two streams: either along the ramp in the direction of the grove which concealed crematoria 2 and 3, or down the central street, skirting the men's camp and the gypsy camp, to the woods and the two farther crematoria, 4 and 5. There was the end of their walk. The entire area was enveloped in clouds of the sickly smell of burning bodies.

Meanwhile, on the ramp the Canada Kommando worked feverishly, carrying out a second selection, the selection of the gassed people's property, supervised by several SS men. Trucks piled high with cases, bags and bundles drove to the depots in Canada, where everything underwent yet another, more detailed selection. A large proportion of these things, in particular foodstuffs and valuables, found their way into the camp.

Once more a time of abundance began. The kitchen used goose grease to cook bread soup. There were tins, fruit, shoes, clothes, fine underwear, down quilts and jewelry. Canada! It did not matter in the least that the crematoria were belching smoke, that in the pits piled with gassed bodies human fat sizzled in the fire. The camp had enough to eat. The camp sighed with relief because the drunken SS men, busy with transports, no longer showed much interest in the prisoners living in the camp. They were looking for gold, and they crammed their pockets with it. They secured their future. So did the workers and prisoners of Canada. They needed these pieces of jewelry in order to make their lives in the camp a little easier. On the orders of the SS, the members of the Sonderkommando sieved the very ashes of the cremated bodies in search of diamonds, which did not melt in the flames. The gold extracted from teeth was melted down into bars and sent into the Reich, to fill the coffers of the disintegrating state. The remains were scattered in fields and ponds. Only the human fat was wasted; in Auschwitz they did not manufacture soap.

The camp exchange experienced severe shocks. Hans, the Kapo

of Canada, was now the most popular person in the camp. Camp senior Danisz smiled at him ingratiatingly, and as for camp Kapo Jupp, he was Hans's old pal, walking arm in arm with him. Hans beamed with happiness and showered presents on everyone. This state of affairs lasted for some weeks, as long as there were transports arriving. Days and weeks went by. How many of these Hungarians had been gassed already? One hundred thousand, two hundred thousand, four hundred thousand, five hundred thousand at least. In the end they must have run out of Jews in Hungary, for the transports grew smaller and arrived less and less often. The ramp was empty. The SS men remembered the camp and came more and more often. The Blockführers rampaged and carried out searches in the blocks. They were looking here for their gold. The Kapos and block seniors ceased paying court to Hans, and Jupp even forgot that not long ago he had walked arm in arm with Hans as though he was his best friend. So what? In his friendship for Hans he even went so far as to search him one fine day. Since he found nothing, he struck him across the face, embittered. "Take that, you Jewish swine! Fucking Jew!"

Canada had ceased to exist and with it half a million human beings.

CHAPTER 70

WHOSE TURN NEXT? The number of attempted escapes rose as summer began. There was hardly a day without somebody attempting to escape. Usually it was Russians. The advancing eastern front gave them courage. Next in number were the Poles. One day three block clerks escaped, all of them old numbers. They crept out of the camp with a Kommando working outside and disappeared. The Lagerführer issued a strict ban on any clerk leaving the camp for any reason whatever. That was a comparatively lenient punishment. We might all have ended up in the penal company. Most of the escapees were from my block. Not surprisingly, almost all of them were Russians from the breakers' yards. I was afraid, as were other block clerks, of being under the watchful eyes of the camp bosses. Meanwhile the day of *our* flight was approaching.

At any rate, I had to do something in order to rid myself of this rather comfortable post. I had to get into a Kommando; otherwise any escape was out of the question.

Edek was growing impatient. Summer was coming, and it was high time for me to join a Kommando. But how was I to do it? I racked my brains. If I were to ask to be relieved of my post as a clerk and request transfer to a Kommando, I would be immediately suspected of having flight plans. I had to do something which would result in my removal from this post as a punishment. At the same time it had to be done in such a way that I would not accidentally end up in the penal company.

On Edek's advice I began mucking up roll calls. However, Kazek Gosk, the responsible clerk, was soon on to my little game. Every time before roll call he carefully checked my report to see whether everything tallied.

"Your arithmetic has been letting you down lately, hasn't it?" he remarked sarcastically, adding, with a flash of inspiration: "It really would be enough reason to dismiss you. I'm not going to, though. I don't want to sit in the bunker later on when you get an overwhelming urge to escape. It has become rather common among you clerks these days."

I was forced to remain a clerk, and I could not get into a Kommando.

What was even worse was a rumor spreading throughout the camp that the SS intended to liquidate all surviving Jews in the near future, and subsequently other nationalities. One had to reckon with this possibility, as we knew only too well. Here in Birkenau anything was possible. Escape from the camp might be our only salvation.

Since we already knew for certain that we could not get a second uniform, we had worked out an alternative plan. Edek, who spoke German quite well, was to be an SS man escorting a prisoner, namely myself, to an outside Kommando—to Budy, for instance, which was a few miles from the camp. This was a fairly

225

common occurrence and unlikely to strike even the watchful eyes of the SS as out of the ordinary.

Our plan was simple enough; all we needed to carry it out was a pass. With this purpose in mind I tried to make contact with the runner of the main office, who had free access to the Blockführers' office by dint of his duties. It would be comparatively easy for him to steal such a document. After a few cautious exploratory talks I left him in peace. The boy, a Slovak, was not suited to this kind of work. Edek went about thoughtful and taciturn. One evening, after a visit to the dentist, we decided to talk. We went to the sick bay block, where one could speak freely. We had lately become more cautious and no longer discussed our secret plans in the block.

Edek began to talk about his relationship with Mala, which had been developing for some time. I was surprised because up to now he had been so discreet and he usually avoided the subject; at any rate, he had never before opened his heart to the extent which he did now. He had known her a long time, he said; he was very attached to her. They were living together and linked very closely; he found it difficult to part with her, particularly since she suffered from malaria. He could not bear the mere thought that sooner or later she would have to share the fate of all the Jews. Now everything is fine, she's even a favorite of Drechsler; everybody likes her, even the SS men. But when the moment comes, she will be the first to be sent to the gas chamber by Drechsler.

He was right. As far as that was concerned I, too, had not the least doubt. But what was Edek's purpose in telling me all this? I assumed then when he spoke of affection he was confessing his love. He loved her, that was clear. I knew him. He did not want to say it in so many words. He would always hide his feelings and try to create the impression of being a cynic. He loved her, and it would be difficult for him to part from her.

I already knew what he intended to say, what moved him so much. I was waiting for the moment when he would suggest that Mala should escape with us. I pushed the thought to one side, but I was convinced, nevertheless, that he had already decided.

"Edek, does Mala know about our plans?" I asked and knew at once what the reply must be.

"No. She knows nothing as yet. And that distresses me. I can't keep her ignorant any longer. I cannot leave her," he said almost in a whisper. "It would not be honest. Mala shall come with us."

"That will be romantic," I tried to be scornful. "If I were to suggest to Halina—"

"Don't be childish," he interrupted. "All that links Halina and you is a flirtation. She would simply laugh at you. Besides, she's not in danger; she's in Quarantine. She may be discharged. Moreover she's not Jewish. You must understand me. I have no obligations towards Mala. I have a plan which may be easily implemented, and to carry it out, it is Mala I need. The plan for our escape remains unchanged. Only there will be an extra person, namely Mala, disguised as a prisoner."

"And the pass?"

"The pass. Mala will be able to get us a pass without great difficulty. She can enter the Blockführer's office at any time, as she is well-known to the SS men. She'll steal the pass without them getting suspicious."

With this pass he put me down. Edek organized everything. I could not even manage a pass. Neither could I manage to get into a Kommando.

"Have you been doubting me, Edzio? Perhaps you no longer count on me, and that's why you suggest this solution," I said, my voice full of bitterness.

"Not at all. But it is a fact that by now you ought to have managed to get yourself into a Kommando. It's high time. Very well, then. The three of us shall go. It'll be a joy ride."

Edek had regained his former vitality. But my misgivings were growing apace.

"You know, basically the plan is good, but with a woman—" I made a last attempt to get him to change his mind. "With a woman, and what's more with one that is delicate like Mala, with bouts of malaria, we won't be able to walk far. We shall have to do at least twenty miles, walking very fast. She won't make it. And can one count on people outside helping us once they see she's Jewish? And, worse still, she could be recognized as a woman even while we're still on this side of the outer cordon." Edek waved his hand disdainfully. "There are risks everywhere, but if

227

one really wants to do a thing, there's always a way out." When he saw that I had exhausted my counter arguments, he held out his hand. "It's all decided, then. Let's shake on it."

We shook hands firmly. As we walked to our block along the dark camp street, Edek kept chuckling and repeating, "It'll be a joy ride," over and over again.

CHAPTER 71

A FEW days later Edek brought me a portrait of Mala, drawn in chalk by a painter in the women's camp.

"Look, does she look Jewish?"

The portrait showed a fairly faithful likeness of Mala's sweet and pretty face. It really was difficult to see any semitic characteristics in it. I expected that Edek had brought this drawing on purpose in order to dispel more convincingly my doubts concerning Mala. I could not remember Mala very well because I had really only seen her on rare occasions. Here she was in black and white.

"And now take a good look at this." With these words, Edek handed me a large, heavy platinum ring set with diamonds. A work of art. Twenty-three stones of at least half a carat each, and the stone in the center bigger still. I was working out in my mind how much food and drink one might buy for it.

"Hide it somewhere, we'll need it on our flight. I bought it from someone for three SS sausages," he explained. "You'll have to organize the sausages." I did not believe this story. I was convinced that this was a present from Mala. But what of it? If she was to come with us, she might as well make an effort. I wrapped the ring in my handkerchief and constantly carried it around with me. That was safer than any hiding place.

I sent a letter to my sister's address in Zakopane. I was afraid to write openly, but I hinted that on her name day towards the end of June she might expect a great and pleasant surprise. She ought to have understood what I was getting at. After our escape from the camp we planned to make for the area round Zakopane, where we intended to leave Mala with my sister and Jurek, her husband, who was a doctor. As for us, we would rest briefly and then make contact with the partisan movement, with whom Jurek doubtless would be in touch. For the time being I was unable to leave the camp. I handed the letter to Jozek, who passed it on to old Szymlak. He would know how to get it to my sister.

I had certain plans regarding Szymlak of which I had informed Edek. Szymlak lived in the village of Kozy at the foot of the Beskids. From the old man's tales I already knew the district quite well. From there it was literally only a few steps into the forest. A splendid place to stop for a rest after our "day trip" out of the camp. Szymlak would make no difficulties; after all, we were such good friends. I would, of course, have to discuss everything with him as soon as I had got myself into a Kommando.

Edek was pleased. "So, I see you're beginning to do something sensible," he said in praise. "I was afraid you might have got cold feet," he added, half-joking.

An almost imperceptible elusive shadow had fallen on our friendship, which had always been innocent and open. Intuitively Edek felt something remained unsaid. His doubts were not altogether unfounded. For some time now a thought was preying on my mind, but as yet I would not reveal what it was.

We stopped having our hair cropped. This was nothing very unusual, especially as many of the old prisoners were given permission to grow their hair. Kazek Gosk was the only one to regard our crew cuts with suspicion, without, however, saying anything.

The fourth anniversary of the arrival in Auschwitz of the first transport was June 14. We decided to celebrate this day as never before. The preparations lasted two days. Each invited guest had to organize some food and drink.

On the evening of June 13, immediately after the lights-out gong, old prisoners crept from almost every block and made their way to the storage depot. Everything was ready. The tables, in the shape of a horseshoe, were laid with cloths, and there were plates, knives and forks. We had almost forgotten how to use these implements. Next to the tables stood several buckets. One contained succulent goulash, the second peeled, boiled potatoes, the third schnapps. The tables were laden with slices of bread, cheese, SS sausage, tins and sardines. For as long as the camp had existed, there had never been anything like it. Fantastic!

And now the first toast. We raised our glasses full of harsh liquid. It was bottoms up all round, schnapps trickling down our chins. The first toast was to freedom; no need to say it out loud.

Quiet, quiet. Jozek wanted to say something. His voice would not obey him. He had already had a quick one before this toast. "How many of us were there in those days? Seven hundred twenty eight. And how many are we now? Thirty, thirty-five?"

Someone interrupted him. "Shut up, we have guests here to-night." He began reeling off their names, but the others quickly interrupted him. "Enough, let's not have a roll call. In a couple of days there'll be even fewer."

Everybody laughed, for one knew what it was all about. Everybody thought about escaping.

In the course of the party spirits rose. "Three cheers for Kukla! How are you going to square all this with the kitchen?"

"I suppose we're guzzling all the SS rations. To hell with them," Edek shouted, exuberant. "Soon we'll have our own board and lodging." Again everyone laughed and exchanged knowing glances.

"When?" one of our guests asked Edek.

"In two weeks' time," Edek replied gravely.

"We, too." The questioner winked at his two fellow escapers.

"Now, look here, fellows, not all at once. Let's settle the dates," somebody said jokingly.

The schnapps bucket was almost empty. Excitement, confusion, laughter, tears, embraces, mutual revelations. It was noisy, much too noisy. Suddenly we fell silent. Standing at the door was a prisoner, our lookout, desperately signaling us to make less noise.

Someone was approaching from the direction of the guard-house. Silence! It turned out to be Blockführer Schneider and Arbeitsdienst Tkocz. They smelled something and were in search of alcohol. All the lights went out. We stood silently, waiting. It was better not to let them know where we were. They would join us for the drinking, but later they might squeal on us. That was all we needed! They got stuck in the block on the opposite side. Jozek went to reconnoiter. When he returned he reported that they were drinking with the block senior. They had inquired where there was booze because they could hear singing from afar.

Fortunately, there was plenty to drink at the block senior's and they decided to stay for a while. How fortunate that it was Schneider who was on duty and not, for instance, Grapatin. He wouldn't have given up so easily. The two of them believed the tale Jozek invented on the spur of the moment, namely that he had seen a few drunks, who must have noticed him and quickly disappeared in the darkness.

We dispersed in small groups. Edek and I departed together. The rest said good-bye, giving us knowing looks. They had understood us, and we them. No one was making a secret of it, anyway. Everybody was preparing his getaway, everybody was thinking of only one thing: freedom.

The Allies were stepping up their air raids; we could not help feeling that the bad times were passing. From Auschwitz the news reached us that the death wall had been abandoned.

CHAPTER 72

MALA WAS a clever girl; she had obtained a pass. She was overjoyed because we intended taking her with us. Edek, too, seemed to be content. I was a little less so. I was of the opinion that the woman would be a drag, that she would bring us bad luck, especially since we had intended to join the partisans and return to the Auschwitz district.

Edek found the identity card of a guard on the ramp. The SS man must have lost it while rifling through the belongings of Jews who had arrived in a transport. It might be useful. For the time being I hid it under the lid of my desk together with my other treasures.

This time I had succeeded. I had made such a good job of messing up roll call that the entire camp had to stand for an hour before the mistake was found. Rapportführer Wolf did not touch me. Grapatin, however, seized the opportunity to hit me in the face. Let him! Soon I would have a chance to retaliate. Actually, they might not have removed me from this post but for the intervention of block senior Bednarek. He appeared as the advocate of the prisoners who, because of my negligence, were made to stand at roll call for such a long time. Why keep a clerk who couldn't count? The whole camp had to suffer Stehappell because of an idiot like that. Hence his complaints to the reports clerk.

So, this was the defender of the enslaved. The arch-villain, the creep. Just to please the SS men, he played the big shot in their presence. Had I not witnessed often enough what he did with prisoners in the penal company? I turned on him furiously and told him to shut up. Some defender! He kept on griping, so I suggested he might care to get screwed. He ran to Danisz to complain.

Immediately after roll call, Danisz ordered a meeting of block clerks. Kapo Jupp and Bednarek were also present. A large group of prisoners stood at some distance, watching what went on. Danisz said quite calmly that he was dismissing me from my clerk's job because apparently I was not suited to it. "Into a Kommando with you! To the spades. That's where you belong."

"What?" Bednarek was outraged. "He ought to be severely punished. Let me have him. I'll teach him obedience and reason. Put him in the penal company." He came very close to me and thrust his fist threateningly under my nose. Then he lifted his arm as if to strike me.

"Just you try and touch me, you asshole. Haven't you finished off enough people? Come on, hit me." I stood boldly facing him as soon as I saw that the group of prisoners had come closer and formed a tight circle around me. I really did not know how it would all have ended, if Danisz had not suddenly pushed Bednarek to one side and me into the lined-up row of clerks.

"At ease," he shouted, taking the worked-up Bednarek firmly by the arm and dragging him away. As he was leaving he once more turned to me and said in Polish, wagging his finger at me: "And you, clerk, stop being clever. Tomorrow you'll work," he added in German. Once again he wagged his finger, but it was obvious that he was playing the affair down. Times had clearly changed.

Edek was beside himself with joy when he learned of this turn of events. At last I would get out of the camp into a Kommando, and that was what mattered. The Arbeitsdienst assigned me to the

232

road-leveling Kommando where Jozek Wasko worked. This did not suit me particularly because I wanted to be as near as possible to Edek. Edek arranged for a transfer with Chamek, a Jew with a bad reputation especially among the Jews. He was Kapo of the road construction Kommando which worked in the women's camp. That suited me best.

Being the labor duties Kapo, Jozek assigned me to this Kommando as clerk. They needed a clerk like a hole in the head, but that was not the point. Next day I was busy "road-building" in the women's camp. There were forty men, Jews, Russians and Poles, in Chamek's Kommando. They worked in the prison hospital sector, which had grown considerably since my time. At present they were building a road between the wooden barracks, as yet unoccupied but in the process of being adapted to the needs of a sick bay. Nevertheless the block staff was already complete, including the block senior, as I noticed. Like every proper Kommando, the road construction Kommando had someone in charge, a Kommandoführer. He was an Oberscharführer, supposedly from the Memel. He was cool, calm and collected. Chamek introduced me to him. He nodded, stood for a while in silence and walked away.

"A fine fellow," said Chamek. "I do what I like with him."

"Get on with your work," he yelled, as in the distance he noticed an SS man on a bicycle. A tall, skinny prisoner with an intelligent face was hanging around. Chamek called him over. The old man stood to attention. Clicking his heels smartly so that his spectacles almost slipped from his nose, he waited, with lean chest thrust out, for his orders. He was obviously a ganger. "Colonel!" Chamek said solemnly. "Everything must be in order. Understood?" "Yes, Herr Oberkapo," came the loud, soldierly reply. "I shall be in this block." Chamek pointed behind him. "In case anything—well, you know, Colonel—at ease."

"Do you know who he is?" He turned to me emphatically, when the alleged colonel had gone. "He was a VIP—with the staff."

In Czarist Russia, I thought. "I've appointed him ganger because he's old and not fit for heavy work. I'm sure if he survives the camp he'll be in the government."

So that was it. Chamek was making sure of his future. I had

233

heard many stories about his being bloodthirsty. Instead he was meek as a lamb, though rather clownish and excitable, as it turned out.

"Come along, clerk," he said to me when he saw me beginning to write down the numbers of prisoners in our Kommando. "Leave that. It'll wait. Come along," he added mysteriously, "I'll show you my fiancée, the most beautiful woman in the world. When you get to know her, you'll see for yourself. And what a temperament!"

As I followed him into the block I thought what a good influence women had even on types like Kapo Chamek. A buffoon, but not dangerous, anyhow. At least that was the impression he created here in the women's camp.

We found the "fiancée" in the women block senior's room. On her chest she wore a red triangle. A Yugoslav, young and pretty. Chamek introduced me with a flourish: "My clerk, a Pole, one of the oldest numbers in the camp."

She greeted me with indifference. It actually seemed to me that she regarded Chamek with undisguised loathing. I began a conversation with a few casual phrases. Meanwhile Chamek put presents on the table: chocolate, sardines and other bits and pieces. Wera appeared not to notice at all. Undeterred, Chamek said ingratiatingly, "And now say 'thank you,' darling."

The girl blushed. He took her in his arms and began to kiss her. She wriggled nimbly out of his embrace and gave his face a resounding slap. Nothing doing! The girl certainly had spirit. So that was what this romance was like.

Someone told me that Halina was in Quarantine. Her eyes had deteriorated. So I was not to see Halina again, not today nor at any other time.

CHAPTER 73

THE DATE for our escape was fixed, Saturday around midday. The conversation was not very pleasant, for there was the constant feeling that I was still keeping something back. At last I explained my point of view. Edek was not at all surprised.

I had worked out a plan whereby Edek and Mala were to go on Saturday, and on Monday, if their escape had been successful, Jozek and I would follow them. Edek and Mala were to make a stop in Kozy. There they were to hand the uniform and the pass to Szymlak, who would have to bring them to where Jozek worked. The rest was as arranged. We would leave the camp in the same manner along the same route. The plan seemed simple. Szymlak would have to be spoken to. I did this on the following day. Szymlak agreed, but without great enthusiasm. He had objections. In the end I persuaded him. The fact that Edek and Mala had reached Kozy would be proof that their escape had succeeded. The SS could not know how they had got out of the camp; therefore the masquerade might be repeated.

This solution was very convenient, for me, needless to say. Edek and Mala were to be the guinea pigs. They were taking the risk, while I took the easy way out and hid behind them. I was backing down, that was quite clear. That I did not want to go with them because there was a woman involved was just an excuse. Ah yes, I wanted them to go first. Edek never let me feel that I was a coward.

Edek had already made a duplicate key to the potato bunker, which was on the escape route. We arranged that I was not to go to work on the following day but to stay in the camp in order to throw them the uniform and the weapon. Edek would wait in the fitters' hut.

CHAPTER 74

THE UNIFORM and weapon were in the potato bunker. Edek let one of his fellow fitters into our escape plans: Jurek Sadczykow was to help Mala change. The guardhouse toilet had also been prepared. Everything was organized down to the last detail. The next day was Saturday, the day of the escape. All night I hardly closed an eye. Edek slept like a log.

In the morning we went to our Kommando as usual. The weather was fine. I was pacing up and down the sick bay, waiting for Edek to turn up. The nearer midday came, the more intolerable the heat grew. That was a good thing. It was just what we had been waiting for. In heat like this the SS men were in the habit of finding a quiet corner somewhere for a snooze. There no longer existed the discipline of the old days.

At last Edek appeared. He was calm and smiling, as always. Mala had been prepared. Everything was ready. "I'll just walk once more through the Blockführers' office," he said, "to keep an eye on the wardresses."

What was all that about? Why was he wandering around like this, I asked myself. Perhaps he didn't know yet who was on duty in the main guardhouse. Surely Mala could have found that out quite easily.

He returned around midday. Blockführer Perschel and an unimportant wardress were on duty. Perschel, a crazy SS man, could be dangerous. One never knew what he might suddenly get into his head. There was the hope, however, that he would not snoop around too thoroughly because he was still limping after an accident with his motorbike. Besides, he would be going to lunch around this time.

We went to Sector B of the women's camp, where Mala lived. She was expecting us in her block. She sat squeezed in between the beds and the table, in the company of the two runners who were supposed to be her cousins. In other words, they, too, knew of the plans. Mala was pale and clearly agitated. Her russet hair was cropped short. Spread across the table was a map, just like in a staff H.Q. They quickly folded this map.

"Edzio, hide this as well," said Mala in bad Polish, handing him a few gold bits and pieces. "The girls brought them to me. We'll need them on our journey," she added, when she noticed Edek making a face. Through the barrack walls came women's voices. "Runner, runner!" they called in chorus.

The girls were wanted at the guardhouse. They flung their arms round Mala's neck, kissing her, weeping and wishing her luck. This scene was taking far too long, so that in the end Edek impatiently took the girls by the arm and forcibly pushed them towards the door.

"Come along, time to go," he said when he saw that Mala was completely dissolved in tears.

I said good-bye to her. She gave me her little hand. It was cold and damp and it trembled.

"Everything is in the hands of God," she said tearfully.

"It'll be okay," I gasped. Somehow it sounded forced. At this moment I felt very sorry for her. I pitied Edek, and I was simply furious with myself. How is he going to make out with this weak girl? Surely she can scarcely walk more than a couple of miles. Just then I was ready to go with them. However, I did not dare suggest it.

"Let's go. And you, Mala, be at the main guardhouse in fifteen minutes. Jurek will be waiting there."

I threw a last glance at Mala. She was standing there, helpless, her face tear-stained, looking like a small girl.

At the barracks door Edek stopped. "Give me your belt, mine's too tight." With these words he opened his overalls, and I saw under them the green SS uniform, and only then the trousers. It really was sheer madness. An unnecessary risk, but quite in style for Edek. He was self-assured and always believed in his lucky stars. I gave him my belt with the handmade gold buckle; mine was longer.

We parted between Sectors A and B of the women's camp, directly opposite the street leading to the guardhouse, where the little Slovak girls were already on duty at the barrier. As though nothing were the matter, we did not even shake hands, just a few words.

"Good-bye. We'll wait for you in Kozy. If there are any changes, I'll let you know by the old man. So long!" He gave a tug at his overalls, tossed his toolbox from one hand to the other and walked straight up to the little guardhouse.

I went Sector A. When I had passed the kitchen and the sauna, I turned round to watch Edek. He walked past the guardpost without any difficulty, reported his departure and proceeded with firm steps down the road, along the ramp, parallel to my sector. Chamek's Kommando worked unhurriedly. The colonel was standing at his post, but fortunately did not see me. I did not feel like talking just at this moment, as I was did not want to lose sight of Edek.

Just a few yards from the main guardhouse, I turned right,

jumped across the ditch and made my way towards a pile of drain pipes that were stacked in this corner. Taking out my rule, I pretended to be measuring the pipes. From this spot I had an excellent vantage point. On the left was the sick bay, behind it the wires and the road along the ramp on which I briefly glimpsed Edek's figure before he disappeared inside the tall gate of the building which straddled the road. After a while I saw him again, this time accompanied by another prisoner, Jurek no doubt. Both in overalls, both carrying toolboxes, they were now walking in my direction towards the women's camp guardhouse. Once they had entered there, I lost sight of them. Apparently Jurek stayed at the guardpost, while from behind the building the solitary figure of Edek emerged, walking quickly towards the potato bunker. Glancing around carefully he caught sight of me, made a vague movement with his hand, then reached into the box, probably to take out the duplicate key. He turned the key in the lock and slipped inside. All this happened so fast that I thought no one could have noticed anything. The heat was intense and nobody was around whose attention might have been attracted by a prisoner fiddling about with the door of the potato bunker.

Mala walked swiftly along the main camp road. As she passed the sick bay a woman who was running along the hospital fence called something to her. With an impatient gesture, Mala indicated that she was in a great hurry. Limping Perschel was just coming out of the guardhouse door. He said something to Mala; she assiduously held his bicycle for him, one of the two propped against the bicycle stand. Swinging his game leg over the bicycle frame, he pressed the pedal with his sound leg and rode off.

So far everything had gone according to plan. Long minutes passed. I glanced at my watch: twenty past twelve. What had happened? Why wasn't she coming? Behind the little window of the bunker I discerned the vague, barely visible outline of Edek. He indicated to me that he was worried. He could not see much from his window and depended entirely on my signs.

At last, they were coming. Stocky Jurek side by side with a short figure in overalls, carrying a heavy lavatory pan. Mala was already bending down under this load. I gave a sign to Edek. He had been waiting for it because moments later he emerged from the bunker. Brushing some invisible dust from his Rottenführer's uniform, he approached the side of the road and waited for the others to reach him. Jurek stopped in front of the SS man at regulation distance, executed a regulation about-face and marched back. Mala stayed behind with Edek. He let Mala walk ahead, while he moved a few steps behind her, casual, normal, as one would often see an SS man escorting a prisoner. Slowly they left the camp. I followed them with my eyes for a good three hundred yards until I lost sight of them because the road turned slightly to the right and disappeared behind the building of the potato bunker.

The worst was behind them. Now all they had to do was to cross the outer cordon, where there was a barrier, and beyond it freedom awaited them. I was damp all over. My knees were weak, my throat was constricted. It took a great deal of courage. No doubt they were by now passing their last obstacle, the barrier at which there was always an SS man on duty. Once they had passed that without being stopped, they were free.

I waited another few minutes. Perschel returned. The road was silent. The worst was behind them. No one was being brought back on the road to Budy. That meant they were already free. But what would happen to me? My heart beat like a hammer. My throat was even tighter. I could not speak, I was so agitated. I saw Chamek saying something to me, but I could not hear his voice. In my mind I was far away, beyond the wires, with them. In two days we would be together. How much longer should I have to wait? I should have gone with them. Ah, this stupid premonition. For them the camp was nothing but a memory now.

The siren was silent. The Kommandos were beginning to get ready for their return. Time to head home. The siren was silent. Apart from a few people, no one knew as yet that there were two missing. There was a jam outside the guardhouse of the men's camp, as usual. They couldn't all get in at once. The SS men counted the incoming prisoners; some were checked. The orchestra played a gay march. One after another, the Kommandos marched back into camp. Now it was our turn.

The building works' Kommando was subdivided into different groups working all over the camp, wherever their services were required. For that reason it usually took quite a long time before everybody had assembled. However, just now they were still unable to arrive at the correct total. They must have discovered that Edek was missing. Tadek P., the glazier, who was responsible for the whole Kommando, saw me marching along and asked what was up with Edek. I shrugged my shoulders. I hadn't a clue, I said. I had seen him in the women's camp during the morning. For a long time Tadek had suspected that we were planning to escape. When he saw me returning with my Kommando, he was a little reassured. He could not imagine that Edek would escape without me. Therefore he went on waiting and did not report to the authorities that one man was missing.

Now all were lined up in rows in front of their blocks ready for roll call; only Tadek's Kommando was still standing outside the guardhouse. From afar I saw that Tadek had finally made up his mind to report one man missing. An SS man struck him in the face, again and again.

Roll call. Block seniors reported numbers in their block to Blockführers. They passed on the reports to Rapportführer Wolf. A loud command, "Company, halt!" rang out. Now Wolf reported to Lagerführer Schwarzhuber. Presently an SS could be seen running in the direction of the Blockführers' office. The siren began to wail. Long, insistent, piercing one's ears. "One missing." We stood at attention. I noticed the Russians giving me surreptitious glances. Jankiel was standing close to me, rigid, looking straight ahead, but I felt his hand squeezing mine. How could they know who was missing? Blockführer Schneider gazed earnestly along the rows of prisoners; his eye rested for a long while on me. Or did it only seem so to me?

I looked blank, without batting an eyelid. With a moan the siren stopped its wailing. We remained standing. The whole camp stood. The Lagerführer left the camp with his retinue and proceeded to the guardhouse. Now all was quiet, the tension partly receding. I managed to turn round in the direction of the women's camp. Their roll call went on, too: no doubt they could not make their figures tally, either. I flinched because the siren's voice began to wail once more. General consternation. Everyone was surprised because there was only one missing, and then the siren indicated that there was one more missing, one more had escaped. "Camp senior, camp senior forward!" The shout came from the direction of the Blockführers' office.

After a while he returned, surrounded by trusties. The camp Kapo yelled: "Dismiss!" End of roll call. So there was to be no Stehappell. The trusties dispersed as well. This time they did not even march out to look for the fugitive inside the outer cordon, as was the usual practice.

Before long the news had spread throughout the camp like wildfire. The person who had escaped from the women's camp was a Jewess, the runner Mally Zimetbaum, No. 19880; from our camp it was the fitter Edward Galinski, No. 531. Schwarzhuber was reported to have said if such an old prisoner had got away, it wasn't worth the trouble looking for him.

After the evening meal I hurried to see Jurek. It took me a long time to get there. Every few steps someone would stop me to inquire, shake me by the hand or wink at me knowingly. And then there were the questions. How is it that you're left behind? When are you off? With a girl, too? Happier than anyone else were the Jews. They drew me into their block, overjoyed, offering me whatever they had.

Chamek took me to Hans, the Canada Kapo, for a drink. He was glad that I had not escaped and that he did not have the problems Tadek did. Hans, wishing to claim some of the glory for himself, declared loudly that Mala was his cousin. I began to be scared of the sudden popularity. Many people asked me straight out when it would be my turn. I might well be summoned to the Political Department. The mere thought sent shivers down my spine. At Jurek's I met Jozek. Without realizing that Jozek and I were planning to escape together, Jurek advised us to wait until the excitement had died down. Jozek advocated the idea of escaping via the bunker. That was the safest way, he maintained. The other plan might not work a second time. I decided to escape whatever happened, and to do so as quickly as possible.

On my way back I caught snatches of conversation. There was only one subject today: Edek and Mala. Their names became symbols of freedom.

It was dark by the time I arrived in Block 4, which meant that I could creep there unseen by nosy and excited acquaintances.

I called out for Jurek Sadczykow; I was very curious to hear

241

how he had got on with Mala. She seemed so agitated. We found a quiet corner where one might talk in peace. Jurek was very cautious. It'd be better for the two of us not to be seen together. Walls have ears.

He recounted what had happened in the Blockführers' office from the moment Mala turned up and Edek went into the potato bunker in order to take off his overalls. From the moment when Perschel climbed on his bicycle to when Mala entered the guard-house, where only one wardress was present, there was a for-tuitous chain of circumstances. Jurek pretended to be repairing a lock in the toilet which previously had been removed by Edek. The lavatory pan had also been left there earlier. After a while Mala appeared. He locked her in the toilet where the toolbox and overalls were ready and waiting her. She had to hurry up, for at any moment someone might come. It was easy for Jurek to talk himself out of the situation; he was, after all, working there. But it would be worse for Mala.

While continuing to look as if he was repairing the lock, Jurek waited impatiently for Mala. Seconds seemed like eternities. Nothing happened. Alarmed by the long silence in the toilet, he opened the door and saw the girl standing there, helpless, pale with fear and completely confused. She looked as if she were unconscious. Without much ado, he locked himself in with Mala, dressed her in the overalls, placed the lavatory pan on her head and literally pushed her outside. Then he propelled her in the direction of the potato bunker. Mala walked obediently, her teeth chattering audibly. It might have been an attack of malaria, the illness from which she suffered.

I had seen the rest myself from my vantage point in the women's camp.

CHAPTER 75

SUNDAY, a rest day, seemed to drag on and on. I never left the block so as to avoid running into the curious. It did not help much, though. Again and again somebody came to pester me.

Camp Kapo Jupp, whom I met on the landing, said nastily: "Well, clerk, how are you? Your pal's hopped it." He made a vague movement with his hand which was meant to indicate that Edek was a long way away. I was growing more and more afraid that I was suspected of having helped him to escape, and that I might suddenly be summoned to the Political Department. Impatiently I waited for the next day. At night I tossed and turned, unable to sleep. My last night in the camp, or was it? I tried not to think of this second possibility, but the picture of this fearful prospect came back, torturing me and filling me with dread.

In the morning I got up early, before the gong. From the hiding place I took cigarettes, a picture of my sister and Mala's portrait. I did not know why I took them. During my Kommando's roll call, I stood as usual in the front row, right next to Chamek. We walked in silence. As we passed the gate to the women's camp, Chamek decided to say something: "Don't you play a dirty trick on me the way Edek did on the glazier. It wasn't too bad for him, but I'm a Jew, remember that."

After a while, when he saw that I did not reply, he added: "Give me your word of honor that if you should consider running away, you won't do it from my Kommando." I gave him my word, but I had not the least intention of keeping it.

I did not worry about Chamek. His hands were not clean, although he had always behaved perfectly correctly towards me. A good hiding wouldn't do him any harm, and surely nothing worse could happen to him. Collective responsibility had been abolished, anyway.

The colonel distributed tools from a large box to the prisoners. The Scharführer spoke to Chamek for a time and disappeared, as usual. After he had given the work orders to the colonel, Chamek did the same. He vanished into the block of his Yugoslav fiancée. He had perseverance, one must grant him that.

Hidden behind the half-open door to the block, I smoked a cigarette and began to chat with the Colonel. Meanwhile one of the little Slovak girls approached and led me to understand that she wanted to talk to me.

The colonel put out his cigarette and went away discreetly. Beaming with happiness and unable to hide her feelings, the girl told me everything that had happened on Saturday. It was not until roll call that Mala's absence had been noticed. Rapportführerin Drechsler ordered a search for her throughout the camp because she thought Mala might suddenly have been taken ill or even fainted. She knew of Mala's bouts with malaria, and it never entered her mind that her absence might be ascribed to anything else.

They looked for Mala everywhere. Roll call, although it had started earlier than in the men's camp, dragged on and on. Finally it proved necessary to sound the siren. It had been discovered that, in addition to Mala, one of the prisoners from the fitters' Kommando, who worked inside the women's camp, was missing. They assumed, correctly, that they must have escaped together.

Drechsler, who had been told off by Mandel in front of the whole camp, was livid with rage. Thousands of women meanwhile rejoiced. "And I'm so happy, too." The Slovak girl concluded her account.

Now it's my turn, I decided. I told the colonel that I should be in the "Pump" in Sector B, in case Chamek were to ask for me. This did not surprise him, for I went there often. He gave me a knowing glance, for he knew that occasionally I would have a drink there.

In the "Pump" I found Zbyszek B. and Lubusch. Could it be that Zbyszek was working on Lubusch, I wondered? Zbyszek, who knew nothing of Lubusch's part in the escape, introduced me as a friend of Edek's. Lubusch grew a little embarrassed, but afterwards he regarded me with interest. In his look there seemed to be a silent plea. Don't give me away. As though he suspected something, Zbyszek did not change the subject.

I left the "Pump" as quickly as possible. I had to get out of the women's camp if I wanted to meet Szymlak, who was sure to be waiting for me at the leveling Kommando where Jozek worked. I was perfectly calm. My nocturnal nightmares had vanished forever. I decided to behave exactly like Edek.

Standing by the guardhouse was the girl runner with whom I had spoken less than an hour ago. She whispered, "Quiet. Keep calm. There are only a couple of wardresses here."

It was always much worse when SS men were on duty. One of them sat on the windowsill, the other was standing outside. They seemed to be very bored. When I reported that I was leaving the camp, I mixed something up; I always had difficulties with my German. I stammered, tried to speak more clearly and clutched my cap in my hand in agitation, which greatly amused the two of them. They laughed coarsely and kept saying something in German which I did not understand. At last the one perched on the windowsill asked me in Polish where I was going and what for. I was prepared for this. With complete equanimity I told her the tale I had worked out. My Kommandoführer was sending me to the Kapo of the Kommando working on the ramp. He was to supply gravel and stones which were needed in order to build the road in the sick bay area. The story was rather probable. The wardress repeated it in German to her colleague, who nodded her head in approval. It still cost me two packets of cigarettes because the one who spoke Polish opened the lid of her desk and inquired whether I smoked. "And now, get lost," she said quickly.

Like an arrow, I darted in the direction of the ramp because I could hear the sound of a car arriving. I had already got as far as the trucks when I heard the screeching of brakes. An elegant chauffeur jumped out of the car and eagerly opened the door for fat Lagerkommandant Kramer, who heaved his bulk through the opening and then held out a hand to his companion, chief wardress Mandel. The wardresses stood at attention with raised arms and saluted their superiors. "Heil Hitler!"

I reached for one of the empty trucks and trundled it past the guardhouse, along the railway track of the Auschwitz-Dziedzice line. Half-way down the road was the leveling Kommando, my destination.

In a little wooden house, which had been constructed hastily, were the storerooms and the office. The foreman, a German, had several civilian workers to help him. In a place where prisoners were digging wide, oblong pits, more store houses were to be built. This whole area was very convenient for contacts with civilians and even with members of the Wehrmacht, who worked not far away in anti-aircraft units. Old Szymlak, who worked in the

SS barracks, did not have far to go in order to get here; that was why we met in this place from time to time. In a sense, Jozek, clerk of the leveling Kommando, acted as our go-between. I met him in a wooden hut where he was apparently relating something very interesting, because a little crowd had gathered round him. "Where is Szymlak?" I asked him.

Jozek spread his hands. "He's not here."

One of the civilians, whom I had not seen before, got up. He glanced at my number, then at me, and then walked slowly towards the exit. I followed him.

"Szymlak's not coming today," he said. "He asked me to give you this." He looked about cautiously to make sure no one was watching us. Reassured, he took off his cap and from it produced a slip of paper. I was surprised because I had not expected it. It was a note from Edek.

"We reached the place without difficulties," I read. "Mala carried the lavatory pan for a couple of miles, brave girl. Beyond Budy we threw it into a cornfield together with the overalls. Across the fields we reached Kozy towards evening. We spent the night in a barn on the edge of the village. Mala is well, but her shoulders are aching. We shall continue this evening. So long."

That was all. I was disappointed. I felt cheated. That's your fault, said an inner voice. You ought to have made up your mind. You were a coward. And now you're looking for someone to blame. What should I do? I was even determined to escape via the bunker, all alone if need be, only let me get away as quickly as possible.

The civilian was watching me and noticed my agitation. "I'm the old man's neighbor," his voice was calm. "I live on the edge of the village. They could not find Szymlak's house and asked the people in the village where the old man lived. The news went quickly round the village that an SS man (Edek continued wearing the SS uniform) was asking for Szymlak. It seemed the old man was afraid he might get into trouble and did not let them spend the night at his house. He sent them to me instead. I also was afraid to give them shelter, so I showed them the barns in my field, quite near to the forest."

246

Now I understood why Edek had not sent back the uniform, the weapon and the pass. We had expected too much of Szymlak. Faced with the reluctance of the villagers to shelter them, Edek decided to do without any further help from Szymlak and did not persuade him to run the risk which doubtless would have been involved in taking back the uniform.

As I tore the letter into tiny pieces I looked about me helplessly. Sensing my consternation, the civilian gave me a friendly slap on the shoulder and said, "Don't worry. The war will be over soon. You'll all be free." It was all very well for him to talk.

Chamek was shouting nervously at his men, beating them and driving them to work. When he saw me he calmed down at once. So I had been the cause of his agitation, for I had been away too long. He feared the worst. Now he needn't fear anything, I thought bitterly. I was alone. Without Edek, would I be able to accomplish anything at all, I asked myself. I felt very lonely. Even Mala and Edek's successful escape failed to please me now.

A strange apathy began to take hold of me. I no longer cared about anything.

CHAPTER 76

THE CAMP had not yet recovered from the romantic flight of Edek and Mala when the next day the siren began to wail again. Two "old" prisoners had gotten away. Faced with this epidemic of escapes, the camp authorities were so helpless that they refrained from any retaliatory measures. Only the Political Department, suspecting an organized campaign, increased its activities. More and more often its members came into the camp and made spot searches. In addition, they employed a large number of spies. There was a spy even among the Russians who worked in Mexico. He lived in our block. Shortly afterwards he had a fatal accident at work; the Russians liquidated him themselves. They continued to escape in groups of three or four, almost daily.

I waited in vain for a message from Edek. There was no news from Szymlak either, and the young civilian had disappeared somehow. I had a parcel and a letter from my sister in Zakopane, but in the letter there was not a single, solitary word about the note I had sent a month ago, let alone anything about Edek. I assumed they had not yet reached Zakopane.

So I just went on waiting for a sign from Edek.

Outside the office of the women's hospital stood a small truck. Prisoners from Auschwitz were bringing medical supplies. I went to give them a hand. One of the prisoners took me to one side and whispered urgently, "Edek and Mala arrested."

At first I simply could not believe it. How was this possible? Now, after so many days. It was unfortunately the awful truth.

Yesterday afternoon they had been taken to Block 11 and locked up in the bunker. Now they were to be interrogated by the Political Department. I was seized by a terrible fear. What would happen if they could not stand the interrogations? I met Jurek immediately after the evening meal. He was as depressed by this disastrous news as I.

"Now there's no time to think about it. We must escape as quickly as possible," Jurek said anxiously.

Undeterred by the failure of Edek and Mala's flight, three Polish prisoners who had been planning to escape for some time managed to get away successfully. There were no reprisals. Weren't there, though? Suddenly, out of the blue, a block senior was hanged. The former trusty of the Auschwitz bunker had been denounced by a German woman prisoner with whom he had had some personal relationship, and he was hanged for listening to the radio and spreading BBC news.

Did it mean that the terror was to begin all over again? Under such circumstances the fate of Edek and Mala seemed to be sealed. But before killing them the Political Department would do everything to extract the truth from them, above all, from whom Edek had obtained the SS uniform and weapon.

I received a stiff from Edek. Strictly speaking Jurek received it with the instruction to convey its contents to me. In it Edek described their failure. In the camp several lurid versions of this theme were making the rounds. One said that Edek had gone into

248

shops in Bielsko, that he actually went into a café, where he had attracted attention by throwing his money about. The other version reported that he had taken Mala to a dentist and offered the man gold to pay for treatment; that, unfortunately, the dentist was a German, and so on.

Apparently Edek was aware of the rumors going about; that was why he briefly described what had happened. They were arrested in the Zywiek Mountains where they had run into a border patrol. They were taken to Bielsko and put in jail without being recognized because Edek continued to wear the SS uniform. At present they were being interrogated daily. The Politicals treated them with unexpected leniency. Mala had even been offered coffee and cake. They wanted to find out how they had escaped and particularly where they had obtained the uniform and weapon. This they would, needless to say, never discover.

This note reassured me up to a point, and I began to console myself with the thought that they would eventually leave them in peace and that the whole business would end with a beating and, at most, with "permanent SK." Jurek, however, did not share my optimism. He maintained that if the Gestapo did not get anything out of them, they would adopt other, more severe, methods in order to make them talk.

"Escape, escape. And as soon as possible, before it is too late," he said anxiously. "I tell you, make up your mind quickly. I've made up mine, and I'm not going back on it."

A few days later Jurek, who had contacts with Auschwitz, brought another note from Edek. It was very brief and had been written in a much more depressed mood. The Politicals had stopped playing with them. Zbyszek, who also had close contacts with Edek, knew accurate details. They beat Edek's bare feet with a metal rod. Mala, too, was no longer handled with kid gloves. Boger was in charge of the interrogations.

Jurek's nerves were no longer able to stand it. That evening he called me for a decisive talk. There were four of them who intended to escape via the bunker in Mexico. I could join them if I wished. Everything was ready. But I could not make up my mind.

Next day two prisoners got away: Jurek and Rudy from the packing room. On the same day, another two from Auschwitz made their escape. Now they were sitting in the underground cave in Mexico, waiting for the right moment to get through the outer cordon. I lay on my bunk, once more reproaching myself for not seizing this opportunity.

In the morning I marched out to work as usual with Chamek's Kommando. Outside the gate on the right, facing the orchestra, the SS men had prepared a special display for the prisoners.

Leaning against spades like scarecrows were the corpses of prisoners shot while attempting to escape, massacred, covered with mud and congealed blood. One of them was Jurek. I did not know the second one; the third was Rudy from the packing room.

The orchestra played a march. An SS man gave the command: "Eyes right." The small group of Blockführers standing next to him watched the reaction on the prisoners' faces with satisfaction. Only the glassy eyes of the dead no longer expressed anything. I was so shocked by this macabre picture that it was not until we were well beyond the gate that I was brought back to reality by Chamek's voice saying, "There you are, that's what happens when you try to escape." Chamek was in constant fear that I might play a dirty trick on him; as he would say, this was a salutary warning.

Providence was watching over me, I thought. At this moment I might be in the bunker or have joined these three. Three? Why three? Hadn't there been four who escaped? And where is the fourth? Either he managed to get away or it was he who betrayed them, I thought in alarm.

Shortly after our arrival in the women's camp, Chamek received news from the Kommandoführer, with whom he was on good terms. Immediately after the discovery of the escape, the SS guards inside the outer cordon were reinforced. The night was exceptionally dark. One of the watchmen saw the prisoners crawling without being seen by them. He waited until they had come quite close and then he opened fire. He bumped off three; the fourth managed to get away.

After Jurek's tragic death, I had no news from Edek for some time. Zbyszek had certain leads which gave us faint hopes that their case might not end in tragedy. He hinted that there were behind-the-scene efforts which, he hoped, would be crowned with success. For this purpose he collected jewelry and had a good source somewhere in the women's camp. He intended using Frau Boger's weakness for these baubles. He had a chance to talk to her from time to time when he did various jobs in her house. He was full of hope, as far as Edek was concerned. Things were not so good for Mala, though. She was a Jew.

One day I joined a Kommando which worked on the new buildings in Auschwitz. From there it was easy to get to the locksmith's shop, where I knew many people. I wanted to see Lubusch. Perhaps I might hear something from him. He was not there. I went in search of Julek and Marian, two of my former mates from Block 28, and ran across them as they were coming out of the bunker. Jakub, the bunker Kapo, was taking special care of Edek and Mala, whose courage and spirit impressed him. He arranged for Julek and Marian to bring extra food into the bunker. Mala and Edek had not betrayed anybody. The Politicals had got nothing out of them. Now they were left alone. Julek and Marian brought extra food, and Jakub allowed them to meet. It was said that the Political Department had sent the case to Breslau for a ruling and the final decision was to come from there. Now they waited for their sentence. Judging by the latest punishments for escape attempts, it might end with transfer to the SK.

This was very much in line with what Zbyszek had said. Considerably reassured, I returned to Birkenau. The penal company was in Birkenau, and I might be able to do something. Bednarek would not dare to harass Edek.

Two or three days later I received another note from Edek. It had been written in an even more somber mood than the one before. He told me that they were waiting for their sentence, that they had betrayed no one, that Mala was keeping up her courage. They expected the worst. But they were determined that the executioner would not get them alive. They knew of Jurek's death. He asked me to reassure Lubusch that he had nothing to fear.

Next morning I awoke bathed in cold sweat. I had had a harrowing dream. I dreamt that the sentence had been pronounced and Edek had been hanged. The dream was long, tormenting and very detailed. I told it to Jankiel.

"It's a good sign. It means everything will end well," decided Jankiel kindly.

251

CHAPTER 77

WHEN WE returned from work as usual, to the strains of the orchestra, I noticed from afar, in the spot next to the kitchen close to the large water tank, a solitary gallows. As a rule there were two or three. My macabre dream was coming true. This time I would be forced to witness the execution of my friend during my waking hours.

After my return to the block I ran across camp Kapo Jupp, who came up to me and, amid much gesticulating, spoke about Edek. I merely understood that Edek had been brought to Birkenau that afternoon. He was kept imprisoned in a small room next to the kitchen, where Jupp had fettered his wrists with wire.

"After roll call," he said. I did not quite know what he meant, although he gave the impression that he had a great deal more to say but no time to say it because roll call was about to begin. Already the Blockführer was chasing the hesitant Russians out of the block into the yard between the blocks, where Jupp lined them up in rows. I noticed Grapatin, who wore a brass badge as a sign that he was on duty. Just in case, I made myself inconspicuous in between the lines of Russians.

Roll call began. Jasinski reported to Grapatin. But Grapatin was not satisfied; he began walking through the rows counting the prisoners himself. He stood in front of me, peered angrily at me, and then he struck me full force in the face. He hit me with his left, then with his right fist. My head veered from side to side like a weathervane. I tasted blood in my mouth. At last he stopped hitting me. My head throbbed and buzzed. I could hear him abusing me as he turned to go. Satisfied, he went on counting prisoners.

Roll call was coming to an end. Now, as was customary on these occasions, all of us went to where the gallows stood and formed a large square around the gallows. I stood as near as possible to the small room from which Edek would be led to his doom. After a while the door opened and Edek appeared. There was complete silence. All that could be heard was the crunching of gravel under the boots of Edek, the condemned man, walking towards the gallows, and Jupp, the executioner. Near the spot where I stood people made way to let the two men pass. I squeezed myself into the front row, hoping that Edek would see me. He walked very tall, pale, his face slightly bloated. His eyes scanned the crowd for faces he knew. I was sure he wanted to see me. I stood there, he almost touched me as he went past. A whisper would have been enough: "Edek." But at that moment I was not capable of even that. I stood as if paralyzed. Edek went past me without noticing me. Now I saw his straight back and his hands, drawn behind his back and bound with wire. This was the work of Jupp, who was mincing after him. Bravely Edek mounted the scaffold and immediately climbed onto the stool that had been placed underneath the gallows. The noose touched his head. The command "Attention" was given. After a while an SS man silently stepped forward and read out the sentence in German. At this moment Edek, standing on the stool, sought the opening of the noose with his head; then he vigorously kicked away the stool and hung. He kept his word. He would not deliver himself alive to the hangman.

But the SS men would not permit such a demonstration. They began to shout, and the camp Kapo understood them at once. Grasping Edek round the middle, he placed him back on the stool and loosened the noose. The German finished reading the sentence in German and began muddling it in Polish. He read fast and unintelligibly. He was in a hurry. Edek waited until he had finished. In a moment of utter silence he suddenly cried in a choking voice: "Long live Poland—" He broke off in the middle of a word. Quickly Jupp drew away the stool, and this time the noose was pulled tight. Edek's body tightened, twitched and then remained hanging limply, his head dropped to one side. He was no longer alive. The body circled slowly and bobbed slightly on the thick rope. The rays of the setting sun cast a bloody hue over the huge black water tank; I could not keep my eyes off this sight. To stop my teeth from chattering, I clenched them till they hurt. The entire camp stood motionless.

Slowly the silent crowd of thousands of prisoners vanished in the falling night. There was deathly silence. A group of SS men withdrew in the direction of the exit.

"Caps off." The Polish command rang out suddenly and un-expectedly from the side of the square where Block 4 stood. I thought I could detect Tadek's voice. The whole camp paid its last respects to the dead man. All at once one of the withdrawing SS men yelled: "Dismiss! Scram, everybody!" Danisz and Jupp shouted: "Scram! Scram!" In a moment the space outside the kitchen was empty. Only Edek was left.

I wept with impotence and pain. No one was surprised. I sat on my bunk. The Russians patted me on the back, trying to comfort me. "Pull yourself together, clerk. They'll pay for everything." Next to me someone was sobbing. It was Jankiel. How strange he looked, dissolved in tears, this decent old Jew who was so devoted to us. Somebody held out a glass to me. I gulped down its contents in one swig. The alcohol calmed me down a little, but in my heart there was a great emptiness.

A runner from the main office in Block 2 appeared in the door-way. He came to fetch me. At first I was horrified. I was certain that I was being called to the Blockführers' office. And that meant I, too, was finished. On our way the runner reassured me. There was not a single SS man in Block 2, only camp senior Danisz, Jupp and roll call clerk Kazek Gosk. There was something they wanted to give me.

In fact, only these three were waiting in the office. I stood anx-iously at the door and looked around in fear. "Come here," Kazek said softly, "don't be afraid."

I still feared some provocation. "Come along. Don't be scared, clerk," Jupp added gently.

Danisz spoke to me in Polish. "This guy Edek, he was your friend. He was a decent fellow, didn't betray anybody." He spoke in short sentences, pausing after each one.

"The camp Kapo bound his hands. Edek asked him to give you this note, and if God were to permit you to get home alive, give it to his father." He handed me a minutely folded note. "And now, go back to your block. Don't say anything to anybody. We mustn't do that. Edek was a good comrade." He got up from his stool. Even he felt sorry for Edek.

Back in the block I examined the contents of the little parcel, in the presence of Jankiel and The Barber. Written on the note were the names of Edek and Mala and their camp numbers: Edward Galinski, No. 531, Mally Zimetbaum, No. 19880. Wrapped in paper was hair, some of Edek's short crop and a golden curl of Mala's. This time all three of us wept. And then we drank. It did not help me much. Once again I was overcome by this indescribable emptiness.

Next day the little Slovak girl runner told me of Mala's execution. Just like Edek, Mala was determined to prevent the SS men from executing the sentence. As she was standing on the scaffold under the gallows, while the sentence was read out, she slashed her wrists with a razor blade. But as with Edek, they would not allow her to die in the way she had chosen. Rapportführer Taube rushed up to her, and she slapped his face with her blood-streaming hands. The enraged SS men almost trampled her to death in front of the whole women's camp.

The sentence was duly executed but not in the way laid down in regulations. She died on her way to the crematorium on the handcart pulled by women prisoners, who were unable to spare her this last suffering. One of these women was the little Slovak. She wept, wiping away her tears with her sleeve. I found no words to comfort her.

CHAPTER 78

THE SIREN wailed. Insistent, long, as it did when there was an air raid warning. I looked at my watch. It was going on eleven. Every day around this time Allied aircraft flew overhead. The hearts of camp inmates overflowed with joy. Hopes rose. Not even the tragic end of the Warsaw uprising could shake their belief in victory. The Russian army, although its advance had been slowed, was not very far away. The fighting was reported to take place along the line of the rivers San, Vistula and Bug. At least that was what the people said, large numbers of whom were transported here after the capitulation of Warsaw.

They were strange transports. The majority of the women to

whom I spoke refused to acknowledge that they were prisoners in a concentration camp. They believed that they had been interned here only temporarily, and that, having taken part in the uprising, they would receive special treatment. They were outraged about conditions in the women's camp. After a brief stay, they were moved on into the interior of the Reich.

With these transports from Warsaw came many children. A special children's block was set up in the women's camp, and one of the brick-built barracks was allocated for them. The yard of this block was fenced in, and a nurse in white overalls could be seen among the crowd of children. She was fair, blonde, young, pretty, flirtatious, quite different from Sylvia or Halina. They bore the marks of camp life. Wanda was frivolous, careless, cynical, corrupt. Nothing was valuable. But I liked her. Unlike the others, she excited me. And she knew it, and flirted all the more outrageously.

At the beginning our relationship was fairly innocent, but as time went on, it became bolder until the moment arrived when I had to prove my manhood. My experience in this direction had been moderate, strictly speaking, nonexistent, but I could not possibly let on. Wanda took the initiative. Behind the children's block was a barrack that seemed almost empty. Lying on bare bunks, between dirty rags and discarded blankets, were dozens who were dead or dying. We did not recoil. We held hands and looked for a suitable place, one that might do. Clasped in each other's arms we kissed passionately. Now, now, just let's slip onto this bunk.

I glanced across and sobered up instantly. Staring at me were round, glassy eyes. These eyes were literally popping out of their sockets, huge, full of appalling terror. From the chest came a rattling sound; the woman was dying. Wanda clung to me tightly; it was hard to struggle free from this embrace.

"Come away from here, come." I drew her towards the exit. "Yes, now. We can't do it here," I added more calmly. She looked at me as if I had gone out of my mind.

But the next day I went back to her. She mocked me. In an attempt to reestablish myself as a lover, at least to some extent, I promised to find her a suitable spot. We weren't doing anything wicked, were we? After all, others were doing it if they had a chance. Only not in that place where they were dying. It was terrible yesterday.

"Run along. The fat Blockführer's coming," she whispered suddenly. I turned round. He was about thirty yards away. I recognized him, a good-natured old Silesian. Not long ago, yesterday, in fact, he was drinking with Chamek and loudly cursing his service with the SS.

There was no need to be afraid of him. I continued talking with my back to him. But Wanda did not let him out of her sight. "Listen, he's coming here," she said anxiously.

"Don't worry, I know him well," I reassured her self-confidently. "He probably wants a cigarette." Behind my back I heard his heavy step.

"Blast you, are you blind or deaf?" he hissed furiously. "And couldn't you warn him, you slut, that I was coming?" And he struck her with his stick. Before he could hit her again, she had disappeared.

"Goddammit, cap off!" Instead of taking off my cap I stared into his bloated face, which was purple with rage. He brought his stick down on my head. Instinctively I put up my hand to protect myself. I did not understand at all. What was the matter with him?

"Blast you, I'll kill you, are you blind or something?" He struck and struck again. Blood was spurting from the hand with which I had sought to protect myself.

"Mandel! Can't you see, you stupid idiot?" His eyes slid in the direction of the camp street, where the head wardress, in the company of a colleague, stood with legs apart, watching the scene.

"Damn you, fuck off, can't you?"

At last I got the message. In a flash I ran off to the washroom. The swellings on my head were nothing compared to my arm. If only I could at least have had a jacket to soften the blows. My left forearm was beaten to a pulp, one bleeding wound.

"What happened to you?" Chamek inquired. I did not have to keep anything back. I told him what had happened. "I'll go and tell the boss, he'll settle the matter."

"Leave it," I said, "it was my fault. I behaved like a fool."

On the other hand, I thought, he didn't have to hit me quite so hard.

CHAPTER 79

In the camp there was at this time a strange atmosphere of unrest, excitement and waiting for something that was bound to come and bring with it important changes—the calm before the storm. After the huge transports of Hungarian Jews were liquidated, the crematoria were working more slowly. Transports arrived less often. Selections, too, had become a little less vicious, and consequently the number of prisoners in the camp increased significantly. With increasing frequency transports were sent to other camps which were situated in the Reich. Bombed to pieces, Germany needed hands to do the work.

One evening my name was called out as one of a number of prisoners who were to report at once at the washroom block, where a transport for the concentration camp in Flossenburg was assembled. Some one thousand prisoners had already gathered, mainly Russians. There were also some Jews of different nationalities and Poles. I had no intention of leaving Auschwitz. Kazek Gosk was gracious and struck me off the list. I gave him Ici Mayer's number in place of mine. This time he did leave, one spy less in the camp.

Of late the SS barracks had been put on strict alert. There had been suspicious movements in the areas adjacent to the camp, dark figures who at night crept close to the outer cordon. They were thought to be partisans or Allied parachute troops dropped behind the lines. The news spread throughout the camp like a flash. It was not surprising that there was a state of tension and expectation.

In addition to all this news, there was something else: the camp was to be dissolved. In any case, there were no further extensions. Mexico, the giant new camp sector, suddenly ceased to exist.

Many transports were taking prisoners away from the women's camp. Small wonder then that speculations concerning the liquidation of the camp were rife, especially since the eastern front had long since crossed the San line. The prisoners had gradually become resigned to the thought of having to move to another camp. There were other speculations, too. We began to fear that at some point the SS might liquidate us. Surely that would be simpler than a laborious transport into the Reich.

One day the news went round—it sounded simply incredible—that there was to be a film show for prisoners. The performance was to take place in the sauna next to crematorium 4. Camp senior Danisz ordered all block seniors to choose a few dozen prisoners from each block worthy to enjoy this unusual entertainment.

Naturally I was one of these fortunates. With "a song on my lips," I marched with my fellow prisoners in the direction of the grove where the sauna was. As we entered the crematorium 4 area—in order to get to the sauna one had to go past the crematorium—a terrible thought struck me. Now they could easily liquidate us.

I looked around fearfully. No, what a crazy thought. Next to me walked Schneider, his hands in his pockets, chatting amicably to a block senior. There were only three or four Blockführers altogether, but they did not carry machine pistols, only bayonets on their belts.

The crematorium looked harmless. No smoke rose from the chimney. The cremation pits on either side of the road were covered by partly rotten osier hurdles, evidence of the fact that they had not been used for a long time.

Immediately outside the sauna there was a slight commotion. Although the door was wide open, some of the prisoners were hesitant to step inside. I was among the last whom Danisz finally hustled into the room. As a precaution I placed myself next to the door. A civilian wearing a Tyrolean hat operated the projector; the SS men sat next to him. The performance began. I could not see much of the film because the people standing in front of me were blocking my view. I could not understand the words either. Somehow I found the light music exciting, particularly as it seemed to me that I could hear the humming of aircraft outside. At moments when the actress playing the lead displayed her shapely legs and thighs during a dance, there were in the hall appreciative whispers, heaving sighs and much clicking of tongues; the sort of reaction one might have heard in any flea pit before the war. Here it was possibly even more striking, and one

259

of the Blockführers turned round and shouted, "Shut up." The excited murmuring stopped obediently. From the screen another simple and sentimental melody rang out, easy on the ear. My feet were killing me, because if I wanted to see anything I had to stand on tiptoe. The sentimental film had a depressing effect on me. I waited impatiently for the end of the performance, which had been full of beautiful women, elegant men and superb mountain landscapes.

At last it was all over. Outside it was getting to be dusk. Silently we lined up in rows of five. Outside the gate stood Lagerführer Schwarz with Mohl, who was in charge of the crematoria.

"Caps off, eyes right!" We marched past them smartly.

"Come on, come on, faster!" Mohl hurried us along. "On the double, march!"

The column of the Sonderkommando marched past us by crematorium 4. The night shift. In the yard stood a Red Cross ambulance. When we had swung into the road leading to our camp at right angles, I turned round. Far behind the sauna, in the grove separating crematoria 3 and 4, a crowd of people carrying bundles stood waiting, men, women and children. There were so many of them that they disappeared somewhere in the dense woods and the approaching darkness. They had been ordered to wait until we had left the area, which was exclusively reserved for them. They perished without witnesses. The Sonderkommando did not count. That night the reek of evil-smelling, sickly sweet smoke, the smell we knew so well, penetrated through the cracks into the barrack where I lay.

CHAPTER 80

A PART of our Kommando worked on the ramp, carrying gravel in trucks from a pit not far away. The afternoon was soporific, windless and very warm for early October. It was late 1944. Suddenly we heard a dull explosion and carbine shots. A column of smoke which could not have come from the crematorium chimney rose above the woods. At first I thought that it might be an unexpected air attack. Bullets came whistling over the ramp. The uncoordinated shooting increased minute by minute. Armed SS men on motorbikes and bicycles raced down the main road past the ramp. Limping Perschel rushed from the guardhouse, called out something to us, climbed on his bike and rode as fast as he could in the direction of the crematoria. Again a stray bullet whistled above my head. I leapt into the nearest empty truck. Others did the same. With bated breath, I waited to see what would happen next. Could it be that a group of partisans, of whom there had been much open talk lately, had come into the camp?

What a good thing it was that I had got for myself a pair of comfortable boots, high lace-up boots with double soles, trousers and a civilian jacket with thin red stripes that would easily wash off. I felt that "it" would have to come. I was ready for "it," but now one would have to sit out this shooting in the iron trucks until the moment when they would storm the camp.

What a pity that Edek did not live to experience this exhilarating moment. Gradually the shooting stopped and moved in the direction of Harmensee. The camp fireguard arrived from Auschwitz. Crematorium 4 was on fire. There were no more shots. Apparently the partisans, having carried out their task, were withdrawing. Then it was not yet the "it" I had been waiting for every day.

Disappointed, I struggled clumsily from my hiding place. The Kapo called his men together. The Kommandoführer orderd a roll call. No one was missing. By the time we returned into the camp we knew more or less the reason for the shooting, a revolt in crematoria 2 and 4. Karol from Canada had been correct when, some time ago, he told me that the Sonderkommando was organizing a revolt. They were convinced that one day the SS intended to liquidate them all.

I went to see Karol. He was thoroughly depressed. He maintained that the revolt had ended this way because of treachery. Someone in the crew of crematorium 4 had betrayed the Sonderkommando's preparations. In consequence they had had no choice but to start the revolt without communicating with the crews of the other crematoria. The consequences were tragic. All who did not die during their flight perished in the yard of crematorium 4, shot dead immediately after the suppression of the revolt. At this moment the crews of crematoria 3 and 5, who had not taken part in the revolt, were cremating them in the ovens.

Some stayed alive to serve the well-known purposes of the Political Department. When they began to "sing," many more prisoners would lose their lives.

"Let us flee," Karol whispered, almost imploringly.

I no longer considered escaping. Now I even began to doubt the possibility of liberation by the partisans. I had resigned myself to the idea of removal to another camp. Transports left almost daily. I might be in one of them any day.

On the following day I no longer marched out to work. I was on the transport list like many others. I took from out of my hiding place my treasured possessions: Mala's portrait, the photograph of my sister, her last letter, the folded note with the locks of Edek and Mala, and one of the notes Edek had sent me from the bunker, which accidentally I had not destroyed.

Some things I burned. Julek K. offered to keep the rest in his wallet. All I kept of valuables was my own watch, for which I had got permission in those days when I was still block clerk. Marian and Julek were somewhat better prepared for the journey. They possessed a large margarine carton filled with foodstuffs, margarine, sugar and SS sausage. This carton had a double bottom. There we hid a few bits and pieces made of gold and Julek's wallet. During the compulsory bath and disinfection in the sauna, I nearly lost my magnificent boots, which in my dreams were to have helped me when I joined the partisan fighting.

Thanks to David from Canada, I got my boots back, but the trousers were lost. In order to make up for my loss, he procured for me a splendid woolen coat, warm underwear and quite a decent suit. The kitchen issued each of us a loaf of bread, some margarine and a piece of sausage.

Finally we had to line up in the main road in groups of one hundred. A goods train was waiting at the ramp. Boarding it took a long time. We were so crowded that it was scarcely possible to turn round. After a while two guards climbed aboard as well. We were squashed even more closely because the middle of the wagon must be kept free for the guards. Before the train began to move I managed to make a little hole in the wall. Our wagon stood directly opposite the women's hospital. Outside one of the blocks a few women in white overalls were patiently waiting for the train to leave. A Scharführer now entered the carriage, once more counted us carefully and then ordered the guards to push the door shut.

Slowly we left the ramp. Nothing more could be seen through the gaps between the boards. Outside it was already dark. The train was gathering speed. As we went round a bend, the wheels screeched excruciatingly, just like four and a half years ago when I came here.

Farewell, Auschwitz. I've survived you. But what would become of us? The wagon wheels rattled rhythmically. Everyone was silent. I was sure they were thinking what I was thinking: what would become of us?

CHAPTER 81

ONE OF the guards, sprawled carelessly occupying the whole of the center section of the wagon, was asleep. The other one, who sat on a stool, was struggling against sleep but still awake. A small railway lamp hanging from the ceiling swung back and forth, casting its dim light over the prisoners standing on either side of the wagon. The provisional wire fence, which was to separate us from the space allocated to the guards, gave us no support. My feet hurt cruelly. I stuck a pocketknife in the hole I had made. Holding onto it with one hand I had the illusion of leaning against it. More and more I was tormented by thirst. My eyelids felt leaden. As for my coat it seemed to weigh a ton. My shoulders ached, and below my shoulder blades there was a stabbing pain. I recalled the Stehbunker, but even there I had managed somehow. At least there had been those chamberpots for me to sit on. The dubious support provided by the pocketknife brought no relief either.

The train traveled through various towns and housing estates, but we never managed to read their names. We only knew that we were in Germany, but we did not know where we were going. The guards said nothing.

Some prisoners could no longer control their bowels. The resulting stench put the guards in a foul mood. They became hostile and vicious and beat us with their carbine butts at every opportunity. We were no longer allowed to peep through the small gaps in the wagon walls. In this way we passed the twenty-four hours after our departure from Auschwitz. Outside it was night once again. The wheels of the advancing train rattled over the gaps in the tracks.

For some time now we had been standing in a station. The guards were whispering among themselves; I caught the word Berlin.

So that's where we were, in the capital of Hitler's "invincible" Germany. Once more I pricked up my ears, for the guards were now talking about the camp to which we were going. Oranienburg. That meant we had almost arrived at our destination. One of the prisoners started a conversation with the guards and—wonders never cease—received a fairly courteous reply. We would arrive within the hour. But it took a long time before we began to move again. The train dawdled terribly. Every few minutes it stopped; a few times it went backwards. We thought that several hours must have gone by. We were dead tired. Oranienburg had a bad reputation, but now we longed to get there. At last we stopped in a siding.

The door was suddenly flung open. The harsh beams of searchlights completely blinded us. We stood crowded together in the door, clutching our bundles, undecided as to what we were to do. All at once someone standing close shouted: "Come on, get out." A prisoner, apparently a trusty, judging from the huge stick which he wielded skillfully, jumped into the wagon yelling: "All parcels stay here!" A frightful confusion ensued, because some prisoners went back obediently in order to deposit their parcels inside the wagon, while others, driven by an SS man, sought to get quickly out of his reach and leapt over the heads of the ones trying to get back. Hanging on to my parcel with food from Auschwitz, I waited for a suitable moment to jump out of the wagon without being struck by the SS man. At the same time I had no intention of losing what little food I had in my bundle. I was too old a prisoner to be outwitted by the order of a Kapo.

At the moment which I judged to be most advantageous, I leapt down from the wagon. Busy snatching a parcel from some hapless prisoner, the Kapo would not devote his attention to me. I ran the gauntlet of a dozen guards, consisting of SS men who kicked us, tried to trip us up and waved their sticks at us. Once again I was blinded by this diabolical searchlight, but I evaded their blows as if guided by some animal instinct. I leapt like a hare, ducking before the sticks, and finally got out of the range of the searchlight. Ahead of me was the huge, wide-open gate leading into a hall. Just another few yards, but at this very moment I received a fearful blow with something hard right on my face. I was flung back by the force of this blow. I lost my balance and would have fallen down had I not been thrown forward by yet another blow, this time from behind. I attempted one step but stumbled because someone was tripping me up. I fell forward. At the last moment the prisoner running behind me jumped over me, and then a dog, urged on by an SS man, flung himself on me. With a threatening growl he tore at my coat. Above my head I heard again the whistle of a whip. With an almost superhuman effort I jumped up and bounded forward. Behind me the dog yelped. As I leapt up, I had apparently kicked the dog in the neck with my hobnailed boots.

I heard cursing and the dreaded switch of the whip, but I was already beyond their reach at the door of a vast factory shed. A Kapo who was pushing me into line gave me a strange look. I clutched my bundle still more tightly. With my free hand I tried to wipe my nose. Blood? Only now I remembered that someone had struck me across the mouth with a stick. Suddenly I felt a dull, persistent, unbearable pain. I ran my hand over my mouth. No doubt about it, my lips and nose were swollen, and I felt the swelling increasing all the time. My hand was bloodstained; across the back of my hand ran a clear blue bruise. I flexed my fingers. Not broken. They only hurt when I bent them. I must have managed at the last moment to protect myself instinctively from the blow to my face. My hand caught the full force of it.

Perhaps that was why I had not lost my teeth. I checked with my tongue and felt that they were all there, albeit loose, particularly the front teeth in my upper gums. I spat blood.

Damn! I turned to the prisoner next to me. "Hey, you, what do I look like?" He looked at me in surprise, because instead of words all he could hear was some unintelligible mumbling. However, he guessed what it was I wanted to know.

"They certainly gave you a good going-over," he said pityingly.

I took a handkerchief out of my coat pocket and looked around for my people. They were standing in the second row, a few steps away from me.

"Whatever's the matter with you," inquired the ever-concerned Ludwik when he noticed me holding the handkerchief pressed to my mouth. I could not speak but removed the handkerchief. "Oh, my God, did they ever beat you up."

Full of self-pity, I sniffed and swallowed a lump of congealed blood. I felt sick. Ludwik, who spoke German, asked the Kapo if I might go to the washroom to clean myself up. It was the same Kapo who earlier had looked at me so strangely. I thought then that he wanted to take away my parcel.

"Yes, yes, go along," he now said not ungently, pointing to a washroom opposite. The ice-cold water refreshed me a little. Somebody lent me a piece of mirror. Blue-black lips, horribly distended, particularly the upper lip, which almost touched the nose, which was also swollen. Eyes that were nothing but narrow slits. I looked like a scarecrow. The swelling spread across my face. My head was almost bursting with pain. And while I still had my teeth, I feared they might drop out if I pushed against them with my tongue. Hell! They had really beaten me up. My first taste of Oranienburg.

CHAPTER 82

ROLL CALL. In spite of earlier portents, roll call went off quickly and painlessly. At last we were told where we were. Before going to the Oranienburg camp, which was only a few hundred yards away, we would have to go through a period of quarantine here in this shed. It was one of the aircraft hangars belonging to the Heinkel works which had been prepared to provide temporary accommodation for us. Half of the hangar was occupied by a few hundred three-tiered bunks. Lying on each bunk were a straw mattress and two blankets. There were about two thousand prisoners; in other words, there was one bed for every two prisoners. Considering the cold in this shed and the small number of blankets, sharing a bed was perhaps not such a bad thing, after all.

I, however, was really in a bad way. My aching face was still swelling. I had shivering fits and most certainly ran a temperature. But tiredness overcame pain; I fell asleep. Next morning I felt a little better, and after two more days the facial swelling had subsided, my lips were beginning to heal up and even the teeth seemed to wobble a little less. As I got better, I also recovered my appetite. We never went to work, but lay about for hours in between air attacks, gossiping and eating up our meager food supplies. The revolting food they gave us was not enough to assuage our hunger. Some prisoners began to barter with the gold trifles they had smuggled out of Auschwitz. The trusties, who cheated us of our minute portions, were delighted to acquire these things. However, they came very quickly to the conclusion that this sort of bartering was not worthwhile. They therefore ordered a roll call, during the course of which each one of us was painstakingly searched. They enriched themselves in the process, but we began to starve. Their greedy eyes did not fail to detect Marian and Julek's margarine carton. All they returned to us were our personal mementos, among them my watch and Julek's watch, for which we held permits from the authorities in Auschwitz. Julek sold his watch soon afterwards. In return he received a piece of bread, some cigarettes and a few bowls of soup. He shared everything like a good comrade. The Kapo who had treated me quite kindly when my face was painful and swollen noticed my watch. It was not a very good watch at all, but here at Heinkel's it had a certain value. For that reason I haggled for a long time in order to get as much food as possible for it.

To begin with I got half a loaf of bread and some coarse tobacco, and I was also supposed to receive an extra bowl of snail

267

soup daily until the end of our quarantine. In fact, all I had was a few second helpings and perhaps three bowls of revolting, stinking, heavily salted snails. If one washed it all down with herbal tea or even just water, one could appease one's hunger a little by filling one's stomach with this pig swill.

Although we did not work here, our lives were very varied. Every day and night there were a couple of air raids. During these nocturnal attacks we watched the glare of the fire over Berlin. The fiercer it was, the more we rejoiced and hoped for an early end to the war.

On sunny days we would sit for hours in a nearby pine grove. So frequent were the air attacks that at times no sooner had the "all clear" signal appeared than the next air raid warning sounded. In the afternoons it was usually quiet. It was then that German aircraft would appear in the sky. Our attention was drawn to one particular aircraft which took off from a nearby airfield. After it had reached a considerable height, a second, much smaller plane with short and very wide wings detached itself from underneath the wings of the mother plane. This little plane, incredibly maneuverable and fast, stayed in the air for some minutes, carrying out a series of maneuvers after which it prepared for landing at the airport. The most interesting aspect was the fact that this aircraft made no noise while flying. It appeared to have no motor.

Ludwik, being omniscient, asserted that this was a new kind of V-missile, which was steered by means of radio waves. Even here in the camp there were repeated rumors about a weird new weapon that was soon to decide the outcome of this war.

CHAPTER 83

THE "DEALERS" had arrived, those slave traders. They were the representatives of German firms who hired craftsmen to work in different branches of concentration camps set up near factories and mines.

We weren't eager. One never knew where one might end up.

Our camp motto was: never be first, but never be last either. Already a few groups consisting of two dozen prisoners were departing with their "patrons." One had to decide what kind of craftsman one ought to pretend to be.

"If only they were looking for well drillers," groaned Edek F., who, in Birkenau, had worked in a seven-man well drillers' Kommando.

But the miracle did happen. One of the civilians, who had been conferring with our Lagerführer, called quite clearly for well drillers to come forward. Edek, who could not believe his ears, stepped forward and glanced uncertainly back to the row where we were lined up.

"Any more? Are there any more?"

We stepped forward and joined Edek, who was standing there all by himself. They took down our numbers.

We were to depart in a week's time. I was convinced that well drilling was a good trade. No doubt we would work either somewhere on country estates, where of course it would be an easy matter to procure food, or at worst in bombed-out cities, which did not seem to be any too bad either. We went to sleep full of these delightful prospects.

Next day Edek was in terrible pain. They took him to the hospital in Oranienburg where they removed his appendix, which was badly festering. What bad luck! We were overcome by fear since, apart from Edek, none of us knew anything about well drilling.

That afternoon we were lined up for roll call as usual. A tall, slim "dealer" with a nice face, wearing a Tyrolean hat and a Party badge in his lapel, was looking for electricians. He needed about sixty. His inquiry was urgent. Departure would have to take place today. A genuine mechanic was the first to come forward; he was an engineer, an old Auschwitz inmate. After a brief conversation with the civilian, he began to select his team of electricians himself. He fetched out the whole old guard. We came forward, too. Marian, Jedrek, Ludwik, Czesiek and Wojtek; failed well drillers all, but first-class "electricians."

And once again our numbers were taken down, and we were ordered to line up at the bottom of the steps leading to the office, where our dealer installed himself. We had to appear before him, one by one. There were too many applicants; therefore, he decided to make a selection.

He interviewed everyone concerning his knowledge of the trade. Before our turn came we managed to find out who he was and where he came from. He was an engineer. His name was Siemers, a Nazi who was hiring us for the Philips works.

Now it was our turn. Luckily the interview took place in the presence of our engineer, which gave me a certain advantage because we knew each other well.

"Trade?"

"Electrician."

"How old are you?"

"Twenty-three."

"Occupation before the war?"

"Schoolboy."

"Not another one."

Siemers shook his head; he seemed already to have some doubts concerning our qualifications. He asked me a few more questions, made some notes and dismissed me. On my way out, I passed the next candidate in the door.

Our whole group qualified for departure. True, our skill as electricians equaled our skill as well drillers, but our instinct told us that it was best to be skilled in the field of electricity, the more so since Herr Siemers's attitude to us was quite friendly and his treatment of us humane. It was obvious from his behavior that he wanted us for a job not for liquidation. We were anxious to leave as soon as possible in order to avoid the accidental discovery that we had earlier presented ourselves as expert craftsmen in well drilling. Next morning we left the large and uncomfortable hangar, followed by the envious glances of those who had failed their test. Ever precise, Julek entered in his notebook: "November 14, 1944, Departure for Sachsenhausen."

It was quite warm for mid-November. We marched briskly, in rows of five, through the streets of a pretty little town. Passersby turned away with revulsion and pointedly held their noses. No doubt we stank.

Between the rows of trees on either side of the road children were playing with fallen leaves. At the sight of us their worried mothers fetched them away in a panic. The older ones pelted us with chestnuts. A little farther on, some young people wearing Hitler Youth armbands were drilling. As our column drew near, they interrupted what they were doing. The came at us, circling round the column like hounds, threatening and abusing us.

The bolder among them came closer and began spitting at us or pelting us with stones, sticks, chestnuts or anything else they could find, making horrible faces at us. Smiling indulgently, the guards allowed the young people their little games. Ludwik, the omniscient one, whispered, "We're marching through the Olympic village. That's what's left after the magnificent games." He ducked hastily to dodge a stone.

"Shut up," cried the guard. We marched on silently through the clean streets of this pretty little town. Shortly afterwards we passed through the great gate of Sachsenhausen camp. After a bath and a delousing we were sent to a barrack where we were to wait before continuing our journey to the Philips works.

CHAPTER 84

TWO DAYS later we traveled westward, luxuriously sitting in a passenger coach which gave us the illusion of no longer being prisoners. The soldiers accompanying us treated us well, actually allowing us to smoke. Unfortunately, we had absolutely nothing to smoke. One of the guards, an older man, finished his cigar. He dropped the stump on the floor and, for once, did not crush it with his boot as the SS men would from sheer spite. He pretended to be watching the houses rushing past the windows with absorbed interest. But before I had time to bend down, another hand had snapped up this tempting morsel. I had to be satisfied with a fag end which Marian gave me. I inhaled deeply and passed it on to Jurek, who after a puff handed it to Jedrek, who, trying to extract all he could from the stub, promptly burned his lip. It was on this occasion that I decided to make cigarette holders because it was a pity to waste even this little tobacco.

The train was racing through a densely built-up area. We traveled past several transports going east with heavy weapons and soldiers.

Mountains appeared on the horizon. But before we came close to them we stopped in the picturesque town of Minden, whose panorama with its many church steeples reminded us of Cracov. After we had left Minden, we traveled another few miles and stopped not far from the foot of the steep, wooded mountains. We were unloaded at the goods station of a small town bearing the strange name of *Porta Westfalica*. Our surprise increased still more when we saw this sleepy little town, which stretched up the mountainside along both banks of the river, its houses typical holiday cottages without any sign of industrial activity. Where on earth were these Philips works where we were supposed to work?

Having crossed a handsome suspension bridge over the river Weser, we went uphill along a road planted with old trees, turned into a narrow lane and found ourselves outside a large wooden building which looked a little like an ancient synagogue, except for the fact that it was encircled with barbed wire and had a watchtower at each corner. Could this be our concentration camp? As if in confirmation of our suspicions, a group of trusties with armbands spilled out of the gate. Among them was a red-haired prisoner with a camp senior's armband on his blue jacket, who was conspicuous on account of his incessant yelling. It was getting dark; therefore, we were quickly counted and hustled inside the strange building, which turned out to be the municipal theater. Here we were lined up in rows of five and, as usual, instructed about camp regulations.

The hall was not heated, so it was as cold indoors as outside. Our bunks were on the north wall, precisely in the coldest spot. But first we had our hair shaved off in a weird fashion: they ran the clippers across the center of the head, from the forehead to the back of the neck, thus forming a path which someone facetiously called louse avenue. Not at all a misnomer, as we discovered before long, for the place was crawling with lice, fleas and bugs. We lay down on the top bunks on the fourth tier, always two to a straw mattress. We thought that up here it would be a little warmer and there might be fewer fleas. Moreover, from the top it was easier to survey what was going on down below. On the other hand, it turned out later that sleeping right at the top had its disadvantages, too. The constant chill to which the body was exposed affected the bladder, and frequent visits to the toilet in the yard became necessary. To complete our happiness, we were not allowed to go outside at night wearing our clothing and shoes; this was a security measure to stop people from escaping.

That same evening I almost lost my precious shoes, which so far I had guarded from the Kapos' greedy eyes. As I returned from the latrine barefoot, I discovered that my shoes had disappeared. I just stood there, desperate and furious, looking round helplessly. An emaciated prisoner on the bed next to mine pointed to the annex opposite the kitchen. Peering through the window, I saw that it was a shoemaker's shop. Sitting on a stool was the Kapo, calmly trying on my shoes. Standing next to him was another Kapo, who noticed me behind the glass pane and gave me a sign to come in. The seated Kapo with a foxy face asked in an ingratiating tone: "Are those your shoes? Great, aren't they?" He praised them and showed them off on his skinny legs. "From today they're my shoes, isn't that right?" He addressed himself to me with a false smile and a menacing tone in his voice. As no reply was forthcoming, he took a pair of wooden clogs from a shelf, handed them to me and said, "Take these, wooden clogs are best here." However, he met determined resistance from me. Thereupon he changed his tactics. "Ah, you silly fool. I want to buy them. Many cigarettes, a lot of bread and something to eat."

"Stop messing about," the other Kapo interrupted him. "Give it a rest," he added and took hold of the shoes, which the shoemaker had quickly taken off. "There you are. Take them, go to sleep and don't worry."

I bolted as quickly as possible, surprised at the Kapo's magnanimity. In a similar situation in Auschwitz one might have paid for it with one's life.

My shoes were just the beginning of my troubles. The next day, the same Kapo who yesterday had taken my part with the shoemaker suggested to me that *he* would like to buy my desirable shoes. He was honest, he said, and would pay me well, whereas the shoemaker was an old swindler and a thief. Once again I resisted. But in order to keep him pleasant, I told him that I wanted to think it over. To be on the safe side, I applied some black shoe polish I had found at work to my beautiful tan lace-up boots so as to make them less conspicuous. In fact it was a good thing I did, because it made them waterproof. Water, snow and mud were hazards I encountered continually, because I was assigned to a transport column whose main daily labors took place under an autumnal-wintery gray sky. My illusions of clean, light work at Philips vanished.

The camp in Porta Westfalica was a branch of camp Neuengamme. For this reason our numbers were changed again, this time into five figures above 66,260. As new arrivals we were treated accordingly by the camp authorities as well as by our fellow prisoners, who were of many nationalities. The majority came from the Ukraine, from somewhere in the Don region. They had come to work in Germany either voluntarily or under duress. On account of all sorts of crime—sabotage, theft and escape attempts—they had been sentenced to a limited period in a concentration camp. They were not political prisoners, unlike the minority, who were Poles, Danes, Dutchmen, Frenchmen, Norwegians, a few Russians and one Swiss. Because of the Ukranians' numerical superiority as well as on account of their ruthless and brutal attitude to those weaker than themselves—in particular towards the Danes, whose Red Cross parcels they stole—they were the favorites of the German trusties, who did not respect the rights of other prisoners. The few Russians who had come from Auschwitz with us refused to have anything to do with this undisciplined gang, which terrorized the cultured, weak, undernourished Danes.

CHAPTER 85

As THE penetrating whine of the siren announcing the "all-clear" ceased, the disagreeable sound of the getting-up bell rang out. At the same time a ventilator in the vault of the *Circus*—as we had come to call our abode—was switched on and with its loud humming helped to wake up sleepy prisoners.

Slowly the four-tiered beds began to stir with prisoners flinging on their clothes. Half-dressed, we raced to the washroom. Steam billowed from the door which opened into the yard. Outside there was a hard frost. In the washroom there was, as usual, no one apart from the Auschwitz lot.

The camp authorities tolerated dirt and delapidation. No sooner had we returned and made our beds than the room orderlies chased everybody out into the yard. Then we were allowed to come back indoors one by one for breakfast, which consisted of a bowl of hot (fortunately) herbal tea or rye coffee. Thus fortified, after a one-hour wait in the cold, we lined up for roll call. When the Oberscharführer had taken roll call, we were assigned to our Kommando, and the main gate was opened, behind which our army escorts were waiting for us.

In rows of five, arm in arm, for those were our orders, we lined up in the narrow lane outside the theater, which ran very steeply down to the main street. It was difficult to stay on one's feet in the dark, particularly since the ground was covered with a layer of frozen snow. We started on our way down, dragging ourselves along, side by side. The black silhouettes of the houses stood out against the sky, which was turning to delicate pink in th east; a sharp and penetrating wind blew straight into our faces. As we turned to the right, we were in the worst part of the road, for the wind blew unrestrained and with full force. We were in the open terrain of the Weser Valley, which was not more than half a mile wide. As usual, we stopped by the river bank, where we were divided up into little groups in order to cross the bridge. It took a very long time before everybody had gone across. Frozen to the marrow, we huddled together in a small flock to warm ourselves with our own bodies and shield ourselves from the biting wind. It was rapidly getting light. The violet mountains on the opposite bank seemed to grow darker against the background of a sky that was turning more and more intensely pink. The lights of the lamps cast a flickering reflection on the wind-ruffled water. They sparkled up the slope of a steep and rocky mountain along the track of a mountain railway extending half-way up the incline. It was within the mountain that the nine levels of the Philips works were accommodated. There we did maintenance work. Opposite the brake incline, on a cone-shaped mountain crowned by a huge

275

iron statue, the rays of the rising sun bathed the stone in a bright red hue. Swiftly the red light slid down, creeping over the forest of ancient beech trees and suddenly reappeared as dozens of bright dots in the windows of the sleeping houses down in the valley. The view was so magical that for a while we forgot our hunger and cold.

"Come along, get a move on!" We stepped onto a bridge, which rocked rhythmically under our weight. The wind whistled ominously in the rigging of the bridge. Down below rushed the dark water. Pieces of ice splintered against the sides of river barges, moored along the bank and enveloped in mists rising from the steaming ice. Snaking along under the viaduct was the long line of a goods train, carrying a variety of heavy arms. The train was traveling to the west. "The offensive's coming," Ludwik whispered excitedly.

In fact, for some days now, similar trains had been traveling in the same direction, indicating a major troop concentration in that area. After another few dozen yards, we had arrived at the foot of the brake incline. Here there was an indescribable hive of activity. Narrow-gauge trains drove through a tunnel into the interior of the mountain, where other trains load with lumps of rock could be seen enveloped in clouds of steam. A few dozen workers were struggling to drag huge containers into the tunnel. Others were setting up a giant compressor, which was soon to blow hot air into the tunnel.

The work went on day and night without interruption. Among the workers were representatives of all nations, those that were enslaved and those belonging to the Axis powers. But the majority were Germans, mainly soldiers drafted from the front to rebuild the disintegrated industry of the Reich, and sent to work here. These demobilized soldiers were eager to do the work, often well beyond their strength, in order to postpone the day when they would have to return to the battlefield.

Outside the entrance into the tunnel the Kapos took charge of their Kommandos and proceeded to their places of work. A large number stayed outside, employed in loading building materials, excavations or road works; others went deeper into the many tremendously long corridors of the still unfinished synthetic petrol factory, where they labored shoulder to shoulder with civilians from all over the world.

Meanwhile we, the Philips experts, went into our tunnel, which was about half-way up the mountain, at a height of some four hundred fifty to six hundred feet. Since by now it was almost completely light, we were ordered, so as not to waste time waiting for the return of the lift [a sort of platform on wheels, placed on tracks and pulled by means of a steel rope; as one platform moved down, the other was pulled up] to walk up the steep, very slippery slope. We often indulged in this sort of physical exercise; hence we knew what to expect and had come well prepared. I had tied round my shoes special straps, thickly studded with nails, which stopped me from slipping.

Half-way up the hill we were so hot despite the frost that by the time we got to the top our shirts were sticking to our bodies. This summit was a kind of spacious terrace from which, through an opening in the rock a few yards wide, one entered into the tunnel. From the terrace one had a splendid view over the river Weser, which was now glittering in the sun like a silver ribbon. It wound its way between the mountains to the flat valley, the ancient town of Minden with its church steeples only a few miles away. Somewhere in the distance on the horizon, where the blue of the friendly sky met the snow-covered plain and a number of dark spots, which were small towns and housing estates, lay close together, there was, dissected by the straight line of a canal, the town of Hanover.

But now was not the time to admire beautiful landscapes because the Kapo had arrived on the lift, accompanied by the foreman. We proceeded to the first corridor of the tunnel. Having been counted, we were assigned to our jobs. In a lift which served every floor of the factory, we went up to the radio valve department on the fourth floor, where we had to erect machines weighing several tons. We had laboriously brought these machines from the distant goods station a day before. The transport column to which I belonged consisted of ten people including the Kapo, a young Dutchman with a pleasant and intelligent face but who was

277

basically a fool, vicious, mulish and a coward. His assistant was Zygmunt, a decent boy while in Auschwitz, but here turning out much like his boss. The second foreman was Kuzik from Warsaw, tremendously tall and skinny, with a nose as long as an elephant's trunk, staunch as a mate, cheerful, courageous and shrewd; or, to put it another way, a splendid fellow in every sense of the word.

It did not take us long to do the work. We already had experience. Incidentally, when the foreman was present we had to work properly. Inside the tunnel it was as cold as the grave. Therefore it was better, despite the frost, to work outside, the more so since the day promised to be fine and we expected an air raid, which would provide us with a chance to organize some food and cigarettes. All we had to do was to get rid of the Dutchman. This was comparatively easy, because he preferred hanging about in the corridors or just warming himself in a corner by an electric fire.

We took the narrow-gauge railway to the bottom, and then it was about three-quarters of a mile to the goods station. We had to unload heavy machines from wagons which, of late, kept arriving in increasing numbers from the dismantled Philips factory in Holland. The Germans, fearing that Holland might soon become a battle area, were making haste.

Herr Siemers, the engineer, was already there. These were precision machines, and he ordered us to handle them with great care. Lately he had noticed that they arrived in a damaged condition. The railway people blamed us, while we maintained that the machines were damaged on arrival. The truth was somewhere in between the two. We knew that the employees of the railways stole certain parts, especially when they were made of niccolite; we were keen on those, too. Our buyer was our Head Kapo, an old, crafty villain. He had connections with the civilian population of the village and would trade the niccolite, in the form of heating appliances for alcohol. In turn, he would give each of us a cigarette.

Towards midday we unloaded a large truck. The Italians harnessed themselves to it in order to pull it to the brake incline. These Italians, former soldiers of the Berlin-Rome Axis, now worked together with us prisoners in a transport column. If they had not been of much use to the Germans as fighting men at the front, in this place they were even more useless. Cursing Mussolini and Hitler, they quite openly sabotaged their forced labor. Our shared misfortune brought us closer together. We understood each other. We knew that it would take them a few hours to get their machines to the foot of the brake incline, where we relieved them after we had enjoyed a good rest during this time.

CHAPTER 86

THE AIR raid announced by the sirens was right on time, as usual. We raced to one of the caves at the foot of the rocks, where during air attacks the frightened population of the little town would take shelter, carrying suitcases, blankets, baskets of food and screaming children. Trembling with fear for their houses and their goods, which might become the target of Allied airplanes, they thronged deep into the labyrinth of rocky passages, ducking at each slightly louder bomb explosion.

It was on these occasions that Kazio applied his well-tested psychological approach. He remained courageously at the entrance to the cave, giving exaggerated reports about the consequences of an attack, while we mingled with the crowd, our suffering expressions conveying the message that we were poor, starving prisoners. As a rule it was the women who would notice our distress, and that was why many of us were given some food. At times we even managed to collect a few cigarettes, surreptitiously slipped to us by one of the older German men. However, we did not always succeed in softening their hearts. Occasionally it happened that there was among the Germans some valiant young hero who would wreck all our work. There would then be an atmosphere of hostility among the refugees, and we'd have to make ourselves scarce. On such days we acted in a ruthless manner. We had no scruples whatever and we stole things. As soon as we had managed to con someone out of some food, we would beat it fast.

279

Days and weeks passed. We had already grown used to the Circus and to the heavy work. The lack of food and the constant cold during work, which pushed us far beyond our strength and had to be carried out in snow, frost or rain, resulted in a slow but steady deterioration of our health. Although outwardly we looked different from the other Circus inmates, underneath our worn but clean clothing we were so thin that we were only skin and bones. We only just managed to keep alive and tried to withstand this cruel fate.

During one of the major air raids I caught a severe chill. Bad luck would have it that I had no shoes, having given them to be mended. There was a hard frost; still we were chased out of the Circus into the beech grove, where we were to wait quietly for the end of the air attack. It would not have been too bad but for the fact that I was in my socks, because the shoemaker Kapo had not returned my boots.

I was so terribly cold that I could no longer feel my legs. Taking pity on me, Marian sat on a rock, of which there were many, and with great unselfishness offered me the warmest spot he possessed. He simply opened the front of his trousers and slipped in my feet, this preventing them from being severely frostbitten. After the alert was over, the shoemaker, under pressure from my friends, finally returned my boots, but ordered me to pay for the repair with cigarettes. Luckily I had a few in reserve. I had earned them with my cigarette holders, some of which I managed to sell. The rest were supplied by my mates.

During the night I started to have shivering bouts. I felt that I had a high temperature. A tormenting cough was literally tearing my lungs apart. I noticed with horror that I was spitting blood. In the morning I reported sick. However, I failed to get admitted to the hospital because my temperature was not high enough, only 101.3 degrees. Perhaps it was just as well. The room which, rather grandiosely, went by the name of sick bay was situated next to the latrine. It was a typical place of liquidation. It was there that the poor Danes and Dutchmen who had diarrhea were dying a slow death. They received parcels. Since these parcels had a way of disappearing during the night, they forced themselves to eat up everything in one round. This meant certain death. The body, unused to digesting fat, could not cope with this overburdening of the system. Only those whose parcels got lost stayed alive. Such was the irony of fate.

After a few days' recuperation I began to feel better. My work now was the setting up of machines under the supervision of a retired engineer, a citizen of the little town, who had been recalled due to shortage of staff. He was a funny old bird. At first he treated us ruthlessly, but as time went on he grew less cold-hearted, merely grumbling and getting worked up over the least trifle. He was so preoccupied with politics that he absolutely had to have someone with whom to discuss things. Kazek, who spoke German well, was the one with whom he would converse. During their discussions he forgot that he was talking to a prisoner. Every day he brought fresh news he had heard on the German radio or read in the papers. He bragged that the Germans would soon be victorious. In reply, Kazek gave him the latest news of the BBC. Our informant was a civilian, a Pole from Warsaw, who was employed here setting up machines. The old man would grow angry and threaten to report everything to the authorities. He never did, though.

After some time he got used to us to such an extent that whenever someone was absent he would inquire what the matter was with him, hoping he wasn't ill. We exploited his naïvety and his basically good heart. One of us would simply hide somewhere, and granddad noticed immediately that he was missing. "What's happened to him?" he would ask anxiously. Then we said something like that the person was ill or weak from hunger. And then he would accidentally leave the packet with sandwiches for his lunch in some place or other. He never quite finished his beloved cigars. They belonged to us. But he never ever actually gave anything to any of us. Perhaps he was scared, or thought he would demean himself.

A few dozen German girls worked on the fourth floor winding coils. The finished coils were placed in large cases, which were very heavy. The girls had to take the cases to the lift from where we collected them. Officially, we prisoners were not admitted to

281

the fourth floor. But despite this strict rule, our granddad secretly employed us for this work. The girls reciprocated by leaving behind a ten-quart thermos container of soup. We took it with us into the lift, and the one-armed lift attendant—a Croat and former Wehrmacht soldier who had lost his arm at the eastern front and was well-disposed towards us—stopped the lift between floors so that we could satisfy our hunger undisturbed.

One day in March there was an exceptionally large amount of soup. The reason for this unexpected bonanza was, paradoxically, a major air attack which had taken place on the previous day. Some of the girls who came from nearby Minden to work the second shift had lost their lives during the heavy bombing. Almost every one of the girls had lost somebody, and even if that was not the case, each no longer had a roof over her head. It was therefore not surprising that they had no appetite. And that was why we had an abundance of soup on the following day.

Now everyone on the fourth floor was in mourning. No doubt, the girls, their eyes red from weeping, had had enough of the war. We felt sorry for them because they had been friendly to us. But deep down in our hearts there flickered a spark of satisfaction. Let them experience what war tasted like when it was their own loved ones who were killed.

CHAPTER 87

THERE WAS great bitterness among the prisoners from Auschwitz. Not only did we have to work every Sunday, but now they told us that we would have to go to work tomorrow, Easter Day. In the morning we were woken up, as always, by the humming of the ventilator and the shrilling of the bell. However, miracles will happen; much to our delight we did not march out at all. The Scharführer was running nervously to and fro. Finally he conferred for a long time with Red, our camp senior, who grew grave and suddenly confined all of us to bed. So we climbed back onto our bunks, commenting on the extraordinary conduct of our superiors.

Some two hours passed in this way. All at once we heard an unusual din coming from outside, something like street noises with the volume turned up as far as it will go. What could it be? We pricked up our ears. One could quite clearly hear the engines of dozens of cars. Later there came the sound of carriage wheels loudly scraping against the curb. Finally there was the hum of the voices of hundreds of people marching through the streets near the Circus. Red went outside, together with the Scharführer, and did not come back for a long time. The Kapos left the gate slightly ajar and peeped out interestedly. Unable to resist the temptation, Ludwik joined them. After a while he returned, extremely agitated, with feverish red blotches on his face. For a while he was unable to speak, but in the end he blurted out: "They're refugees. Whole crowds of German refugees. Old men, women, children, - laden with their worldly goods. On foot, in horse-drawn carts, delivery vans, anything at all, along the whole width of the road. They're fleeing, do you hear me, they're fleeing, just like us in 1939. The Americans have occupied Bielefeld—in two, three hours they'll be here—listen, fellows, we're free!"

Tears ran down my sunken, burning cheeks. It was scarcely credible. Just like that, without any announcement, out of the blue. The Americans were barely thirty-one miles away from our camp. Surely it was impossible. Red returned with the Scharführer. Roll call.

"The camp is being evacuated," the Lagerführer announced calmly. The kitchen will issue dry provisions. Everyone get back onto your beds and don't move. During roll call everybody will take his blanket and bowl. Wait quietly for further orders. Disobedience will carry the death penalty."

When the Scharführer had left, Red, after he had assembled his Kapos, went into his hut. From the height of our four-tiered bunks we watched them go into the kitchen and quietly begin to bring out provisions, which they hid under their jackets. So that's what the issue of dry provisions to us looked like.

From the beds of the hapless Danes on the opposite side there came the sound of groans; they were having their parcels taken away. It was an unequal struggle. They were outnumbered ten to one. Now they were lying in wait because the kitchen orderlies began to roll out barrels and cases of provisions. They flung themselves on these like locusts. In no time they had smashed open the barrels and devoured the contents then and there. All that was left were the remains of carrots and the odd scraps of rotten cabbage and turnips on the floor.

More barrels were rolled out from the kitchen storeroom. One of the barrels fell apart. Snails! Julek could contain himself no longer. With one leap he was down there among the milling and fighting throng; Jedrek was right behind him, bowl in hand. They returned with well-filled bowls, incredibly filthy, tattered and torn, but triumphant.

Before anybody else, encouraged by the success of these two, had a chance to join in the fray, several Kapos came running into the hall, using poles or whatever else they could lay their hands on to thrash the thieves. However, even this would have been of no avail, had not the SS men arrived to restore order. A few shots were fired in the air by the enraged Scharführer, which achieved just that. The remainder of the rescued provisions were now rolled across the Circus and piled up outside. There were no difficulties when it came to distributing underwear and clothing; for none of it was very attractive. In fact, it did not differ from what we owned in the way of apparel. Our new garments were just as torn, filthy and teeming with lice. While we busied ourselves with picking up the salted snails, we waited for further events.

We spent all day waiting, followed by a nervous, sleepless night. Next morning we were lined up in rows of five and led out into the deserted street. There was no one about but us. We only saw some soldiers when we came to the bridge. On either side of the bridge, at the pedestrian crossings, rows of wired-up boxes had been placed every few meters. Dynamite! Clearly the Americans must be very, very near. Under the brake incline all was silent. Work had ceased completely. There was nobody about either. Waiting at the station was a long goods train into which we were loaded. We listened hard in case we might hear the explosion of the bridge being blown up, but there was nothing apart from the rattling of the wheels.

And yet, we had been so close to happiness. As the train rounded a curve, we glimpsed for the last time the fast receding mountains shimmering in the mist of a spring morning. On one of the peaks we caught a brief sight of the statue.

Down below was our hated camp. And where would the next one be? And might it not be worse still? It wouldn't be long now. But would I hold out to the end? As always in such moments I left everything to Providence. I began to pray with all my heart.

CHAPTER 88

WE HAD been traveling for five days since we left the camp. We had no idea where they were taking us. We passed through many places over and over again, and we assumed that we were simply going round in circles. Finding out where we were was made more difficult because for safety reasons we traveled mainly at night. We had made ingenious sleeping arrangements: From our blankets we had fashioned something like hammocks, fastening their ends to the hooks which protruded from the wagon walls. Attached to these hooks were rings for tethering cattle. Thanks to several such improvised beds there was a little more room on the floor, enabling those who were too late to do what we had done at least to sit or lie down. The soldiers traveling as our guards paid no attention to us. They were preoccupied with their own thoughts and kept chewing the last few pieces of bread from the dwindling stocks.

For five days, we had eaten practically nothing at all. Every day we were given some coffee—whenever we stopped long enough to make coffee somewhere—and one slice of bread that could not have been more than two ounces. It was not surprising, then, that the sight of soldiers chewing bread made our stomachs turn over.

We stopped in a small place near Brunswick. It was early one beautiful warm spring day, after a terrible night's stay in a half-derelict building where sleep had been out of the question on account of the vermin, which attacked us immediately. We marched in a long column down a country lane, flanked by fields and meadows that were already green. During the course of the morning we got to a large meadow near a farmstead where cows were grazing. A little farther away there were factory buildings, judging from the tall chimney towering above the flat building. Suddenly the head man of the column stopped. The SS men glanced nervously into the sky and strained their ears.

They flew high as usual, in threes, leaving behind them a trail of white vapor which hung in the air for a long time. We were ordered to spread out over the meadow and lie on the ground without moving. Lying in the delicate young green grass—with here and there an early daisy making a colorful splash—I enjoyed the unexpected but welcome rest. Falling bombs whistled past our heads. They fell not far from us, precisely where the factory was. Dense smoke enveloped it completely. The cows, frightened by the exploding bombs, ran all over the meadow and came straight at us, their tails held high. So much meat! Why couldn't they have dropped one of their bombs on these cows instead of on this factory, I thought. My stomach was very empty, and I felt quite sick with hunger.

For some time now the air had been quiet, but we were still lying in the meadow. The bombed-out factory was burning in front of our eyes. We marched on. In the empty field stood a narrow-gauge railway, a few diesel engines and several dozen wagons. Jammed in these deep little wagons, we saw nothing but the vaulted sky. Anyway, by now we no longer cared where we went. All we wanted was something to eat and drink.

It began to rain. Now they herded us across marshland, heavy as lead, to a small camp, which consisted of some dozen barracks and was enclosed by a temporary fence. Straddling the corners were the watchtowers. Over the gate was the inscription SCHAN-DELACH LABOR CAMP. At a little distance from the camp was a factory.

The camp was filthy and gloomy. I sniffed like a hunting dog, for from the kitchen came the smell of cooked food. Roll call. Now the rain was coming down quite heavily. At last they gave us a slice of bread and a little cup of thin soup, which stank of rotten turnips. But even this gave us some sustenance. We were allowed into the block. A smoke would have been nice. I broke my wooden cigarette holder in half, and with the help of a piece of glass, I gently scraped the nicotine-saturated surface. Julek had cigarette papers. Everyone took a few puffs. The stuff was so strong, it nearly knocked us sideways.

We had hung up our wet clothes. Perhaps they would dry out a bit by next morning. Sleeping was difficult because of the bugs.

Despite the designation "labor camp," no one did any work, nor did anybody force us to work. Some people did, in fact, work, but they were a lucky few who worked in the kitchen. At times, they needed people to fetch turnips or parsnips which were outside our camp in close proximity to the factory.

Anyone wanting to get into one of these Kommandos had to look at least passable. One also needed a little strength. In addition, one needed a little luck to get past the Kapos' strict selection. Marian and Julek managed it somehow. I was rejected right away. I did not resign myself, however, and when the Kommando was lined up, ready to march off, I surreptitiously—at least so I thought—joined those on whom fortune had smiled.

The Kapo recognized me at once. I had not had such a beating for a long time. I fell into the mud and tried with difficulty to get up again. And then the Kapo turned to me in surprise and said, "Oh, it's you! And you still have the boots."

Now I recognized him, too. He was the same Kapo who had wanted to buy my shoes in Porta Westfalica.

"Come and see me after roll call," he said casually and marched off with his Kommando.

After I had polished the boots so that one could see one's face in them and laced them up loosely, I made my way to the block where the Kapos lived. From the open window came the sound of many voices. I took off my boots and timidly drew near to the window. Inside, the room was dark and thick with cigarette smoke. The Kapo, his face flushed, peered at the boots for a long time and shook his head, displeased. After a while he gave me half a packet of tobacco and a piece of bread. He must have read the surprise and disappointment in my face, for he produced two butts scented with plums. In addition, before disappearing inside the dark room, the Kapo promised me a bowl of soup every day. But then, while I was busy concealing the bread under my armpit, he remembered that he was supposed to give me a pair of gum boots. He called me back to the window.

I turned my head in the direction whence the voice had come, and at that moment I received a vicious blow between the eyes. I shot away from the window and behind me came two gum boots. Still rather dazed by the unexpected blow, I grabbed the boots and ran away as fast as my feet would carry me. Not until I was back in my barrack did I notice that I had two left boots. Fortunately they were large enough so that I could manage to walk in them.

CHAPTER 89

ON APRIL 10, 1945, we took advantage of the spring-like day to lie in the sun outside the block. All round us were the fences, in the corner the watchtower and in it the old guard with his machine gun. He could speak Polish, for he listened to our conversation and from time to time threw in an observation of his own: "Jesus Christ, you people are really swarming with bugs."

The sun beat down strongly. We had stripped to the waist and were displaying our fearfully emancipated bodies, pitted with insect bites. Julek and Marian, who on the previous day had managed to come by a little salted fish, were busy cleaning it. Since there was no water, the coarse salt was shaken off the fish. They were edible, including the heads. It mattered little that the salt crunched between the teeth. To make up for this minor inconvenience, one had a definite taste in one's mouth, and one's empty belly was at least a little assuaged.

For some time now a butterfly, a sure harbinger of spring, was circling above our heads. At last, put off by our very unflowerlike stench, it fluttered across the fence in search of nectar.

In the country lane, on the other side of the fence, a strange procession came into sight. As it approached, one could make out trucks loaded with belongings. It looked like moving day. A few minutes later there were more trucks, one after another, a whole cavalcade. On one of them sat a soldier with a bandaged head. Our guard began fidgeting in his tower. One of the bolder ones among us inquired what the meaning was of all this and why they were running away. The answer exceeded our wildest expectations. The Americans were only ten miles away. At any moment we might be free.

Meanwhile a roll call was ordered for the whole camp. We were to be evacuated and were only waiting for orders to march off. There were no SS men about; even the watchtowers were empty. However, nobody escaped. What was the point, when the Americans were so near? Some prisoners rushed into the kitchen, but the kitchen was empty.

The Kapo, with my beautifully polished boots on his feet, quietly called our Kommando together. We walked out of the camp throught the unguarded gate. Our destination was the factory, or, more correctly, the carrots and turnips which were stored there. We were allowed to take as much as we wanted. Taking off his armband ostentatiously and pointing at his red triangle, the Kapo suggested that we should occupy the factory in the name of the prisoners and hand it over to the Allies, who might be here at any moment.

It was an odd sight, this well-fed Kapo inciting the emaciated prisoners whom he had beaten only yesterday; positive proof were the bruises across my back. The Kapo talked, and I went on filling my shirt and trousers with large roots, intent on satisfying my hunger and nothing else. After a while the Kapo had nobody left to talk to. For everyone, after collecting as many of the root vegetables as he could carry, returned to the now unguarded camp.

Meanwhile the camp was preparing for departure. Suddenly, no one knew from where, SS men returned, surrounding us and leading us gently but firmly out of the camp and in the direction of a forest, through which ran a single-track railway. As soon as it was dark, we were loaded into wagons, and the train left. It was the second time that we were running away from the Americans.

The next day we arrived at the station in Madgeburg, where utter confusion reigned. The frightened population of the bombed city had left their houses and tried, with air raids going on all the time, to board some train, any train, which would take them to safety. We sat watching all this unmoved, chewing our carrots, the only food we possessed. This day we were given no food at all. It was indeed fortunate that we had managed to secure a supply of carrots. Chewing them made one's jaws ache, it was true, but they did quench one's thirst and slightly lessened the feeling of hunger.

Every day our strength ebbed a little more. We were given almost nothing to eat; what was the use of a small piece of bread when it had to last twenty-four hours? Our stock of carrots was running low, too.

It was night when we traveled on. We no longer cared where. We were merely waiting for morning and a chance, at some stop on our way, for a bowl of rye coffee to quench our raging thirst. The coffee grounds might even fool our hunger-twisted stomachs into believing we were getting food.

Now we were standing in a station in Stendal. Goods trains completely blocked every track. Next to us was a cattle train crammed with prisoners from Oranienburg. Just like us, they did not know where they were going, but their mood was much better. Besides they looked better; compared to them we were Mussulmen. They were luckier than us, too. At one station a nearby train had been destroyed in an air raid. The train was carrying tobacco, cigarettes, cigars and alcohol. The only thing lacking was bread. They had got a rich haul. Now they wanted to barter with us, but all we had were a few carrots that were left because they made our gums bleed. Much to our joy the carrots proved acceptable bargain counters. At least now we could smoke. We left Stendal to the sound of heavy gunfire.

In the afternoon we reached the suburbs of Wittenberg, which was enveloped in black smoke after an air raid. The air was buzzing with fighters strafing artillery positions. From beyond the river came the growl of heavy gunfire. Slowly we crossed an iron bridge spanning the wide Elbe, which linked the suburbe with the city center. The city was in flames. The shooting was growing more intense. Now machine pistols began to rattle near the still visible bridge.

From time to time single shots could be heard. Suddenly a huge detonation shook the air. The guards, who had been extremely agitated, seemed to sigh with relief. From their whispers it was clear that the bridge had been blown up. The river now formed a natural barrier against attacking Allied troops. For the third time we had succeeded at the last moment to escape from the Americans.

CHAPTER 90

On a cold and foggy morning we found ourselves in a pine forest. We were ordered to remove everything we possessed from the wagons. Everything, including blankets, which were already in rags, and bowls, if anyone still had them. We were lined up in rows of five and counted, including the dead, who had to be taken along. Surrounded by guards with dogs on leashes, we were taken to an open space on the edge of the woods. So this was the end of our five days' journey. Thank God!

There was nothing better than a camp, after all. At least they'd give us something to eat. Our new camp looked a little like the beginnings of Birkenau in 1941 and 1942, the only difference being that instead of mud we now had marshy sand. A few low brick barracks were crammed with thousands of terribly undernourished prisoners of many nationalities, mainly Russian. Nobody worked, as we soon discovered, and almost nobody had anything to eat. Although the kitchen did its best and distributed food once a day, this distribution took place in such a way that only those ate who had enough strength and the cunning to get to the kettles first, while the meal was being handed out.

The sick and the weak wasted away, sentenced to death by starvation. There were many corpses. Heaps of skeletons, piled up to the roof, lay outside one of the barracks. The heaps grew higher daily, and many rats ran about among them. The authorities were not in the least interested in what happened in the camp. They left us to ourselves. They guarded us only to make sure that no one escaped. At the corners of the wire-encircled camp stood watchtowers on which SS men sat, armed with machine pistols.

After staying in this camp for a few days we turned into Mussulmen and looked like the rest of the inmates. Ludwik was struck with fever. He lay on his bunk, his sunken cheeks covered with bright red blotches, whispering in his weak voice that the end of the war was near and that he would return to his beloved wife. Jedrek, ragged and unbelievably neglected, loudly raved about food, constantly scratching his ulcerous body. I was preoccupied with sewing large patches, torn from my blanket and meant to serve as deep pockets, to the inside of my striped prison garb. In my fevered imagination I filled them with bread, which I had come by in a mysterious manner. Julek and Marian drifted to the kitchen, waiting for a favorable moment when they might steal some food. They did not succeed. They returned, groggy from having had a beating, but empty-handed.

However, they learned that the Kapos were looking for strong men to fetch carrots, turnips and even potatoes for the kitchen from outside the camp. We had to get ourselves up to create a good impression with the Kapos. Spruced up with difficulty, we dragged ourselves to the assembly point. By a lucky accident Marian and I were assigned to the trucks. We agreed that on returning with the loaded truck we would try to get as close as possible to the blocks where Jedrek, Ludwik, Czesiek and Julek were. Our friends would pick up the potatoes we would attempt to throw down from the truck. Pushing the loaded truck across the camp, we made our way to the kitchen. In front of us walked several Kapos, clearing a path among hundreds of starving prisoners who were trying to snatch at least one potato as we rolled past.

At the corner of the last block, not far from the kitchen, our friends stood waiting. At a prearranged signal Marian and I began to throw down whole handfuls of potatoes. The Kapos noticed this and hit us with poles. Disregarding the blows, we went on throwing. Our buddies picked up the potatoes, putting them inside their shirts, filling their trousers and pockets. Taking advantage of the general commotion, we did the same. Before the Kapos, with the help of the kitchen staff, managed to restore order, we fled with our booty. Doubling back between the barracks, we reached our huts at long last.

We laid the potatoes in our bunks and guarded them zealously.

Now we were no longer threatened with death from starvation. That same evening we managed to get a bucket of water. Julek stole it from the camp kitchen. On a fire that we had lit in a little dug-out hollow near the block, we boiled the peeled potatoes. It was the first time in many days that we had full stomachs. I filled the pockets of my striped prison clothes with the peelings; they would soon be needed. What are twenty-four or twenty-five pounds of potatoes to five almost completely starved prisoners?

When I emptied the peelings into the bucket, I failed to notice that a small piece of soap I kept concealed in my clothing had also dropped in. We were puzzled as to why there should be so much foam on the boiling soup. I skimmed it off carefully and in the end realized that the foam was in fact my soap. Luckily it was only a very small piece. Needless to say I did not reveal to my friends what had happened. The "soup" stank of soapy foam, but we ate half a bucketful all the same. The rest we generously passed on to some Mussulmen, whose eyes were almost popping out as they watched us eat. This, however, was the end of our food stocks. Once more hunger stared us in the face.

It was during a roll call that the authorities were again looking for prisoners willing and able to work. Although we were afraid that we might be recognized as the potato thieves, all five of us reported. We assumed that we would go to work right away. Instead we were transferred to another camp, a few hundred yards from this camp, which we had thought to be an SS barracks. The name on the entrance gate was WEBELING LABOR CAMP. The camp was small, with only a few barracks, quite decently equipped with windows and beds. Compared to our previous camp, this one seemed positively comfortable. There was even a washroom with taps, from which flowed clean water.

This abundance of water was possibly the cause of my diarrhea. My body longed for water; that was why, unthinkingly, I drank again and again, quenching my constant thirst. At any rate, we did not starve quite as desperately as in the previous camp.

Our place of work was not far away. It was the spot where two or three days earlier we had loaded the potatoes that had saved us from dying of starvation. Now we cleared out the turnips, carrots and potatoes and loaded them into goods wagons. Our beds were full of potatoes. After work we prepared them in various ways. On account of my diarrhea, I roasted them on charcoal. It did not do me much good, though. My diarrhea was very debilitating. My strength was rapidly decreasing, and I noticed moreover that my legs were so badly swollen that I was forced to slit the legs of my gum boots because I could not get my swollen legs into them. Next day I was horrified to see that what had been normal diarrhea had turned into dysentery.

So this was the end. I knew from experience that I had only another three or four days left, for I had observed the dysentery patients in Auschwitz. My sole salvation lay in a strict fast and charcoal, since under present circumstances there was no question of medication of any kind. A two-day fast and large quantities of blackened bread did the trick. My dysentery subsided, but my legs were still immensely swollen. I was so weak that I could move them only with difficulty. I did not go to work but hid under the bed because I knew what would happen if I were discovered. It worked. During the course of the day I felt a definite improvement. At night I actually ate a few potatoes, which I had roasted on the little iron stove.

Somehow we could not get to sleep that night. From afar came the rumble of artillery. Above the dark horizon the bright beams of searchlights moved across the sky.

The next morning we no longer went to work. Around midday we were lined up for departure from the camp. We distributed our potato rations among the five of us. They would have to last for a few days. We did not march far. Waiting in the pine forest was a long goods train. It was the same place where, two weeks earlier, we had been unloaded after our five-day journey. A few dozen cattle trucks were already filled with prisoners from the previous camp.

They crammed us into one of the large wagons near the engine. Immediately we made ourselves at home and hung our hammocks across the wagon. As always, the center section was occupied by SS men. There were two of them. The older one was fat and had the good-natured face of a Bavarian peasant; the younger one looked sullen and vicious. It was easy to see that these two disliked one another. They sat on a long bench which blocked the open door of the truck. Under the bench lay a dog to whom the younger SS man talked affectionately, tempting him with pieces of raw meat, of which he had a whole bucket. In reply to the request by one of my friends for a few of these scraps, the SS man growled like a vicious dog and went on feeding his greedy pet, which turned its head away from the meat held out by its master.

At last the dog began to burp and then vomited. We had to clean up after it. The Bavarian regarded his comrade and the overfed dog with undisguised hate and loathing. As soon as it was dark, the train started to move. Tired from a sleepless night we quickly dropped off to sleep.

CHAPTER 91

WE WERE awoken by the chill of the morning. To our great surprise we discovered that we were still in the same place where we had been herded into the cattle train the night before. We were ordered to get out, and after a while we were back in the large camp that reminded us of Birkenau. The camp was overcrowded. Since we had been transferred to the labor camp, thousands of prisoners from all over the place had been brought there.

The majority of the prisoners camped in the field. Some crowded round the fire; permission to light one had been given by the authorities. Others walked around in gangs, stalking prisoners who had arrived that night from a camp where they had been given Red Cross parcels. Anyone who would not surrender his parcel voluntarily had it taken away by force. Those who had already eaten most of the contents of their parcels sat in the latrines tormented by diarrhea. Their bodies were unable to cope with all the rich food. However, their suffering did not prevent them from trying to finish what was left of their gift parcels. The roaming gangs, crazed with hunger, stormed the latrines, where, after a brief and merciless struggle, they captured anything that had not been eaten up and then drowned the hapless prisoners in the cesspools.

There were those who contented themselves with the corpses

which were lying about all over the place. Just then the Kapos were taking one of these cannibals to the heap of dead bodies, one of which had had its buttocks cut off: a victim of a man-eater. Some time later his corpse lay next to the one he had mutilated. One of the prisoners took off the man's boots, which were still wearable. Complete anarchy reigned in this camp. After the Kapos had killed the man-eater, they vanished somewhere. The SS men in their towers could not care less what happened in the camp.

More and more campfires were lit. It was not hard to guess where the prisoners got their wood. We trailed them and in a short while we had dismantled one of the bunks in a deserted block. We found a space in the farthest sector of the camp and lit a fire. The smell of potatoes frying immediately attracted a gang, which surrounded us in a tight circle. They prowled around us like starving jackals, waiting for a chance to pounce. Armed with huge wooden wedges, we defended our grub courageously and determinedly. Our weapons as well as our resolution gained us respect. Several of our assailants retreated, battered and bruised. Suddenly they once more flung themselves on us. This time we used burning torches to repel the attack. Defeated and scorched, they gave up the fight and went away to look for less pugnacious victims.

A few prisoners with parcels, who had managed to save themselves, decided that our campfire was a safe place for them. They noticed that we were boiling water in a bucket and offered to barter. Filled with rich food, they were now plagued by a raging thirst. In return for a bowl of boiling water, we could get anything we wanted. Before long we had butter, lard, tins of meat and fish as well as dozens of American cigarettes, and all this because we had supplied ourselves with water—though it must be said that this was neither easy nor altogether without danger. But now we had a feast. Disregarding my still somewhat weak stomach, I tried a little of everything. I only stopped eating when I began to retch.

At last my friends, too, could not eat another morsel. We lay around the fire, which was slowly burning down, filled as never before, and smoked real, strong cigarettes, which made our heads spin. The sun shone pleasantly on my back; waves of warm air from the ashes of the fire were coming towards me. I nodded off. I was awoken by a strange commotion in the camp: "They're coming, they're coming!"

Marching down the road on the other side of the fence was a group of people in striped clothes. When they were only a few hundred yards away, we noticed, not without surprise, that they were women being led into the labor camp. Shortly afterwards the Kapos appeared and summoned all prisoners to roll call next to the camp exit. At the gate stood the Scharführer in the company of a large group of SS men. He announced that anyone who was willing and strong enough could go to another camp a few miles away, where conditions were better than here because the camp was supplied by the Red Cross. He said that only healthy and strong prisoners need report, because they would have to walk all the way.

About four thousand people reported. We decided to stay where we were. Our intuition and long camp experience told us so. If the Red Cross was only a few miles away, it would soon be here, we argued. So why trudge through the woods to a camp supervised by the SS? We stayed behind.

It was midday and the weather was warm. All around there was a soporific, uninterrupted calm. Suddenly a loud detonation broke the silence. At the spot where the road came out of the forest, a column of fire and smoke rose in the air. Crouched figures were running away. Two large vehicles appeared between the trees. Good God, tanks! Hidden behind the rising ground close to our campfire and trembling all over, we watched them rapidly approaching. Now they were driving alongside the fence. From the mobile turrets protruded gun barrels, which were trained in our direction.

But what was this? The nearest watchtower was empty. The guard was hurriedly climbing down the ladder. He was unarmed. Now he ran towards the nearest shrubbery as fast as he could.

The vehicles slowed down. They were not tanks; they were huge armored cars. The flaps in the turrets opened. American soldiers were leaning out and waving their helmets. Painted on the side of the armored car were large white stars. Americans!

We ran quickly to the wires, our throats tight with emotion.

297

From the mouths of thousands of dying human beings rose a shout of happiness. Hurrah, hurrah! Three cheers! Freedom! Someone tore at the barbed wire with his bare hands. Several jeeps with the Red Cross symbol emblazoned on their sides came racing down the road. They turned into the lane and entered the camp through the gate, which was no longer there. They stopped by the first barracks outside, where a pile of corpses lay. The very last hunger victim of the camp, the man-eater, lay on the top.

It was impossible to get close to the jeeps. One of the officers climbed onto the hood and tried to speak. Impossible. The screaming crowd of prisoners, crazed with happiness, pressing forward, threatened to suffocate the soldiers in their cars. However, the Americans knew what to do. They began throwing oranges, chocolates, cigarettes, food tins. Thousands of feet whirled in the dust. People scrambled and fought for these gifts, thus loosening the tight circle around the cars.

One of the prisoners who spoke English translated the officer's words: "You are free. However, the war goes on. This is the very edge of the front line. Stay in the camp until the regular army arrives; that will be safest. The woods around here are teeming with Germans. The army has already reached Ludwigslust, three miles from here. The Red Cross will look after you. Where's the hospital? Where are the sick?"

The prisoner who was acting as interpreter pointed to the barracks and the heap of corpses which rose to the roof. The officer turned in the direction the prisoner had pointed.

"Good heavens." He clutched his head. "This is terrible," he added in a low voice.

The others took snapshots. Presently they all drove off. A motorized army column appeared on the road, flanked by fast and nimble motor bicycles. From the woods around us came the chattering of machine pistols.

The prisoners meanwhile threw themselves on the food stores inside the wagons, which were standing in a car between the two camps. They returned with bread, sugar, flour and tins. We, too, must stock up with food. One never knew what might happen. Although we were free, we were quite unable to grasp it all. The war went on; the most obvious proof of this was the shooting in our immediate neighborhood. We were not yet safe. What if the Germans were to come back?

We had no choice but to supply ourselves with foods, lots of food. Then, at night, as soon as things calmed down, we must try to get to Ludwigslust where the Americans were. There we would be safe.

I was almost trampled to death. I was determined to come by some sugar, and there was plenty in one of the wagons. All we needed was sugar; we had everything else. Swept along by the avalanche of prisoners, I found myself inside a goods truck full of flour. Nothing could be seen but clouds of white dust. It was a miracle that I managed to get out of this miller's shop, half squashed to death and drenched with sweat. In order not to come back empty-handed I picked up a couple of loaves that were lying on the ground. On my way back I came upon a prisoner who used his shirt as a bag in which he carried a large quantity of sugar. He flatly refused to consider any kind of barter. I was stronger than he. He defended his sugar with determination, but I managed to fill my cap with it, since I had no other receptacle handy. During the struggle his shirt tore and the sugar spilled out. With his bony hands the prisoner, squatting on the ground, scraped his precious sugar together. I placed the loaves, which I no longer needed, next to it. We were even. Giving me a look full of hatred, he pushed the bread away disdainfully. He appeared not to share my opinion. Even before reaching the camp gate, I had already eaten some of the sugar. I lost the rest when the man from whom I had stolen it came at me from behind and made me drop my cap.

My friends were waiting for me. They remembered the women who had arrived that morning and decided to visit them in the labor camp. Perhaps there were some acquaintances from Auschwitz among them. In the SS barracks next to the labor camp, we found clean underwear and lots of soap. This gave us the idea that we might benefit by tidying ourselves up a little. I discarded my uncomfortable gum boots. Women now occupied our former block, but there were none among them that we knew. They originally came from Auschwitz but had last been in Ravensbrück, awkward old women. We gave them some of our food, and they reciprocated with hot water. Washed, shaved, full, wearing clean clothes, we suddenly felt—for the first time in ages—like human beings.

CHAPTER 92

AN AMERICAN patrol appeared on the road which ran along the other side of the fence and which had been empty for some considerable time. Their jeep drove very slowly. Next to it walked soldiers who were looking around watchfully, pistols ready. Suddenly they halted, hid behind some trees by the roadside and began to shoot. Their fire was directed at a clearing between two sections of the forest. In reply, several bullets came whistling above our heads; then all was quiet. The silence was interrupted from time to time by distant machine-gun fire. The Americans were leaning against tree trunks; their jaws moved incessantly, chewing gum, an activity which, at this tense and dangerous moment, seemed somehow odd and lacking in seriousness.

Several tanks with clusters of soldiers clinging to them rumbled past. They saluted us, waving their pistols and throwing packets of cigarettes, chewing gum and chocolates.

Only now did the soldiers leaning against the trees notice us. The one sitting at the wheel of the jeep called out cheerfully, "Hello, boys," and then he asked something which even Czesiek did not understand, although he spoke some English. We rushed towards the fences. Julek was first to get out. With an axe he had picked up somewhere, he hacked an opening in the fence. and ran to the jeep. Weeping, he embraced and kissed the driver who was taken by surprise at this outburst.

"Long live America! Long live freedom!" we shouted, weeping with boundless happiness.

"Are you Poles?" the American soldier asked, freeing himself from Julek's embrace. "I'm a Pole too. Hello." He turned to a black soldier who flashed very white teeth when he laughed. "Polish," he said pointing at us. "Concentration camp." The black soldier, always smiling, picked up little Czesiek and lifted him like a feather. "Polish. Concentration camp," he said earnestly. "Germans kaputt. Hitler kaputt."

We could not believe it. The Pole explained everything to us. It was true. Hitler had been dead for two days. Berlin was occupied by Soviet troops. And at this moment the Russians were only a few miles from here. In this sector of the front the Wehrmacht had laid down its arms. Members of the SS were hiding in the forests around here.

As if in confirmation of these words, one of the soldiers who had been observing the terrain all this time noticed some movement in the forest and immediately sent a long burst from his machine pistol after the Germans, who beat a hasty retreat into the forest.

At this point several passenger cars marked with white tarpaulins appeared on the road. Two motorcycles of the military police, taking up positions across the road, barred their way. The cars stopped obediently. Sitting in the black BMW at the head of the column were several officers of the Wehrmacht.

With an unequivocal motion of the hand, the motorcyclist holding a pistol ordered them to get out. The officers climbed out without protest and straightened their elegant and immaculate uniforms. They clicked their heels, stood at attention and saluted. The American contemptuously shrugged his shoulders and without interrupting his chewing ordered them to take off their belts from which hung their bayonets. They were obviously looking for pistols. Encouraged by our Pole, we began to search the officers. One of them, flushed with rage, barked at me: "Take your dirty hands off me. I'm a German officer." He pulled away and threw an appealing look at the American soldier. The American calmly chewed his gum and tucked another confiscated pistol into his belt. One of the officers wore a handsomely decorated dagger at his side. When I tried to get this dagger from him I was brutally pushed away. Before the American had time to deal with the situation, one of our people socked the officer on the jaw so that his fine pince-nez dropped to the ground. The women prisoners,

301

who had been standing quietly to one side watching this scene, seemed to have been waiting for this moment. Screaming hysterically, they flung themselves at the officers, tearing off their insignia, scratching, spitting and kicking.

"If you recognize anyone who's a member of the SS, give him to me here in the ditch," laughed the soldier, amused by the sight of the hate-crazed women.

But for the presence of the military police, who fired shots into the air, the women would have torn these officers to pieces. We proceeded to search the inside of the cars. Strapped on the luggage racks at the back were large boxes and dust-covered trunks. With one motion of my newly acquired dagger I severed the thick cord. The trunks were locked, and the officers ignored us quite pointedly. Therefore I went from trunk to trunk, slashing the leather lids with my sharp dagger. There was a small pistol concealed in one of the trunks; the rest contained only large rolled-up sheets of ordnance survey maps. So they were captured staff officers, no doubt very high-ranking ones at that. In the end, they were ordered to get back into their cars and directed to drive to Ludwigslust, escorted by the MPs on motor bicycles. They left behind, lying in the dusty road, dozens of German maps and several trunks, which the women were now rummaging through.

A solitary pedestrian came walking down the road from the direction of Ludwigslust, a small bundle dangling from a stick across his shoulder. We were standing under a tree, talking to the Polish-American. He advised us to make our way to Ludwigslust as quickly as possible because from there we might have a chance of a lift in an Allied car away from the battle zone, that is to say, to the other side of the Elbe. As he passed, the pedestrian bid us a polite "Good morning." Modestly dressed, he gave the impression of a local person going home. Asked where he came from and where he was going, he replied steadily that he lived not far from here and was returning to his village. This seemed a little odd to us, and we began to search him. Meanwhile the women crowded round us curiously, observing the glum face of the tall, broadshouldered stranger.

Suddenly one of the women shrieked, "Surely that's our Lager-

302

führer." As if on command, the women hurled themselves on the German. He grew pale and tried to get away, but it was already too late. The American ordered him to put up his hands and led him to the jeeps that were parked not far away. He was taken to Ludwigslust immediately.

From the opposite direction came several horse-drawn vehicles, covered with tarpaulins and looking very much like a group of gypsies on the move. The Americans, who were by now a quarter of a mile away from us, allowed the vehicles to pass. As they approached us, they increased their speed, passing us at a full gallop without stopping when challenged to do so. I managed to cling to the last vehicle, which as it turned out was full of army bread. I ran after the cart and, holding on with one hand, threw down loaves of bread with the other. The driver lashed out at me with his whip, catching me from time to time and inflicting considerable stinging pain on me. My swollen, tired legs were giving out, but I was afraid to let go of the vehicle, which was now hurtling forward at breakneck speed. The driver lashed out furiously, first at his horses, then at me. Leaning far out of his cart, he succeeded in bringing down the whip handle across my hand, desperately clinging to the vehicle. I let go immediately and rolled into the nearest ditch. The driver cracked his whip in the air and left me in the ditch with a guffaw. Limping and cursing, I returned. There was no bread left on the road. The women had picked it all up to the last crumb.

Marian, Julek and Czesiek were waiting for me outside the little brick cottage, which had always roused our curiosity when, not long ago, we were working quite close to it. Somebody had been there ahead of us, for the rooms presented a pitiful sight. All that was left was a large number of antlers hanging on the walls; surprisingly the unknown vandals had not touched them.

We climbed up into the loft on a ladder. In the brine tubs were large pieces of meat. We did not take them because we had found a bag full of tins in a corner. Quite by accident we found the entrance to the cellar. With the light of a candle we discovered four large packing cases with crystal, porcelain and silver cutlery. We brought away as much as we could carry and took everything to the women who lived in the barracks. They were delighted with the lovely tableware and offered to cook a splendid dinner for us. The offer was tempting, but remembering the American soldier's advice that we ought to get into town by evening, we left on the pretext of wanting to collect some more bits and pieces that were supposed to have been left in the mysterious house.

As we passed the big camp we noticed that the kitchen was in operation. Prisoners wearing white armbands and carrying carbines were patrolling inside the camp. So they had got themselves organized and were waiting for the Red Cross to arrive. We quickened our steps, for we were anxious to leave behind us the deserted cordon and the long rows of barbed wire of our last concentration camp. We were free, free to go wherever we turned our gaze. What a fantastic feeling! Our hearts were filled with joy. Spread out before our eyes was the world in all its tempting, colorful beauty, a world which until now had been invisible and unattainable.

The unforgettable day of our freedom was the second of May.

American patrols, which passed us every few minutes, were pleased to see us. They showered us with sweets and cigarettes, shouting: "Hello, boys! Hello, concentration camp."

It was almost dark when we reached the residential outskirts of Ludwigslust. Once the sun had gone down, there was an impenetrable darkness all round us. We had to grope our way to the center of the town, going solely by noises, for we could discern the regular humming of car engines and the movements of a crowd of several thousand people coming from there.

CHAPTER 93

"HALT! HANDS UP!" We stood rooted to the spot, rigid from terror. Germans! The harsh beam of the searchlight slowly slid over our trembling bodies.

"Ah, concentration camp!"

We breathed huge sighs of relief. These were Americans. Once

304

again Czesiek's linguistic abilities proved to be our salvation. It was hard going, but somehow he managed to make himself understood with the MPs. They advised us to return to the camp, because we might well be swallowed up in the crowd of German soldiers being captured.

After being stopped another few times by MP patrols, we finally left the town. In complete darkness we joined the stream of German soldiers, who made their way in vehicles or on foot. This was neither wise nor safe. Luckily the Germans were far too preoccupied with their own fate to notice that marching side by side with them were four prisoners in striped concentration camp garb. To be on the safe side, we spoke only in whispers or not at all. Our eyes were slowly getting used to the darkness. On either side of the road, which was overcrowded with military equipment and people, was an immense forest.

It was growing cold. The straps of our heavy bags cut into our aching shoulders; our legs, tired from marching, began to flag. And yet there, right next to us, were thousands of Germans with their tanks, armored cars, private cars, motorbikes and bubble cars.

They were driving into captivity. We were making our arduous way to freedom on foot. Even now they outdid us. We were absolutely furious, as every few minutes we had to step aside if we did not want to get run over.

When at last we came out of the forest, we were enveloped by moist, cold, pervasive fog. However, walking became less strenuous because all of a sudden the road was empty. At midnight we reached a small forester's lodge on the edge of the continuing forest. We pondered spending the night there. Nothing doing. The barns were filled with refugees, as was the forester's lodge. There was nothing to be had to quench our thirst; not one drop of water was left in the well.

A bucket hit the dry bottom. Julek began to rage. We obtained a bowl of unboiled milk and continued on our way. The milk quenched our thirst, but the consequences were dire and immediate. Our stomachs, incredibly overtaxed by the day's overeating, rebelled. My condition was worse than that of the others. I had only just recovered from a severe bout of diarrhea, and now this milk just about finished me off. I spent more time squatting in ditches than marching on the road. My friends were furious with me because at this rate we would not get far. In the end we were absolutely bushed. Had it not been for the damp and the cold, we would have slunk off into the bushes to sleep there until the morning.

Slowly, step by step, we once again emerged from the forest. Now it was a little lighter. We could see in front of us the vague outlines of buildings. Shadowy figures were moving about by feeble, scarcely burning campfires.

Germans? Americans? Our tired and sleepy eyes failed to see very much. It was all the same to us. A private car was standing in the ditch. There was nobody in the car. It was undamaged, not broken down. What it seemed to lack was gasoline. Someone had moved it off the road so that it would not be in the way.

We flopped onto the soft seats. It was a relief to rest our weary legs. Before long the windows steamed up. It actually grew quite warm. We were overcome by sleep. An unquiet, tormenting sleep since our warm bodies were itching fiercely: we had become infested with vast numbers of lice.

Damn! Sleep was out of the question. And that was not all. Things were getting cramped, because every one of us began to scratch and fidget about. An evil demon rose inside us and made us quarrel, our first quarrel since time immemorial. Each one annoyed the other, each one was in the other's way, each one shoved, wanting as much room for himself as possible; and I was easily the most objectionable and disagreeable of all.

Meanwhile night slowly made way for the blue morning. When the windows were wiped clean, we clearly saw someone creep up on us, pistol ready. An American. Czesiek rolled down the window, popped out his shaven head and squeaked in a weak and frightened little voice, "We are here boys from concentration camp. Polish," he added, a little more confident when he saw the smile of the soldier, who was covered at some distance by two more.

We had an extraordinary stroke of luck. They were all of Polish origin. They sat us down by their fire, wrapped us in warm blankets and gave us hot, strong coffee.

Later there was a sumptuous breakfast. Immediately afterwards I had to make a dash for the ditch. As far as the eye could see, on either side of the now empty road, the ditches were crammed with weapons of all kinds, especially grenades and anti-tank rocket launchers. My God! I might have been blown up twenty times during the night while I was using the ditches like any other decent pedestrian. It was safer in the forest. When I returned, the soldiers gave me some tablets, which, as it turned out later, saved my life. They also gave us warm underwear, and after a thorough wash, sprinkled us with DDT, which we were told was a powerful insecticide.

Thus began our second day of freedom, the unforgettable third of May. The first Germans began to appear on the road. This day pedestrians predominated, but there were a few vehicles, cars and cyclists.

We were standing right across the road with the soldiers, looking for SS men among the Wehrmacht soldiers. The huge black man next to me waited impatiently for us to find one, for he had sworn to shoot any SS man on sight, after he had listened to our stories, translated by his fellow soldiers. From time to time he looked tenderly at my skinny frame. He struck with his pistol butt any slightly more prosperous-looking German who fell into his hands, never disturbing the rhythm of his gum chewing. He would stick out his jaw and hiss, "Concentration camp." And, wham, the hapless German got another blow across the back.

We did not allow any vehicles except carts to pass. They could walk into captivity. A pile of bicycles was slowly accumulating for us in the meadow. All we needed now were some large knapsacks, because we could no longer get all the foodstuffs we were given into our bags. We simply took away the knapsacks of some Germans and, at the same time, confiscated the food they were carrying, I really do not know why. There was no SS, and in this way we revenged ourselves only on the Wehrmacht.

He came walking straight at me, limping, ragged and barefoot. A small bundle and a pair of army boots hung from his stick. In his hand he held a piece of bread, from which he took bites as he went along. In a moment of fury I knocked the bread out of his hand and ripped away the stick that held his bundle and boots.

"You bastard!"

He was very young, sixteen at the most. With his watery, pale blue eyes he looked at me, skinny and intimidated, like a beaten stray dog.

Suddenly his chin, with its sparse as yet unshaven growth of hair, began to tremble, and childish tears flowed down his grimy cheeks. He continued to sob, his shoulders hunched, his head drooping, his bare and bleeding feet leaving behind a wet trail on the asphalt. For a while I looked at these swollen, bleeding feet, at the stooping, weak shoulders shaking with sobs of this infant member of the Wehrmacht, and all at once something inside me broke. The feeling of fury vanished and shame took over.

"Here, you," I gasped. My throat was tight in a sudden burst of pity.

He cowered still more, as if he expected to be struck, but did not stop. Quickly I grabbed one of the bulging knapsacks, picked up the small bundle and the shoes lying by the wayside and caught up with the limping boy, shouting, "Hey, you there!" Running was not easy for me; my legs were still swollen. He looked at me with such an expression in his eyes that I nearly burst into tears myself.

I've done the right thing, haven't I? I thought on my way back. The black man looked at me quizzically and rolled his black eyes. What was he thinking about me at this moment? Probably that I was crazy, especially when, a moment later, I mercilessly dragged a German from his bicycle. It was a lady's bike. I bet the German had confiscated it from somebody else, possibly even under cruel circumstances. I kept this bicycle for myself and traveled on it during the journey lasting several days which the four of us were to begin presently.

I did not see the young member of the Wehrmacht again. Perhaps somebody gave him a lift on a cart. Instead we overtook a few of the Germans whose bicycles we had taken away. Their threats and curses followed us.

Cheerfully and determinedly we pedaled on.

CHAPTER 94

"HEY! WHERE are you off to in such a hurry?" someone shouted as we passed a large cart covered by a tarpaulin and drawn by horses. Ludwik! And there was sleepy Jedrek, poking his head from under the tarpaulin. We had lost sight of them when we were transferred from the train into the big camp. It turned out that they had got away through the fences as soon as they noticed the SS men leaving their watchtowers. They had obtained a horse-drawn cart and were now on their leisurely way to Denmark to go on a milk diet, as they informed us earnestly. The mere thought of milk made my stomach turn. We said good-bye, assuming that we would meet them again at the rendezvous at the river Elbe. A few miles farther on the road forked. We were supposed to turn to the south, but the MPs directed us westward, while the Germans had to go to the south.

At night we reached a large village. A farmer allowed us to stay for the night at his mill. He implored us not to smoke because the mill, with its dozens of flour bags that were going to serve as our beds, might burn down. When he had bid us good night, he locked us in, not suspecting that we might have to relieve ourselves during the night. His fault! We covered the traces of our misdemeanors. But no doubt one day he'd find them and say, "Those Polish pigs."

We could not get to the Elbe, not on this day nor on the next. Fortunately it was early May, beautifully sunny and warm. Every hour, every day our strength returned. We were in no hurry and looked upon our bicycle journey as a wonderful and interesting jaunt. We roamed about without finding the right road, but we did not much mind. The countryside was delightful, sparsely populated and therefore quiet. If one did not hear the distant thunder of artillery fire, one might even conclude that there was no war.

At last on the third day we got onto the right road. The weather was not very good, for it rained. Thousands of people, all kinds of vehicles and arms of every possible make littered the main street, which was flanked by large trees showing the first tiny shoots of young green leaves. The road led directly to a slight hill, where it forked in three directions.

Stretching on either side of the hill were extensive fields and meadows, which were covered with the accumulated military materiel of the defeated enemy. The crush was worst next to the camp of French prisoners of war. The ex-prisoners rushed about among the Germans, who were the prisoners now. The French searched for cars belonging to German officers, whose insignia they tore off. They were also looking for SS men.

With difficulty we squeezed through this crowd, always looking for even the tiniest gaps between the vehicles to maneuver our bikes through. We were always in danger of being crushed at any moment by the caterpillars of tanks or other heavy military equipment.

It was at this least suitable place that my bicycle chain slipped. Since I was the last to squeeze through on my bicycle, my friends, who were going ahead of me, failed to notice that they had left me behind. I tried to catch up with them, but the wretched chain kept slipping, and in the end I gave up because I had to get off and push the bike. I hoped fervently that they might wait for me at the spot where the road forked. But when I got there, I found that I could not stop.

The Americans directing the traffic at these crossroads dealt quickly and efficiently with the never-ending throng. German prisoners of war to the right; civilian population and refugees to the left; former inmates of concentration camps and prisoner-of-war camps straight ahead into the small town, where the rendezvous had been arranged. Large numbers of prisoners from various camps had congregated in the marketplace. There were people from Auschwitz among them, but when I asked whether they had seen my pals, they were unable to give me a straight answer. They advised me to stay in this little town, as my friends were sure to turn up. The place, its streets teeming with striped prison uniforms, reminded me too much of camp, and I could not imagine that my friends would wish to stay here. My opinion was shared by a congenial former Auschwitz inmate to whom I talked for some time. Tadek even recalled three cyclists carrying knap-

310

sacks who had stayed in the marketplace for a while, after which they had left for an unknown destination.

When Tadek had ascertained from the local people the shortest route to the Elbe, he suggested that he accompany me in my search for my friends. I agreed. We cycled through empty country lanes, across forests, groves and villages. There was no doubt that we were getting nearer to the Elbe, but unfortunately we had to find somewhere to spend the night because night came swiftly on this dull and rainy day. We spent the night in a school with many people stretched out on the floor.

Next morning, not having had a good night's rest on account of fleas, we rode on. It was going to be a fine day. May sunshine made the world look more colorful. Flowering meadows and shrubs shimmered everywhere. We were in excellent spirits, as we knew we were near the great river, the goal of our journey. Towards midday, on the edge of a village on the right bank of the river Elbe, we came across a deserted and annihilated remnant of the German army. As far as the eye could see, thousands of people camped here under the open sky, waiting to cross the river. The bridge had been destroyed in an act of war. The Allies built a temporary pontoon bridge, but they would not allow anyone across. I was certain that Julek, Marian and Czesiek were here, but how was I to find them in this crowd? The day passed without my finding the least trace of them.

During the night I could not sleep. The barn in which we had set up our quarters was a place where couples went to make love. There were no prisoners here. We were physically much too weak to think of such matters. It was only towards morning that things quieted down a little. As dawn broke we were woken up by music. The camping place was equipped with a radio. In the intervals between music, the Allies broadcast news. It was announced that no one was allowed to cross over to the other side of the river, but the Allied authorities were organizing a series of assembly points on this side, offering maximum welfare services. Everybody was asked to proceed to these assembly points. Transport to take people to these points was being arranged. In other words, we were back where we had come from.

311

Resigned, we were just about to climb on one of the large waiting trucks when quite unexpectedly I saw Marian. Julek, Marian and Czesiek had taken up residence in a dilapidated farmhouse. They took us joyously into their circle after a hot bath, a change of underwear and a thorough delousing. We resolved to stay by the river Elbe until the Americans decided to let us cross to the other side. We built a splendid tent, with tarpaulins, which we had requisitioned from the Germans, topped by a red and white flag, with a cardboard sign above the entrance bearing the following inscription in Polish: WE ARE FIVE BOYS FROM AUSCHWITZ, and in English: HERE ARE LIVING FIVE BOYS FROM KL AUSCHWITZ, as translated by our linguist Czesiek.

A fire was burning outside the tent. The aroma of the chicken I was roasting wafted from the pot. Nobody wanted to touch it, for it was inedible.

We went to bed early, lying on comfortable divans in our large tent. The steady sound of drizzle, which had been coming down for some time, made us sleepy. It was growing dark.

In the morning we leapt up, roused suddenly from a deep, healthy sleep. The feeble morning sun was battling its way through the fog floating above the meadows. There was some shooting by the river. A weird cry from thousands of throats drowned the news broadcast in English from the loudspeaker. Above our heads rockets burst with a hiss.

We ran outside our tent to find out what had happened. Czesiek was the first to understand: "Boys," he cried enthusiastically.

The Germans had signed an unconditional surrender. The war was over. Hurray! Long live freedom! Long live peace!

Weeping, we embraced one another.